The Price Guide To
ANTIQUE SILVER

The Price Guide To ANTIQUE SILVER

2nd Edition

Peter Waldron

Antique Collectors' Club

First edition 1969 by Ian Harris
Second edition 1982 by Peter Waldron
Reprinted with new prices 1985, 1992 (reprinted 1994)

ISBN 1 85149 165 1

British Library Cataloguing in Publication Data:
A catalogue record for this book is available from the British Library

Printed in England
on Consort Royal Satin paper from Donside Mills, Aberdeen, Scotland, by the
Antique Collectors' Club, Woodbridge, Suffolk IP12 1DS

The Antique Collectors' Club

The Antique Collectors' Club was formed in 1966 and now has a five figure membership spread throughout the world. It publishes the only independently run monthly antiques magazine, *Antique Collecting*, which caters for those collectors who are interested in widening their knowledge of antiques, both by greater awareness of quality and by discussion of the factors which influence the price that is likely to be asked. The Antique Collectors' Club pioneered the provision of information on prices for collectors and the magazine still leads in the provision of detailed articles on a variety of subjects.

It was in response to the enormous demand for information on 'what to pay' that the price guide series was introduced in 1968 with the first edition of *The Price Guide to Antique Furniture* (completely revised 1978 and 1989), a book which broke new ground by illustrating the more common types of antique furniture, the sort that collectors could buy in shops and at auctions rather than the rare museum pieces which had previously been used (and still to a large extent are used) to make up the limited amount of illustrations in books published by commercial publishers. Many other price guides have followed, all copiously illustrated, and greatly appreciated by collectors for the valuable information they contain, quite apart from prices. The Antique Collectors' Club also publishes other books on antiques (including horology and art), garden history and architecture, and a full book list is available.

Club membership, open to all collectors, costs little. Members receive free of charge *Antique Collecting*, the Club's magazine (published ten times a year), which contains well-illustrated articles dealing with the practical aspects of collecting not normally dealt with by magazines. Prices, features of value, investment potential, fakes and forgeries are all given prominence in the magazine.

Among other facilities available to members are private buying and selling facilities, the longest list of 'For Sales' of any antiques magazine, an annual ceramics conference and the opportunity to meet other collectors at their local antique collectors' clubs. There are over eighty in Britain and more than a dozen overseas. Members may also buy the Club's publications at special pre-publication prices.

As its motto implies, the Club is an organisation designed to help collectors get the most out of their hobby: it is informal and friendly and gives enormous enjoyment to all concerned.

For Collectors —By Collectors —About Collecting

Price Revision List

Published annually

The usefulness of a book containing prices rapidly diminishes as market values change.

In order to keep the prices in this book updated, a price revision list will be issued each year. This will record the major price changes in the values of the items covered under the various headings in the book.

To ensure you receive the price revision list complete the pro forma invoice inserted in this book and send it to the address below:

ANTIQUE COLLECTORS' CLUB
5 CHURCH STREET, WOODBRIDGE, SUFFOLK IP12 1DS

Acknowledgements

The Author is grateful to numerous people for help, advice and information. In particular thanks are due to John Culme and the staff of the Silver Department of Sotheby's Belgravia, and to my colleagues in the Silver Department of Sotheby's, 34-35 New Bond Street. Thanks also to Sotheby Parke Bernet and Co. for allowing me to draw on photographic archives, and to my wife Ann who has worked tirelessly typing and sorting my work.

Contents

Introduction

Until the latter part of the 19th century most silver was bought for use in the household and not thought of as 'collectable' in the modern sense of the word; today it is collected as avidly as any other work of art. It is possible to build up a representative collection with quite modest means and, as long as one chooses carefully, it will be a good investment. If investing in antique silver, however, it is imperative that one becomes interested in the subject. Do not just dream of how much money can be made, but try to understand quality and design. We are fortunate that English silver is very easily dated by the well regimented hallmarking system. There are a number of publications available which are easy to use and set out all the various hallmarks. This should be top of the shopping list for any aspiring collector of silver.

This book is intended to be a working manual to assist the collector in his purchases, although it is hoped that it will also be a pleasurable book through which to browse. It is not necessarily meant to be read from cover to cover in one sitting. The main objective has been to try and provide answers to questions which may arise when buying an item of silver and to give guidance about the price being asked. It is also hoped that it will assist the buyer to identify a piece as far as date and style are concerned. The pieces are arranged alphabetically and chronologically under main headings, with sub-divisions also arranged, for the most part, alphabetically. This may have led on occasion to some rather arbitrary juxtaposition of items but then so does any method of arrangement. The index will of course overcome any problems the reader may have in determining under what heading he will find any particular item for which he is looking. Each section gives a general introduction followed by notes on what to look for with regard to condition, hallmarks, and, in most cases, details of the most obvious fakes one may come across and how to spot them.

Good patination is perhaps one of the most important factors which make a 'fine' piece. As on other metalware and, indeed, on furniture, this is something which builds up over the years and is practically impossible to imitate. Patina is caused by the wear of successive generations, when small scratches and pitting come together to give a fine velvet-like appearance which reflects a blue-grey colour in the silver. A modern piece of silver has a mirror-like surface which is easily marked or scratched, whereas a piece with old patination withstands these marks. Occasionally you may come across a piece of antique silver which has been 'buffed' so that it looks brand new. The colour will be much nearer to white than blue-grey just as it is when a piece has been repaired. The majority of dealers and collectors will not buy a piece in that state and, therefore, anything that has been subjected to this treatment will not be as good an investment as an 'untouched' piece. The importance of good patination cannot be emphasised too strongly. The recognition of the original may be complicated by the possibilities of electroplating or a superimposed fake patination, which is not easy for the novice to detect. The former can usually be detected by any signs of bubbling or flaking in small areas, and the latter by a very even surface of scratches and pitting as opposed to the irregularities one normally finds.

Personal taste is, perhaps, bound to dominate one's purchase of antique silver, just as in any other areas of collecting. One collector would not buy a particular piece of silver at any price, whilst another would consider it a fine addition to his collection. Fashions come and go in much the same way as in any other field and what may be considered 'out' one year may be very much 'in' another, with consequent alteration in the price one is asked to pay. The problems of pricing are occasionally shown up by events, thus proving the fallibility of the author. Auction sales have occurred and no doubt will continue to occur where items which are illustrated in this book fetch prices far in excess or far below the most up-to-date price guide range. It is only sensible to give prices as accurate as possible based on the market at the time. Inevitably not every example of the items illustrated comes to the market with regularity; thus a certain amount of the carefully considered adjustments are based on general trends. Occasionally the price of an item will rise or fall dramatically in the updated price listing. These changes do not necessarily reflect a boom or slump in that type of item but are based on fact where a similar or the same item that is illustrated has sold for a price very different to the one previously quoted. The annual publication of a price revision list is designed to give the most up-to-date and accurate information possible.

The most important considerations when buying silver are that you like the piece; that you are satisfied it is what it is purported to be, that is, not a fake or altered in any way, and that the price is in line with the price bands in this book. It is advisable to form one's own opinion about date and style before confirming this by reference to the book.

The prices quoted for each piece may appear in some cases to have a wide range. The actual price that should be paid depends on many factors — condition, quality and rarity being the foremost considerations, followed by personal appeal. The lower valuation is my opinion of an average retail price for a piece in fair condition or a top auction price for a piece in very good condition. The higher price is applicable to a piece in good condition when purchased from a dealer. On some occasions this higher price may be applicable to an auction which is of the highest standard and attracts an international audience of collectors and dealers. There is of course no fixed price for *any* item of silver and therefore it is likely that two dealers might mark the same item completely differently. They will both know how much a piece of silver is worth to them in their own particular situation and consequently how much they can sell it for. This makes the task of compiling a price guide extremely difficult. Until the 1950s silver was sold by the ounce indicating that there was more value in the metal than in the object itself. This has always been the case in respect of some items which are difficult to sell but it has never applied to pieces which have assets of desirability, quality and rarity, which outweigh their metal value, and I have not therefore thought it necessary slavishly to quote the size and weight of each piece. However, weight may be used as a gauge of quality between two outwardly similar items. Two salvers, for instance, of the same date, measurement and style will be priced very differently if one is twice the weight of the other and in the salver section the price is most often expressed in terms of £s per oz.

Weight may occasionally influence the price of a piece of silver; its dimensions do not and, although an attempt has been made within the spread of two pages to illustrate items in such a way that the largest is the largest, the size ratio cannot be followed. For example p.130 shows a christening plate, which is only a fraction of the size of the two chargers shown with it. If we adhered to the correct scale, the christening plate would be shown so small that it would have been impossible to appreciate the fine detail of the engraving.

As far as makers are concerned, everyone has his own favourites, and the most popular makers will of course influence the price accordingly. A list of some of the better known makers appears later in this book. A piece made by one of these makers may be more highly priced than a similar piece by a lesser known maker and in many instances the quality and craftsmanship will justify the higher price, but this is not always the case. The Bateman family for example have in recent years become very popular but their work is not necessarily any more accomplished than many of their contemporaries. Most pieces made by the Batemans will command higher prices because their name is 'known' and the demand for their work is there. Conversely almost any item made by Paul de Lamerie will be sought after, and thus highly priced, *because* of the quality and superb craftsmanship, not merely because he has become a fashionable name to collect.

There is no way of generalising about variations in value between one assay office and another as in the end quality normally overrides all else, except in the extreme cases where the hallmark is the rarest feature.

Armorials and crests on silver could justify a book to themselves and are, indeed, a fascinating subject, but I have only been able to give a general indication within the scope of this book of what to look for and what to avoid. The section of Salvers gives advice on the detailed examination necessary of a piece bearing armorials, and equally important, if it is not engraved, how to spot if they have been removed. The chronological order shows how the different styles and fashions developed, and it is important that a coat of arms or cartouche is contemporary and, therefore, in the right style when judging the value of a piece. It is not always generally realised that it is folly to remove contemporary engraving simply because it has no bearing on one's own particular family, and that any erasure will have a very marked effect on the price obtained should one later try to resell.

Where does one buy silver? Armed with a little knowledge of hallmarks, dates and styles and a wary eye for possible fakes as outlined in each section of this book, there are a number of options open to the collector. The main London auction houses hold regular sales where silver will be accurately described, as it will be when sold by reputable dealers. Never be afraid to ask for help and advice. You will only find out whether the advice is reliable or not by experience but all reputable auctioneers and dealers will give an unbiased opinion. The law provides more protection than it did twenty-five years ago, and there is also an increased public knowledge of antique silver, so that the possibility of being sold a fake has become less likely. At the other end of the scale a lucky collector might find something of value at the local jumble sale!

World wide inflation is here to stay and we all look for some form of protection for our savings. Although a collection of silver does not pay annual dividends, it is very pleasurable to own and many discerning collectors, when coming to sell a piece, have been able to recoup ten or more times the original outlay in as many years. The British passion for collecting is certainly very much alive, and antique silver provides ample opportunities for expressing this, giving the collector satisfaction, and perhaps re-kindling a childhood interest in history.

Argyles

An Argyle is a gravy pot, thought to have been invented by one of the Dukes of Argyll, perhaps the third Duke as the earliest recorded example is 1755, although they are not commonly found before the 1770s. They worked on the principle that hot water was put into a jacket which surrounded an inner container so that whilst the gravy was on its long journey from kitchen to dining room there was a chance that it kept warm. Some examples, instead of having a hot water jacket around the outside have a cylindrical or conical insulator in the middle which can either be filled with hot water, a heating iron, or possibly charcoal.

Hallmarks: no set rules, but make sure all detachable parts are marked.

Condition: apart from a careful general examination, look especially at the handle sockets and junction of the spout.

Fakes: I have never come across any fake Argyles, although there are bound to be some. It is possible that you might be sold one with its water jacket removed as a 'rare bachelor's teapot'. Look out for this.

1

2

1. A cylindrical example with conical insulator rather than hot water jacket. The lids at this date are detachable and should be hallmarked with maker's mark and lion passant. The conical insulator will also have a detachable lid, which should also bear a lion passant.
c.1770 *£2,000 — £4,000*

2. A cylindrical example with hot water jacket, the filling point for the jacket being in the top handle socket. The engraved contemporary armorials will add to the value, but the rather outsized and ugly spout will most certainly detract.
c.1780 *£2,000 — £4,000*

3. An unusual Irish example with hot water insulator from the base to the waist, filled through an aperture on the opposite side to the spout. The scroll handle, although figured with beading and gadroons, would probably have had a wicker covering (unless the butler had asbestos hands!).
c.1780 *£2,250 — £4,500*

3

4. A vase shaped example (the handle is hidden behind) with hot water jacket and extremely slender spout, which would be no good for the thickened gravy of today, but of course long ago flour was not used and it would have been just the juices from the meat which were put in the Argyle.
c.1790 *£1,800 — £3,500*

5. A cylindrical example with gadrooned borders, quite similar in style to the first example with the handle at right angles to the spout, and the water jacket has its separate filling and pouring spout with a hinged cover.
c.1820 *£1,400 — £2,300*

6. Strangely enough Argyles were not produced in great quantities and there are very few 19th century examples in existence. At the beginning of the 20th century however a number of reproductions in late Georgian style were made. This one has a hot water jacket filled through a small spout on the opposite side of the body to the main spout.
c.1910 *£1,000 — £1,500*

4

5

6

Bells

Small table bells are uncommon and were made either as separate pieces or to fit especially on an inkstand. The average size is 4½ins. to 5½ins. high and weight normally around 5oz. to 8oz.

Hallmarks: they should be marked either on the outside near the lower rim, or on the corresponding place on the inside, and they should bear four hallmarks before 1784 and five marks afterwards.

Condition: the first place to examine is the interior. Occasionally the original clapper, which was silver, has been changed for a harder metal one and this could obviously irretrievably damage the interior surface if it were rung vigorously. Sometimes you may find that the hallmarks have been struck with such firmness that a small split or hole has appeared behind. Other than this, general examination for wear and tear, discoloration and patches should be made.

Fakes: some early inkstands have had their bells sold as separate items and a new bell has been made. This will of course not be hallmarked, but will undoubtedly have been given a fake patination and perhaps an engraved crest to make it look old. However, one should steer clear of a bell that is not marked unless it is as inexpensive as a modern example. I have seen the odd example with fake marks, but they are usually quite easy to detect.

7. This is the traditional shape for the table bell and here has applied girdles on the body and handle. This example is hallmarked inside.
c.1730 *£2,750 — £5,000*

8. This slightly later example is very similar, but a little bolder. It has a longer handle and is hallmarked on the outside.
c.1750 *£2,250 — £5,000*

9. George III table bells are usually much lighter in weight than the early examples (about 6oz. as opposed to about 7oz.), but again the form is very much the same.
c.1800 *£1,000 — £1,500*

7

8

9

10. At coronations a canopy is held above the sovereign by the representative Barons of the Cinque Ports and at the end of each canopy pole there was a specially made silver bell. This example, dated 1820, was used at the coronation of George IV and is very elaborate. These are obviously very rare but, should the collector come across one with any royal associations, this may have been the use.
c.1820 *£4,000+*

11. An unusual table bell designed by Henry Fitz-Cook and with the maker's mark of C.T. and G. Fox. A pleasing and quite amusing piece with finely modelled cherub.
c.1870 *£1,500 — £2,500*

12. A mechanical bell produced by Garrards. The firm's signature can be seen on the base. The well modelled elephant, as with other models of animals, will set the price quite high.
c.1870 *£1,000 — £1,750*

13. Hundreds of this Old Mother Hubbard model are made in brass, and can be seen in many 'antique' or curio shops. Silver ones are uncommon. The head of the old lady is attached to the top of the clapper so that her head has to be shaken to ring the bell.
c.1890 *£750 — £1,250*

10

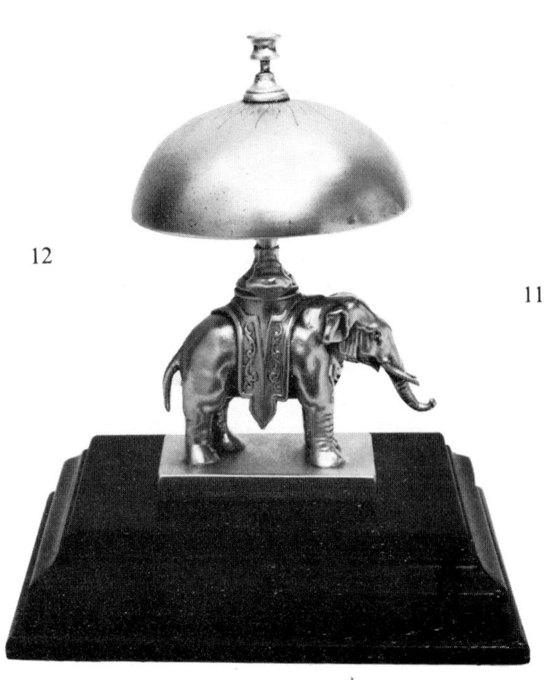
12

11

13

Bowls

Bleeding Bowls

Opinion as to the use of these bowls is divided. In America they are usually described as porringers and it is perhaps more likely that they were used as a vessel for eating from, especially for feeding the sick, than for letting blood. The form is circular with a pierced single handle, and some of the earliest ones could in fact have been skillet covers (see **Brandy and other Saucepans,** No. 84).

Hallmarks: these will either be hallmarked around the rim, or in the centre of the base, either underneath or on the interior. They should also have a lion passant on the handle.

Condition: general examination for any splits, patches or wear should be made. Look carefully at the handle junction to make sure that it has not been torn away or repaired. The soldering on the underside of the handle is often left rough and this should not put you off, unless it obviously looks like a repair.

Fakes: these bowls were only made in England between 1625 and 1730 and any outside this date should be treated with caution. The author has never in fact come across a fake, although no doubt they do exist.

16

14. The earliest types have straight sides, as shown here, with no other decoration apart from an occasional crest or coat of arms. As mentioned in the introduction, this could have been a skillet (small pan) cover which may have doubled as a dish in which to serve the contents of the skillet.
c.1650 *£6,000 — £9,000*

15. This later example is marked on the interior of the base, and the handle is engraved with a coat of arms of a later date. The sides are now more bulbous and have a thin narrow band at the rim. Skillets were not made at this date, so there is no possibility that it is a cover.
c.1690 *£2,500 — £3,800*

16. The sides of the bleeding bowl become less bulbous after this date. The form however is still much the same.
c.1700 *£2,250 — £3,250*

14

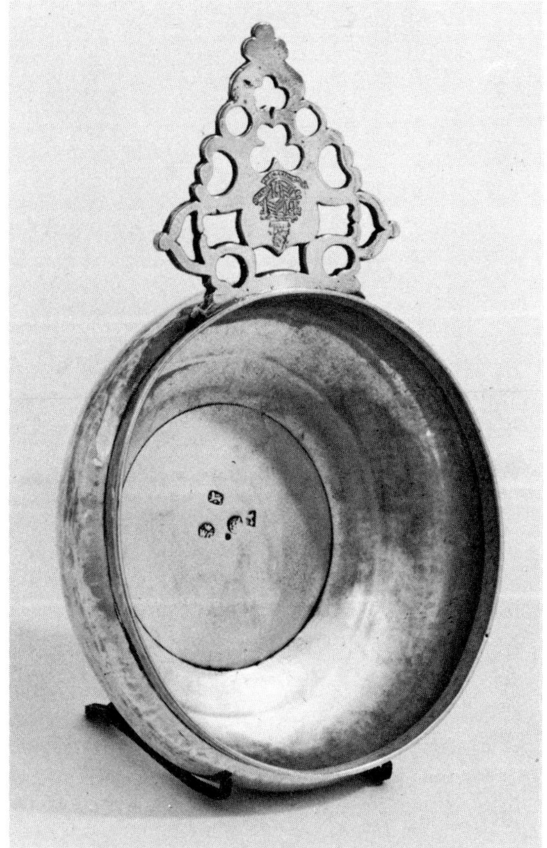

15

Punch Bowls

A small bowl made from a dish, betrayed by the hallmarks which are upside down (shown in detail below).

The silver punch bowl was not common in England until the late seventeenth century, and even examples at this date are rare. The earliest type often had a detachable rim shaped to hold the foot of a glass and was called a Monteith. Any bowl more than 9ins. in diameter may be termed a punch bowl, but from the late nineteenth century examples are often called rose bowls as they were sold with a wire mesh grille to fit over the top.

Hallmarks: the earliest examples are usually marked on the side and if they have detachable Monteith rims, these should be fully marked. The majority of eighteenth century bowls are marked underneath, but in the nineteenth century they are again marked on the side. The marks will be in a straight line if on the side, or at the points of the compass if on the base.

Condition: the rim should always be examined for any splits or repairs, the body for any erasures of armorials. The foot will be separately applied with solder and one should look for damage where this may have been dropped. Do not be too worried if the solder on the underside looks rather rough as silversmiths did not clean this away in areas where it was not visible.

Fakes: the most common fakes are those where the hallmarks have been let into the side of the body, or where dishes or plates have been raised to form a bowl. The small bowl illustrated left shows hallmarks for 1755, but all the hallmarks are upside down. This has been raised from a dish. Apart from the fact that the decoration is a mixture of that found on early Monteiths and late Victorian rose bowls, the rather curious placing of the hallmarks should immediately arouse one's suspicions.

17

17. This is the earliest type of punch bowl, sometimes called a Monteith because of the notched rim, which is reputedly supposed to have been derived from the scalloped edge of a cloak worn by a Scot of that name. These notches have been described as being used for hanging the foot of a wine glass over, whilst the bowl of the glass cools in the bowl containing iced water. The chinoiserie decoration nearly trebles the value, and the applied foliate motifs at the rim are typical of this type of bowl.

c.1685 *£60,000 — £95,000*
a plain example £25,000 — £40,000

18. A large bowl with detachable rim. This is perhaps the most commonly illustrated variety with lion mask and drop ring handles. The rim is detachable so that it can either be used as a Monteith or a punch bowl, and as you can see, there is a full set of hallmarks on the rim (as there will be on the body). A finely engraved contemporary coat of arms.
c.1695 *£30,000 — £50,000*

19. This small example has the typical shallow fluting of the period and may have had a Monteith rim originally. It is unusual that there is no cartouche or space left in the chasing for an armorial engraving. The small crest is probably a later addition.
c.1700 *£10,000 — £15,000*

20. An unusually heavy Irish punch bowl which is on the same lines as the small bowls with deep sides one finds made in Dublin. This plain design is more popular than the preceding example and the fine contemporary engraving makes this piece.
c.1710 *£35,000 — £60,000*

21. Another punch bowl with detachable Monteith rim. This plain type of bowl is found up until about 1740, but usually without a Monteith rim.
c.1720 *£25,000 — £40,000*

21

20

18

19

22

22. A small circular punch bowl on the same lines as the last example, attractively engraved below the applied wire rim with ovals enclosing an infant Bacchus astride a barrel. Any unusual or fine contemporary engraving can add substantially to the value of a piece, and this is a case in point.
c.1730 *£15,000 — £20,000*

23. This unusual shallow bowl with flattened rim was perhaps intended for use as a small washing bowl or finger bowl in the dining room. The centre is engraved with the armorials of George Booth, Earl of Warrington, whose patronage of the arts, particularly silversmithing, was renowned. The quality is almost certain to be first class if a piece bears his coat of arms.
c.1730 *£15,000 — £20,000*

24. Very few punch bowls were produced in the latter half of the 18th century, but this example is particularly fine and is engraved with the city arms of Chester, and was presented to Gabriel Smith, who was mayor in 1780. The proportions of the piece are now much taller than earlier examples, with a higher foot and extra curve in the body, making the piece nearly as tall as it is wide.
c.1780 *£15,000 — £20,000*

23

24

25. Even during the excesses of the late George III and Regency periods, the punch bowl took a back seat. This example is of traditional shape and is a presentation piece. The finely engraved cartouche with banners and weapons gives added interest to a very simple piece of silver. It was in fact made in Edinburgh and is fairly typical of Scottish punch bowls of the period.
c.1805 *£8,500 — £12,500*

26. Plain punch bowls like this are popular even though their design and decoration is far from appealing. This is again a Scottish made example on a plain rim foot.
c.1810 *£6,000 — £10,000*

27. A large circular punch bowl embossed and chased with Bacchanalian cherubs, fruit and scrolling foliage.
c.1820 *£8,000 — £12,000*

28. This presentation bowl was perhaps made for the retiring master of a hunt. It is of large size and with the cover weighs 192oz. The finial illustrating the kill is cast and chased, as are the applied fox masks and hunting horns.
c.1860 *Per oz. £45 — £75*

25

26

28

27

29

29. This profusely decorated bowl is in the same pattern as some ewers (see No.1127) and goblets made at this period (sometimes called the "Cellini" pattern for obvious reasons). The later inscription around the foot is fairly discreet and will not necessarily affect the value.
c.1870 *Per oz. £40 — £70*

30. This large bowl was probably originally designed as a racing trophy and has the lion mask and drop ring handles found on early Monteiths. The plinth has a plaque with a later presentation inscription.
c.1870 *Per oz. £40 — £70*

31. The chased band of lobes is a typical feature on late Victorian punch or rose bowls, rarely found on earlier examples. This one has an additional feature of lion mask and drop ring handles.
c.1880 *Per oz. £30 — £45*

32. Another late Victorian bowl echoing the shaped rim of the early Monteith bowls, this time chased with lobes and shallow curved flutes, an alternative type of decoration found as often as the straight lobes on No. 31.
c.1885 *Per oz. £30 — £45*

30

31

32

33. A much simpler example by Messrs. Barnards with the same lobes and flutes. Look out for any erased inscriptions as these were quite often presentation pieces originally.
c.1890 *Per oz. £30 — £45*

34. Perhaps a fruit bowl rather than a rose bowl or punch bowl, with simple piercing of pales reminiscent of the 1780s and fitted here with a blue glass liner. A smaller amount of silver is used for this item than for a solid example of a similar size and the price will therefore be a little higher per ounce.
c.1895 *Per oz. £32 — £48*

35. An unusual bowl by Gilbert Marks, whose expertise in chasing realistic flowers and leaves is rarely surpassed.
c.1900 *Per oz. £75 — £150*

36. A Birmingham assayed bowl from Elkington and Co. The decoration in the art nouveau style will add to the price somewhat, but this is a commercially, rather than an individually, produced design.
c.1900 *Per oz. £35 — £50*

36

35

33

34

37

37. A rose bowl or centrepiece bowl with pierced and cast rim and three handles.
c.1905 *Per oz. £35 — £50*

38. Here is a bowl on which you can see the modern hallmarks in a straight line to the right of the cherub's mask in the centre. Slightly further to the right are the remains of mid-18th century hallmarks erased by Goldsmiths' Hall after they had decided the piece was a fake. Bowls of this type were made in the late Victorian period from large plates or dish covers, retaining original 18th century hallmarks. The marks however are normally not where one would expect to find them, and are often distorted. This is the main giveaway, but in fact the form of decoration is highly unlikely to be mid-18th century, and therefore few people are fooled (compare with the fake bowl illustrated in the introduction to this section).
Hallmarked 1977 *Per oz. £18 — £28*

38

Boxes

Boxes in a variety of shapes and sizes have been popular since the seventeenth century. What they were used for is not always obvious, but the majority of types are included in the following pages, though not all the different variations are necessarily shown. The first section deals with boxes designed for a miscellany of purposes arranged in date order, followed by **Snuff Boxes, Snuff Mulls, Vesta Boxes** and **Vinaigrettes,** arranged under separate headings.

Birmingham became the main centre for small workers (including box makers) from the late eighteenth century, and their output was staggering. This is proved by the vast numbers still in existence.

Hallmarks: special peculiarities on boxes in this section are commented on, but in general boxes should be marked both on bases and lids. The base will usually have the full set of marks, as this is the larger part. Occasionally there will be one set of marks on the lip of the box only because the overall decoration does not allow the lid and base to be marked in the normal way without being damaged.

Condition: the hinge is the most important area to examine as it can often be strained, or one or two lugs may have broken away. The base is often more worn than the rest of the box, and special attention should be paid to the corners.

Fakes: the collector should be cautious of boxes marked on the sides as these may have 'let in' marks. If a box has a stamped or cast scene on the lid look at the base to see if it has an initial or crest shield. The absence of one could indicate a later added top covering the original shield.

39

39. This counter box is rather uncommon. It is pierced with leafage and has a portrait of James I on the lid. The counters are die-stamped with further portraits and the coats of arms of the various Kings and Queens of England engraved by Simon de Passe. Usually unmarked.
c.1630 *£2,500 — £4,000*

40. This is an oval casket, sometimes referred to as a sugar box, although there is no certainty that it was used for this. This very simple example is typical of much Commonwealth silver and is basically well made, but not particularly attractive. It measures 8ins. across and is likely to command a high price because it is an unusual item apart from being 17th century and in fine condition.
c.1650 *£35,000+*

40

BOXES

41

41. Tobacco boxes of this oval form with detachable lids were quite popular from the Restoration right up until the reign of George I. They are usually extremely plain except for engraved armorials. Some however do occasionally have lobed or corded borders.

c.1685 *£2,500 — £4,000*

42. Part of a toilet set with two large comb boxes, two scent flasks and several other accoutrements. It is quite possible that one will occasionally come across the odd box from a toilet service and this group gives an indication of the type of items included in one of these. Halve the price if with maker's mark only, and be cautious if completely unmarked.

c.1690

Pin tray	*£1,800 — £3,000*
Pair toilet water bottles	*£7,500 — £10,000*
Pair hair brushes	*£2,500 — £3,500*
Pair oblong comb boxes	*£30,000 — £40,000*
Pin cushion	*£1,800 — £2,800*
Pair large circular boxes	*£6,000 — £10,000*
Pair small circular boxes	*£4,000 — £6,000*
Pair clothes whisks	*£1,500 — £2,000*
Set	*£70,000 — £100,000*

42

43. Nutmeg graters are found from the late 17th century through to the beginning of the 19th century. This example is one of the earliest types and they are usually quite attractively engraved with stylised flowers or leafage, usually with hinged lid and base, steel grater, and space for keeping the whole nutmeg. This and the following example will usually only be found with maker's mark.

c.1690 *£1,000 — £1,500*

44. A cylindrical example used for rasping tobacco, with detachable lid, base and silver grater, which conforms to the shape of the outer case. Although sometimes called nutmeg graters, the silver grater would not make any impression on nutmeg.

c.1700 *£1,000 — £1,600*

43

44

45

45. A tobacco box very similar to that shown as No. 41 though of a slightly later date.
c.1700 *£2,500 — £3,500*

46. Boscobel oak boxes are extremely popular and date between 1690 and 1730. The theme is always the same, showing Charles II hiding in the 'Royal Oak' in Boscobel Wood, whilst Cromwell's men search below.
c.1720 *£1,350 — £2,500*

47. During the latter half of the 18th century there was a great vogue in Ireland, and to a lesser extent in England, for presenting silver (and sometimes gold) boxes with the freedom of a city, corporation or college. This circular example is engraved on the lid with the arms of the City of Dublin, enriched with a mace, sword and tree. The base will be either inscribed or engraved with the recipient's own coat of arms. In addition, there would originally have been a parchment (Freedom paper) recording the presentation with the box.
c.1770 *£2,500 — £4,000*
With Freedom paper £4,000 — £7,000

48. Here are two examples of Cork freedom boxes, the lids engraved with the City arms. The left hand example is bright-cut engraved, and dated from about 1795. The right hand example is circa 1770 and is more formally engraved. Freedom boxes have always been very popular and this is reflected in the price. If the presentation relates to an interesting historical event the value is increased.
Left c.1795 *£2,750 — £4,500*
Right c.1770 *£2,750 — £4,500*
With Freedom paper £4,000 — £7,000

46

47

48

48

49. This is an oblong toothpick or patch box, finely bright-cut engraved. These were originally lined in velvet with a mirror in the interior of the lid. The main exponents of these were Samuel Pemberton of Birmingham, and Phipps and Robinson of London.
c.1780 *£650 — £1,000*

50. A vase shaped nutmeg grater with attractive bright-cut engraving. This type has hinged lid and splits into two halves with another hinge at the base. They will normally be fully marked.
c.1790 *£750 — £1,250*

51. From the late 18th century onwards, many gentlemen would have owned a rosewood or mahogany brass bound dressing case which contained everything one would need when away from home, such as manicure and shaving implements, ointments and medicines. Shown here is a cologne bottle, a shaving jug, a beaker, a vinaigrette, and a mainly mother-of-pearl paper knife, and three boxes, all engraved with the owner's crest. The various items in one of these cases can number as many as forty. The quality will vary tremendously. This set is of top quality with fine engraving and chased and applied borders. Some sets are extremely plain and therefore much less valued and may be bought for as little as a tenth of the price quoted.
c.1815

Cologne bottle	*£250 — £400*	*Vinaigrette*	*£400 — £800*
Shaving jug	*£750 — £1,250*	*Paper knife*	*£250 — £400*
Beaker	*£500 — £800*	*Three boxes*	*£1,800 — £3,000*

A complete set in case £6,000 — £9,500

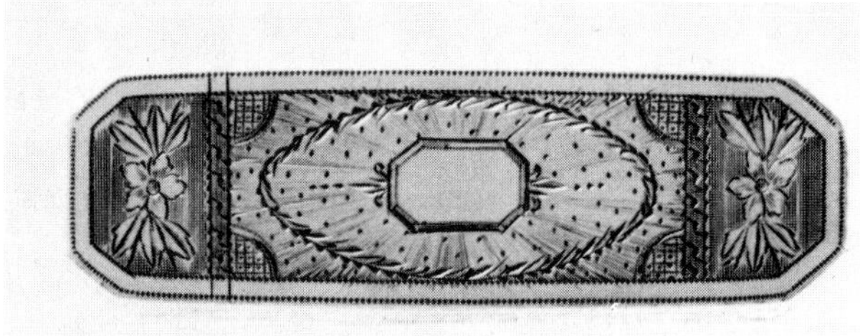

49

50

51

51

52. This London made seal box, the lid embossed with the royal armorials, would have contained a wax seal attached to a parchment, probably confirming a royal appointment. These are quite rare and were obviously made by the royal silversmiths, at this time Rundell, Bridge and Rundell, for whom of course Paul Storr was one of the main craftsmen.
c.1820 *By Paul Storr £7,500 — £12,500*
By John Bridge or Phillip Rundell £5,000 — £8,000

53. The Victorian habit of leaving one's visiting card produced a roaring trade for silver card cases. These are now collected and here are two examples with stamped scenes of buildings, which are the most expensive.
c.1860 *£600 — £1,200*

54. Two more examples with engraved scenes.
c.1870 *£300 — £600*

55. Four late Victorian scent bottles, three in glass with silver mounts, and one entirely encased in silver. The hinged lids fit very tightly and have a cork seal.
c.1880-1900 *£250 — £850*

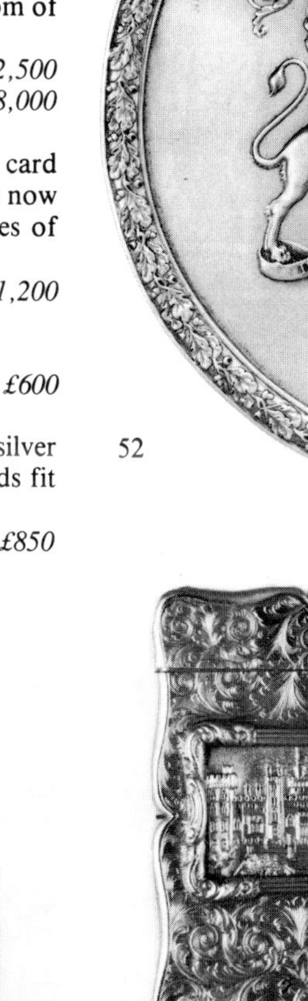

52

53

55

54

Snuff Boxes

56

56. Snuff boxes in the form of a book appear at this date and are usually quite delicately engraved. The hinge is usually concealed and the sides reeded to look like the pages of a book. Smaller boxes became more popular when snuff became available rather than the plugs of tobacco which had to be rasped.
c.1720 *£750 — £1,500*

57. This double compartment snuff box with twin hinged lids is a type that is found during the mid-18th century, and the shape, which is almost like a boat, is presumably designed for comfort of holding in the hand, or putting in the pocket. The lids are nearly always engraved with the owner's coat of arms or initials.
c.1750 *£750 — £1,500*

58. An interesting oblong box with canted corners. The lid is centred by a contemporary inscription within a cartouche of military trophies. Bright-cut engraving to a high standard. This type of decoration is very popular, although as the inscription is not particularly historically pertinent, it will not necessarily bring a top price.
c.1780 *£1,000 — £1,750*

57

58

59. Cowrie shell snuff boxes were popular from 1760 onwards. The most desirable examples are those which have their lids attractively engraved. This is one of the best examples I have come across.
c.1800 *£750 — £1,400*

60. An oblong presentation snuff box made in Edinburgh, although no different from London examples in basic form. This was presented to the captain of a volunteer Scottish regiment and is engraved with his armorials.
c.1800 *£600 — £1,000*

61. An oblong box celebrating Nelson's victory at Trafalgar. Unusual commemorative boxes can command 'unusual' prices.
c.1805 *£1,500 — £2,500*

61

60

59

62. An oblong snuff box, the lid chased with a shell and flowers. A reasonably attractive example, without a lot of character.
c.1810 *£1,250 — £2,000*

63. An unusual oblong silver gilt snuff box of book form with border of various musical instruments, probably made as a presentation piece. Boxes of this type which are of individual design can command very high prices.
c.1810 *£1,500 — £2,500*

64. A fine 18 carat gold snuff box with engine turned decoration which was a very popular and a comparatively cheap method of decoration.
c.1810 *£5,000 — £8,000*

62

63

64

65. A box with a raised and chased mythical scene on the cover. Boxes of this type are more popular than plain ones or examples decorated with flowers and foliage, but perhaps not as popular as the following example.
c.1820 *£1,500 — £2,250*

66. Boxes with scenes of hunting, shooting and fishing are very popular, and this example of hare coursing would be no exception. The scene on the lid is again cast, chased and applied.
c.1820 *£1,800 — £2,500*

67. Mask snuff boxes are very rare. This satyr's mask example was made around 1830 in silver gilt, but is completely unmarked. Other mask boxes include one of the face of Nelson, and the more commonly found fox head mask examples.
c.1830 *£2,500 — £4,000*

67

66

65

68

68. This is called a peddlar snuff box for obvious reasons, and these are very much sought after by collectors.
c.1830 *£3,000 — £5,000*

69. A fairly typical presentation snuff box with foliate snap or thumb grip, which is nearly always an indication of quality.
c.1830 *£400 — £800*

70. This oblong snuff box, although basically fairly plain, has been decorated with a sort of tartan motif. From the 1820s onwards it was a very popular custom to present a snuff box to a colleague, associate or friend, and to record this with an inscription.
c.1835 *£450 — £800*

71. An example somewhat similar to No. 73, but with heavily chased sides as well as a border to the lid. Make sure no inscription has been removed.
c.1840 *£750 — £1,250*

69

71

70

72. This large box (5ins. wide) shows engine turning taken to its limit with amazingly involved scrolling foliage. One cannot help but admire how neatly the hinged lid fits, which is a sign of good condition and craftsmanship.
c.1845 *£700 — £1,250*

73. A rather elaborate early Victorian snuff box, the border of the lid applied with a border of chased floral motifs. The centre may have had an inscription. Look for traces of one having been removed.
c.1845 *£750 — £1,100*

74. A shaped oblong example, of similar size, again with typical Victorian engraved decoration of scrolling foliage and strapwork, the lid centred by a crest.
c.1855 *£700 — £1,250*

75. A scroll bordered oblong snuff box with engine turned decoration.
c.1860 *£400 — £700*

75

74

72

73

Snuff Mulls

76. A bone and lignum vitae snuff mull. This could only be Scottish and in this case has a silver plaque on the lid for a crest or initials.
c.1740 *£450 — £850*

77. Another lignum vitae example with silver mounts.
c.1740 *£400 — £700*

78. An oval silver example. These are comparatively rare made totally from silver, and are quite often of provincial manufacture.
c.1740 *£600 — £1,000*

79. This is the other type of Scottish snuff mull, in this case made in the form of the tip of a ram's horn. The material however is wood and has silver mounts, and is carved with a dog's head holding the hinged cover.
Late 18th century *£350 — £650*

76

78

77

79

80. A ram's horn snuff mull using the tip of the horn which has been applied with a silver rim and hinged lid inset with a cairngorm. This type comes in varying sizes according to the size of the horn, and the earliest appear about 1760 and often have simple mounts.
Early 19th century *£350 — £650*
Less interesting examples £200 — £400

81. This rather amazing item is a ceremonial snuff mull. The snuff goes in the circular box in the centre of the head, the lid of which is inset with a cairngorm. Suspended from a ring in the forehead are a gavel, spike and rake for blending the snuff and a small spoon and rabbit's foot, the first for applying the snuff to the nose, and the latter for wiping the upper lip.
c.1860 *£3,000 — £6,000*

80

81

Vestas

82. Over recent years the Vesta case (matchbox) has become increasingly more collected, and here are eight varying examples. These date between c.1880 and c.1920. They usually have sprung hinged lids and a serrated bottom edge for striking. Many of them were worn on a watch chain, hence the little suspension rings. Some rare designs sell for three or four times the higher price shown here.
c.1880-1920 *£75 — £650*

82

Vinaigrettes

From the late eighteenth century onwards silver vinaigrettes were carried by people and used for inhaling when smells were unpleasant. Inside they have a little sponge which is impregnated with an aromatic substance which is concealed under a pierced and engraved grille. The interiors were always silver gilt as this would not stain in the same way as silver. These are now fervently collected, and examples can be priced up to £500 and over. The most popular are those with topographical scenes, which include Windsor Castle, St. Paul's, the Scott Memorial in Edinburgh, and many other prominent buildings and landmarks. The designs and decoration of vinaigrettes are so various that I will leave it to the reader to see from the illustrated examples how different they can be.

Hallmarks: the majority of these are made in Birmingham, and are marked on the bases, lids and grilles. Some are however only marked on the bases, and in these cases be sure to examine the lids and grilles carefully.

Condition: wear and tear on vinaigrettes is usually fairly obvious, the main areas to examine being the corners and the two hinges.

Fakes: Apart from the odd example I have seen with fake marks, small snuff boxes are sometimes converted to vinaigrettes by the addition of a grille.

83. A selection of various vinaigrettes dating from 1800 to 1870 are shown opposite and overleaf.
£220 — £1,800

83

83

Brandy and other Saucepans

The brandy saucepan varies very little in design from its earliest date in the reign of Queen Anne to its latest appearance in the mid-19th century. They are always flat based with occasionally a slight concave curve. Some have short spouts. They are various sizes, with a tendency to be smaller in size in the early eighteenth century than in the second half when the average capacity is half pint. Skillets, which are much rarer, are distinguishable by their three legs.

Hallmarks: the majority are marked under the base and often the hallmarks are worn because of the excessive cleaning necessary after they have been standing over a burner, which leaves a sooty deposit.

Condition: the most common areas for damage are around the handle socket and around the spout, if there is one. If there is no spout look for splits at the rim. The baluster examples also become damaged around the belly and are sometimes patched.

Fakes: there are no commonly known fakes, but one should always examine the spout as occasionally these have been added later, and some of the straight sided variety are found with the handle removed so that they can be used as a small sugar basin. For a long time small George II baluster saucepans (similar to No. 88), all made in Exeter or Plymouth with simple scroll handles, were considered fakes. They have now been proved to have started life with that type of handle.

84

84. Skillets, not to be confused with brandy saucepans, are found in the 17th century and are extremely rare. This example has lost its original lid, which would have been of bleeding bowl form. The incised triad initials are contemporary, but the coat of arms has been added about one hundred years later and will detract from the value. Even so, the rarity is the main point of value.
c.1650 *£6,000 — £10,000*

85

85. Some fairly large examples of this type are occasionally found early in the century and measure some 3ins. to 4ins. from base to rim. There is a slightly defined lip on this one which was probably added as an afterthought when found not to pour very well.
c.1710 *£2,500 — £4,500*

86

86. This is the most common early 18th century saucepan with straight sides, about 2ins. to 2½ins. high, and will normally be marked under the base. Isolated examples dating as late as 1770 are known, but the sides are usually more flared and the rim foot is a bit higher. This is the type that is occasionally found with its handle removed and used as a sugar basin.
c.1710 *£1,000 — £2,000*

BRANDY AND OTHER SAUCEPANS

87

87. The small baluster body with a short spout at right angles to the handle is found throughout the reign of George II and was one of the most popularly produced of all types of brandy saucepans.
c.1730 *£750 — £1,500*

88. A very plain straight sided example of the type which is often found with a lid.
c.1795 *£700 — £1,400*

89. This is one of the same form as the previous example, but this time slightly larger and with a detachable domed lid which has a hinged projection for covering the spout. There should have been a wooden finial, which has obviously been damaged and not replaced. The engraved initials and coronet probably date from the late 19th century. In its present state this is not a good example, but could easily be improved by a small amount of restoration, which would increase the price by 15% to 20% if successfully completed.
c.1795 *In good condition £1,000 — £2,000*

88

89

90. The attractive shape coupled with a pretty but not over-ornate coat of arms makes this a good example. The detachable lid is here complete with its wooden finial.
c.1800 *£1,000 — £2,000*

91. A large pan which was certainly not used for brandy. It is hallmarked 1913, and is a silver replica of a kitchen saucepan, by no means practicable but presumably used as a serving dish in one of our large stately homes!
1913 *Per oz. £40 — £55*

90

91

Butter Shells and Butter Dishes

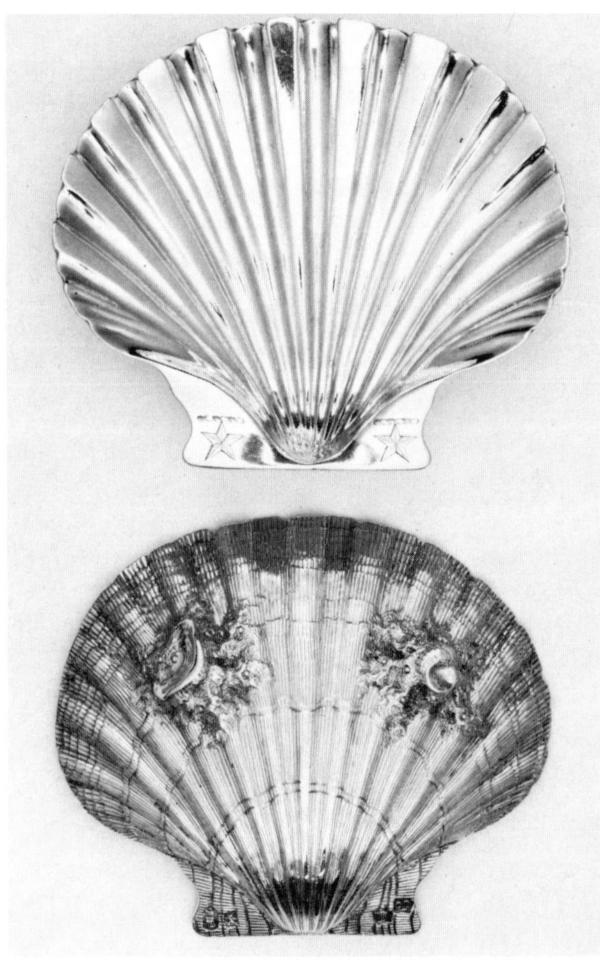

92

93

The escallop shell butter dish is fairly common in English silver from the mid-eighteenth century until the 1830s, although George I and earlier examples do exist. Their form varies very little. The majority are of thin gauge and sometimes have two or three whelk feet. Small examples were made for use as salt cellars. At the end of the 19th century butter shells, copied from 18th century designs but smaller and lighter, were produced, and these might fetch £40 — £80.

The butter dish usually comprises a stand, dish and cover of either oval or circular shape.

Hallmarks: butter shells are usually marked under the plain grip and occasionally down one of the flutes. Butter dishes should be marked on all component parts.

Condition: look for splits in the fluting and on the rims, especially near the grips. With butter dishes examine the feet on the stands carefully, if there are any, and make sure that the finials on covers are both contemporary and have not been altered in any way.

Fakes: I know of no fake butter shells, but they should be examined to see if the hallmarks have been let in. Butter dishes with detachable glass liners are in existence with let in marks around the rim of the base.

92. A superlative pair to start with made by Paul de Lamerie. These are cast and chased, unlike later ones, and are therefore much heavier. All the decoration, which is superbly executed, remains hidden when the shell is in use but both sides can be seen in the illustration. None of the later examples are decorated in this way: they are left plain and occasionally have whelk or ball feet.
c.1740 *Pair £60,000+*

93. One of the plainest examples, which sometimes are found with whelk feet, and are of such thin gauge that they are occasionally split or damaged. The hallmarks are often rubbed because there is no great depth of silver for them to be stamped into, and when hammered back the mark was left very shallow.
c.1750 *Pair £1,500 — £2,750*
Single £600 — £1,000

94. Very similar, but with a larger grip, this time engraved with a crest and motto.
c.1760 *Pair £1,500 — £2,750*
Single £600 — £1,000

95. The applied gadroon border is indicative of a slightly later date and better quality, and because of this such shells are much more popular.
c.1770 *Pair £1,750 — £3,000*
Single £750 — £1,250

96. The more elaborately shaped grip and the border decoration of husks indicate the later date, otherwise the quality is very much the same, although not as heavy, as the preceding example.
c.1790 *Pair £1,500 — £2,750*
Single £600 — £1,000

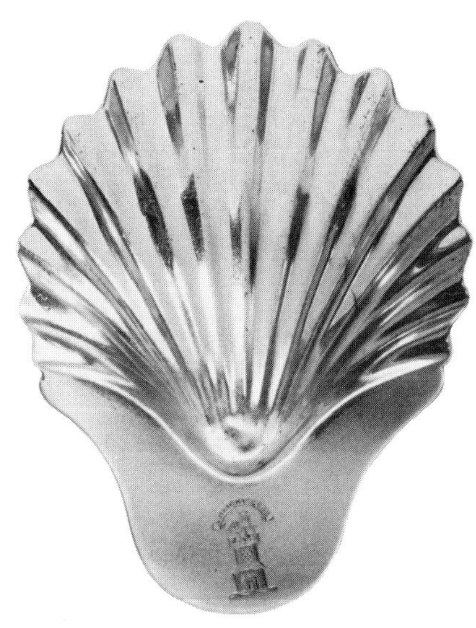

94

96

95

97

97. A fine oval butter dish with stand and cover made by John Emes, a design also used by Paul Storr. All the decoration is cast and applied, but the finial and its base plate are detachable. The anthemions around the dish became a popular motif which was inspired by architectural designs.
c.1805 *£3,000 — £4,500*
If by Paul Storr £7,500 — £12,500

98. The butter dish was popular in Ireland and this later example has typically crude chasing, but the quality is still fine. The matted ground of the chasing is a 19th century feature. Some earlier Irish examples were of oval shape, and pierced and bright cut, but they are fairly unusual.
c.1820 *£2,250 — £3,250*

99. This heavy fluted dish may perhaps have been made for serving something more exotic than butter as it is slightly larger than than some of the other examples illustrated here. The heavy quality with applied shell and foliate motifs is typical of the craftsmen of Rundell, Bridge and Rundell, the royal silversmiths of the day, and this one bears the maker's mark of John Bridge.
c.1825 *£5,000 — £7,500*

98

99

100. A Scottish tub shaped dish imitating the form of a quaich. The lug handles are hollow and soldered on to the body.
c.1830 *£1,000 — £1,500*

101. One of the most commonly found butter dishes is that with a cow finial; the majority of them had glass dishes with silver plate or stand, and silver cover, as this one has. Occasionally just the stands and covers are found alone and, although it would not be impossible to make a glass dish to go with them, the value is halved if this is missing.
c.1840 *£1,000 — £1,500*

102. Echoing the same shape as the preceding example, this is rather more unusual. The pierced matted scroll work is lined with an opaque liner. The detachable lid has an attractive flower finial.
c.1840 *£1,000 — £1,500*

100

101

102

BUTTER SHELLS AND BUTTER DISHES

103

104

105

103. This is perhaps one of the prettiest styles of mid-19th century silver work. The octagonal tub-shaped dish with the matching cover and stand is delicately engraved with diaper and scroll work. This has the maker's mark of C.T. and G. Fox, who are sought-after makers, popular with collectors.
c.1850 *£1,250 — £2,000*

104. The pierced and open-work body was occasionally used with a blue glass liner, and in this case it is coupled with a finely engraved domed lid. Also shown is a butter knife with mother-of-pearl handle. These are sometimes mistaken for odd fish knives, but fish knives and forks were not made until the last quarter of the 19th century.
c.1865 *£700 — £1,000*
Butter knife £60 — £120

105. An unusual circular butter dish with a swing handle. The cast and applied swags and ribbon-tied classical medallions are taken from the 18th century. The piece should be marked on the body as well as on the hinged handle. The frosted glass liner is slightly damaged. If this were badly cracked, or missing altogether, the price would probably go down by 25 to 35%.
c.1865 *£500 — £800*

106. This example is of very simple design, the glass dish with foliate decorated lid and stand.
c.1895 *£400 — £700*

106

Candlesticks

Candlelight is used so often at dinner tables today that there is always a healthy demand for silver candlesticks. There are very few extant that date before the reign of Charles II and therefore this section will cover the late 17th century onwards. The main types are cast candlesticks and loaded candlesticks, the former being cast in sections and soldered together, and the latter being stamped or hammered out in sections and soldered together, then filled with pitch or plaster of Paris to give them body. Further details of different methods of construction are given throughout the section.

It is difficult to make a general statement about the relative size and weight of candlesticks as this can vary tremendously. A rough guide would be:

1700 – 1735	6ins. – 7ins.	20oz. – 30oz.	per pair
1735 – 1760	7½ins. – 9ins.	25oz. – 35oz.	per pair
1760 – 1775	9½ins. – 11½ins.	30oz. – 45oz.	per pair

1775 onwards: too varied to list but many loaded sticks used which are 11ins. – 12ins. between 1775 – 1815 and after this the average reduced to 9ins. – 11ins.

Single sticks are very difficult to sell and they should be avoided if possible. The price will normally be a little above an eighth of the price of a pair.

Hallmarks: the positioning of hallmarks on candlesticks varies tremendously depending upon the date, style and type of manufacture, but in the main cast candlesticks will be marked underneath, with one mark on each angle if they are square based, and if they are circular based they are often grouped together on the inside rim at one point. Ideally a cast candlestick dating before 1784 should have a mark on the sconce as well as on the detachable nozzle, if there is one. There are however occasions when the sconce is not marked, and this may be for one of three reasons: firstly that it was just omitted, as they sometimes are, or that it was so weakly stamped that years of cleaning have rubbed it away, or that the sconce has been damaged and repaired which may have involved replacing the whole sconce. The last should be left well alone. They can usually be easily spotted because the size and form has been changed. Loaded candlesticks are usually marked on one side of the base in a group and on the detachable nozzle.

Condition: cast candlesticks in the main are usually found to be in good condition, but excessive cleaning and wear can give them a very tired look. The casting process occasionally produced some cracks or flaws which the silversmith would tidy up with solder or a patch. These poorly cast candlesticks are not desirable and should be avoided. The sconces should be carefully examined for any damage where the butt of a candle has been forcibly levered out. The sconce rims may be torn, and bad dents or holes found in the sides. The nozzles should be examined to see that they have not been repaired where the bezel joins the drip pan, as these may easily get stuck into the sconce with wax, and when an unsuspecting person tugs very hard they may be torn and damaged. Always check that the bases are not bent or distorted. This may give the effect of the stem leaning to one side or another.

The condition of loaded candlesticks is likely to be less good than that of the cast examples, as the gauge of the silver is so much thinner. Always carefully examine all raised decoration, corners and projections being susceptible to wear during cleaning. It is practically impossible to repair a worn or damaged loaded candlestick successfully as this involves completely dismantling and removing the loading. If the loading is not removed, when one heats the silver to a high temperature to apply solder, the loading explodes and comes out anyway.

Always make sure that pairs *are* pairs. If they have just been matched, this may drastically reduce the value.

Fakes: one should be very careful with cast candlesticks. They may have been cast from an original, with marks and all. Comparison of the positioning of the marks on the bases should give this away, as they will all be in the same position. Also the definition of the hallmarks will be poor. However, as on cast candlesticks, the underside was left very rough, and the marks in any case may be badly struck, but they should have received very little wear as they are usually tucked right out of sight. There are candlesticks which have been cast from earlier examples and then re-hallmarked. This was done occasionally in Ireland and you may find a cast candlestick with mid-eighteenth century London marks underneath and Dublin marks on the edge of the base. Very occasionally examples with marks let into the base turn up, but it should be possible to spot these by breathing on them and looking for any unnecessary seams.

107

107. One of a pair of highly decorated Charles II candlesticks of the type one finds with dressing table sets. These are partly raised and chased from sheet silver, and partly cast. They are therefore not particularly heavy in weight. Sometimes they may have been filled in at a later date to make them heavier and more stable. It is probable that this type will either be unmarked or marked with the maker's mark only. Dressing table sets were made for the very rich and were often specially ordered. The silversmith might, therefore, get away with only having one or two pieces assayed and marked by the hall, usually a casket or box.

c.1670 *Pair unmarked £7,500 — £12,500*
Pair fully marked £20,000 — £30,000

108. A plainer design; the chased fluted stem of square section is much sturdier than the stem on the following example. Again these are raised from sheet silver and would be hollow. The foliate platform above the base is the only cast section. This type is apt to wear at the corners and will often have been split and repaired. This is in very fine condition and has its original nozzle, which is quite rare to find nowadays.

c.1670 *Pair, 25oz. £50,000 — £70,000*
Pair, 45oz. £120,000 — £180,000

109. The most commonly found of 17th century candlesticks with lobed and fluted cylindrical stems. They tend to be much lighter than the preceding examples and the stems are pitch filled to give extra weight.

c.1690 *Pair £12,000 — £15,000*

108

109

110. A variation on the preceding type of candlestick with square base canted at the corners. The upper base is fluted and chased with a scalework cartouche engraved with contemporary armorials.
c.1695 *Pair £9,000 — £13,000*

111. Cast candlesticks first appear at this date. This example is much smaller than the preceding ones, and a pair would probably be used as desk candlesticks. They are cast in two separate sections, the base being one, and the stem in two halves. Occasionally the sconce will also be a separate casting from the stem. Because they are cast they will be heavier in weight than the preceding examples. They are also capable of withstanding greater wear. The knopped and baluster vase-shaped stem survives in varying form right into the second quarter of the 18th century.
c.1685 *Pair £12,500 — £20,000*

112. Two very similar cast candlesticks with lobed and gadroon decoration. Note that the sconces have a mark even though they are not detachable and, therefore, are certain to be original. The majority of candlesticks from 1700 to 1760 will have a lion passant mark on the sconce and this is a plus point with regard to price. More elaborate versions of this type of candlestick exist with lion mask decoration at the shoulder and these may command up to twice the price.
c.1695 *Either pair £15,000 — £22,500*

110

111

112

113

113. One of a set of four of similar basic outline to 112, but without the gadroon decoration, and therefore not as valuable. The candlesticks still have the knopped and baluster vase-shaped stems, but the bases lack the clarity of line.
c.1700 *Set of four £30,000 — £40,000*
Pair £15,000 — £18,000

114. One of a set of four with circular bases. These can sometimes be marked around the rim of the foot and consequently are occasionally found with very rubbed hallmarks. The stems are of octagonal outline and do not follow the line of the base, whereas the preceding examples had octagonal bases and circular stems. Sets are also found of this shape without any decoration at all apart from the obvious mouldings and any armorial engraving. They are rather smaller and lighter than the preceding example.
c.1700 *Set of four £30,000 — £45,000*
Pair £15,000 — £20,000

115. One of a pair of octagonal based candlesticks with diamond facets, the stems now conforming in outline with the bases. Candlesticks of this type may become rather worn on the pointed sections and should therefore be examined for repair. In good condition they are amongst the most desirable of Queen Anne candlesticks.
c.1710 *Pair £15,000 — £25,000*

114

115

116

116. Another example with octagonal base, this time engraved with contemporary armorials. The stem is disproportionately heavy for the bases and would look better without the knop above the foot. Candlesticks in the latter part of the 18th century were made rather taller than at this period. Sometimes candlesticks are heightened by having an extra knop or section inserted.
c.1715 *Pair £15,000 — £20,000*

117. One of a pair of Irish octagonal based candlesticks, again with diamond faceting. Candlesticks of this type were made from the Queen Anne period right up to 1735 in Ireland, and are usually marked on the top of the base in the well. The marks are, therefore, very often badly worn with excessive cleaning. The combination of diamond faceting with a well is almost invariably an Irish feature. Irish candlesticks are usually smaller and lighter than their English counterparts, weighing in the region of 15-20oz., as opposed to 20-28oz.
c.1710-1735 *Pair £6,000 — £10,000*

118. This example has sconce, stem and base all conforming in outline. It is more pleasing than the two preceding examples, the whole design having better balance.
c.1715 *Pair £15,000 — £20,000*

119. A very solid and heavy George I design; this type may weigh up to 40oz. or more a pair. This candlestick has a finely engraved armorial in the well.
c.1720 *Pair £16,000 — £22,000*

120. One of a pair with shell and floral decoration. The decoration is part of the original casting, highlighted by chasing. This example looks rather blotchy, and this is because it is made from silver gilt, which is wearing away in places. Not many of this type are found. The decoration is French in taste and was introduced by the persecuted Huguenots, who came to England with their silversmiths' knowledge of craft and design.
c.1720 *Pair £15,000 — £25,000*

120

119

117

118

121. One of a pair of hexagonal based candlesticks without the well in the base found on the preceding examples. The sconce and stem conform in outline.
c.1720 *Pair £12,000 — £18,000*

122. A square based candlestick with cut corners ribbed at the centre of each angle. James and William Gould were specialist candlestick makers who made large numbers of this type over the following fifteen years.
c.1730 *£7,000 — £9,000*

123. One of a taller and heavier pair with shaped square bases, the stems now being slightly more decorated with bands and ribs. This pair are approximately 45oz. in weight, but smaller pairs of 25oz. are found.
c.1735 *Pair, 45oz. £9,000 — £13,000*
Pair, 25oz. £6,000 — £8,000

124. One of a set of four by Paul de Lamerie, made in the style of No. 112 and displaying lion masks at the shoulder. A very fine set.
c.1735 *Set of four £150,000 — £220,000*
Pair £70,000 — £110,000

121

122

123

124

125. One of a set of four with shaped circular bases, the vase-shaped stem again with more decoration. The detachable nozzle (drip pan) is not original and is too plain for the design. This does not detract materially from price as they are removable, but if the set had the original ones, it might add slightly to the value.
c.1735 *Set of four £12,000 — £16,000*
Pair £5,000 — £8,000

126. Another one of a rather similar pair, but not so heavily decorated, and this time the ribbed nozzle is original and should be marked with the lion passant and maker's mark.
c.1735 *Pair £5,000 — £8,000*

127. One of a set of four with shaped square bases, again with detachable nozzles of the plain circular type (these may be later, as the original ones would have probably conformed in outline). This type was made extensively by both James and William Gould.
c.1735 *Set of four £10,000 — £15,000*
Pair £4,500 — £7,500

128. One of a set of four with shaped square bases decorated with whirlpool motifs at the angles, the panels between alternately plain and decorated with shells. This decoration is repeated on the shoulder. This type is neither common nor of a particularly pleasing design.
c.1740 *Set of four £12,000 — £16,000*
Pair £5,000 — £8,000

129. A frequently illustrated design of candlestick by Paul de Lamerie. Few people however can afford, or are likely to find, a set of this type. The casting and chasing is of the highest quality, and a set of four is likely to command as high a price as the top range of Rolls Royce.
c.1740 *Set of four £200,000 — £250,000*
Pair £100,000 — £150,000

125

126

127

128

129

130

130. One of a pair of finely cast and chased rococo candlesticks with armorial engraved cartouche, which is part of the casting. The detachable nozzle is almost certainly original. Rococo examples like this are not always fully appreciated — there is no doubt that these are very fine and pleasing.
c.1750 *Pair £7,500 — £10,000*

131. One of a pair of demi-figure candlesticks with triform bases. Candlesticks of this type are again cast in several parts and then soldered together. The decoration will then be chased to give the final touches. These are sometimes called caryatid candlesticks, which refers to the half female figure. Look carefully at the bases which, being of an irregular shape, are more likely to have been strained, knocked, damaged or repaired.
c.1750 *Pair £7,500 — £10,000*

132. One of another pair of figure candlesticks based on a late 17th century pair with ball knops and sconces decorated with acanthus leafage. In fact, this pair was made by the royal goldsmith of the time, Thomas Heming, and is extremely fine, weighing in excess of 60oz. for the pair. The open-work bases with applied swags are in good condition, but this sort of applied work can often be damaged. A few pairs of figure candlesticks dating from the late 17th century are known in the form of kneeling blackamoors; these however are rare.
c.1760 *Pair £35,000 — £50,000*

131

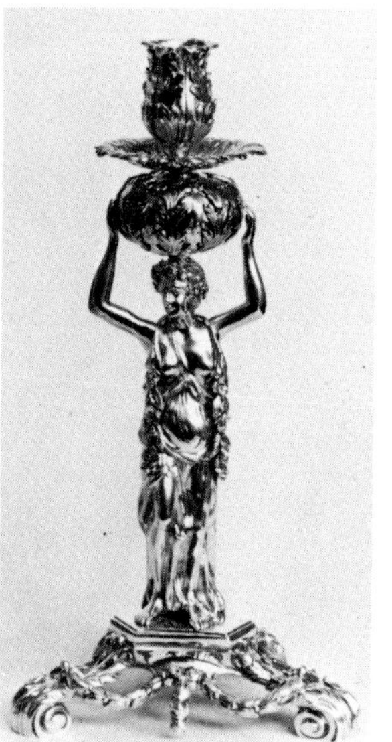

132

133

133. One of the most common types of Georgian candlesticks with shaped square bases decorated with shells at the angles. There are many variations of this type of candlestick which differ only slightly from one to the next, and therefore one must look closely to be certain that any pairs or sets of four match completely. In the 18th century it is quite likely that large houses would have had sets of up to twelve or more, and these could have been split through successive generations without careful matching of pairs. I have seen 20th century castings of this type of candlestick which bear the Georgian hallmarks, having come out quite clearly in the casting. The ground of the mark however does have slight pitting and one can usually detect a later casting.
c.1750 *Set of four £8,000 — £12,000*
Pair £4,000 — £6,000

134. One of a set of four in the same vein as 133 but with a 'sexfoil' shell base. These candlesticks are neither quite as popular nor as common as the square based variety, although the price varies more with quality and condition than style.
c.1755 *Set of four £8,000 — £12,000*
Pair £4,000 — £6,000

135. A slightly later version of the square based shell candlestick. Notice that the base does not spread quite so much, and the candlestick seems to stand rather more smartly to attention.
c.1760 *Set of four £8,000 — £12,000*
Pair £4,000 — £6,000

136. Yet another type without wells in the bases which appear less frequently after the first ten years of the reign of George III. Slightly taller and heavier than the preceding example.
c.1770 *Set of four £8,000 — £12,000*
Pair £4,000 — £6,000

136

135

134

137

137. An example from another pair in the same vein as the preceding set, but slightly more elaborately decorated and engraved with a coat of arms at the base. The corded borders on the sconce and bun-shaped knop will give a good indication of how worn this type of candlestick is. Occasionally you will find one of a pair slightly more worn than the other, and this is not desirable.
c.1770 *Pair £4,000 — £6,000*

138. One of the most popular designs of candlestick of this period, usually of very heavy quality — they vary in weight from 35oz. to 60oz. per pair. It is desirable to have the detachable nozzles, which complete the balance of the candlestick.
c.1760 *Pair £6,000 — £10,000*

139. Another type of cast square-based candlestick which is a popular design. The swirl fluting on the top of the stepped base is repeated on the shoulder and on the detachable nozzle. May weigh between 35oz. and 45 oz.
c.1770 *Pair £5,500 — £8,000*

140. One of a set of four circular based, cast candlesticks displaying Adam motifs with finely finished decoration. The bases are cast separately from the stems and a seam can be seen above the engraved crest where the two have been soldered together.
c.1775 *Set of four £17,500 — £30,000*
Pair £7,500 — £12,500

138

139

140

141. The first loaded candlesticks appear around this period. They are made from sheet, as were some of the late 17th century examples, and not cast. This one comes from a set of four which have fluted columns very similar to William and Mary candlesticks, but differ with heavy fluted square bases, and intricate open-work Corinthian capital sconces. Variations of this design and the following three examples will be found.

c.1765 — *Set of four £6,000 — £8,500*
Pair £2,750 — £4,000

142. Two candlesticks from similar pairs, one initialled, the other crested, with the maker's mark of John Carter, who specialised in candlesticks and salvers. At this time Sheffield, which was granted an assay office in 1773, was pioneering economical methods of manufacture, including stamping out candlesticks in sections which were then soldered together and filled with pitch or plaster of Paris. John Carter was a London silversmith who ordered numerous sets from Sheffield, and you will occasionally find sets where he has had them re-marked in London and signs of the original Sheffield hall-marks can be seen underneath. This was presumably because the silversmith's clients did not feel able to trust different hall-marks from those to which they were accustomed, Sheffield using a crown as the town mark instead of a leopard's head crowned.

c.1775 — *Pair £2,750 — £4,000*

143. An example made in Sheffield, similar to 142, with cluster column stem and papyrus sconce. The base is decorated with the familiar Adam features of rams' masks and husk swags within bold beaded borders. Because candlesticks like this and the preceding two examples are stamped from sheet and use far less silver than the cast type, they are often found in a worn state. The purchaser should examine raised points, like the nose of the ram's mask or the beading, to see if the silver has worn through to the loading.

c.1775 — *£2,750 — £4,000*

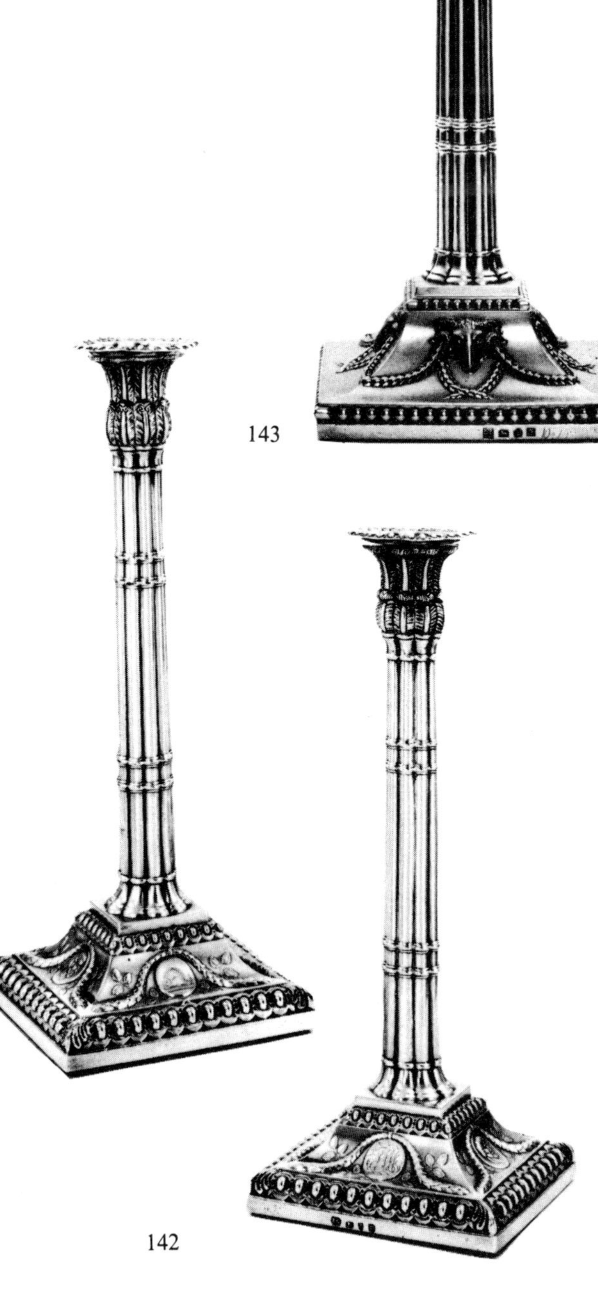

143

142

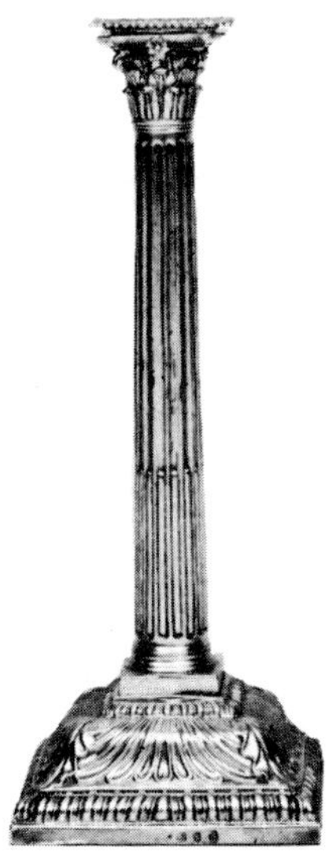

141

144

144. Another die-stamped type of candlestick made in Sheffield, but rather plainer and, perhaps, more pleasing than other examples. The pitch or plaster in the loaded candlesticks will be concealed at the base either by felt, usually green, or by a turned mahogany insert on the better quality examples. Because of the thinness of the metal, these loaded candlesticks should always be examined very carefully for any repair, usually done with soft lead solder. The use of hard solder would damage or break the candlestick unless it was completely unloaded. The higher heat necessary to apply it causes the loading to expand and distort the candlestick.
c.1780 *£2,750 — £4,000*

145

145. A pair of candlesticks by John Schofield, of very fine proportions and with pleasing circular bases engraved with contemporary armorials. A popular design.
c.1780 *Pair £5,000 — £9,000*

146. One of a set of four by the same maker and of similar design. The beading of this type of candlestick should be crisp and clear and not so worn so that the beads run into one another. The narrowest parts should be examined for any splits or strains as these can bend comparatively easily if mishandled. This type are usually not loaded, but do sometimes have mahogany inserts in the base (just to thoroughly confuse the issue!).
c.1780 *Set of four £12,500 — £20,000*
Pair £5,000 — £9,000

147. Heavy silver gilt candlesticks after a design by Robert Adam preserved at the Sir John Soane Museum and executed for William Beckford of Fonthill. The large pair of candlesticks weigh in excess of 50oz. and all are in first-class condition.
c.1780 *Large pair £30,000 — £50,000*
c.1810 *Smaller pairs £15,000 — £20,000*

146

147

148. One of a set of six Sheffield replicas of the Schofield type of candlestick which are loaded and will be made with less silver and die-stamped. The thinness of the gauge of silver can be seen on the edge of the base and, as these are made from thinner sheet, there is more likelihood of the silver wearing through to the loading at the raised points.
c.1785 — *Set of six £12,000 — £18,000*
Pair £3,000 — £4,500

149. One of a pair of very simple, Sheffield made, loaded candlesticks with circular bases. Again because of the thinness of the metal, they should be examined just below the sconce and above the base for any splits or lead solder repairs. A rather utilitarian pair of candlesticks displaying very little artistic design or craftsmanship of merit.
c.1800 — *Pair £2,500 — £3,500*

150. A Sheffield made loaded candlestick with circular base. More highly decorated borders of foliage and flowers are now commonplace and they are much more dumpy and less elegant in proportion than the pre-1800 candlesticks. They are not therefore so popular.
c.1810 — *Pair £2,250 — £3,250*

151. An even more elaborate type which will very often be worn through on the high relief decoration.
c.1815 — *Pair £2,250 — £3,250*

152. One of a pair of demi-figure candlesticks based on the 1750 type (see No. 131) and cast and constructed in the same way.
c.1810 — *Pair £5,000 — £8,000*

152

151

148

149

150

153

154

153. One of a set of four loaded candlesticks, again from the Sheffield factories, with high relief foliage and ribbed and fluted stems.
c.1820 *Set of four £5,000 — £9,000*
Pair £2,250 — £3,500

154. One of a pair of heavy cast and chased candlesticks, in the rococo manner. These, and variations of this type, were made by the firm of Craddock and Reid, sometimes incorporating motifs in the manner of Lamerie. Pairs of this type weigh between 60 and 80oz. and command high prices because of their fine quality.
c.1820 *Pair £12,000 — £16,000*

155. A set of four figure candlesticks of unusual design, cast and chased with two male and two female sticks, all having the same type of floral base and leaf decorated sconces and nozzles.
c.1820 *Set of four £20,000 — £30,000*
Pair £8,000 — £13,000

156. One of a pair of Sheffield made candlesticks based on mid-18th century Georgian originals, but differing from them by being loaded, and therefore stamped from sheet, rather than cast. Without even picking them up however one can tell from a distance that these are the later type by the fatter sconces and slightly shorter proportions. The same comments apply as with other loaded candlesticks. Examine carefully for repairs to the raised points.
c.1835 *Pair £1,500 — £2,500*

155

156

157. One of a set of four cast candlesticks with flat chased decoration of scrolls and foliage. This set was made by Robert Garrard, a popular maker and exponent of good quality craftsmanship.
c.1840 *Set of four £14,000 — £20,000*
Pair £6,500 — £9,500

158. A mid-19th century design showing that neo-Gothic style so typical of this period. This example is die stamped and loaded and made in Sheffield. 10ins. high.
c.1845 *Pair £1,800 — £2,500*

159. A pair of unusual figure candlesticks in the form of medieval knights holding a foliate branch supporting the candle sconce. This pair was made by Charles and George Fox and are parcel gilt (partly gilt).
c.1850 *Pair £6,500 — £9,500*

160. Another cast and chased example showing the popularity of figure candlesticks. This one of a native standing on a foliate and rocky base below a tree is more 'risqué' than one would normally expect in the Victorian era.
c.1860 *Pair £5,000 — £7,500*

160

158

157

159

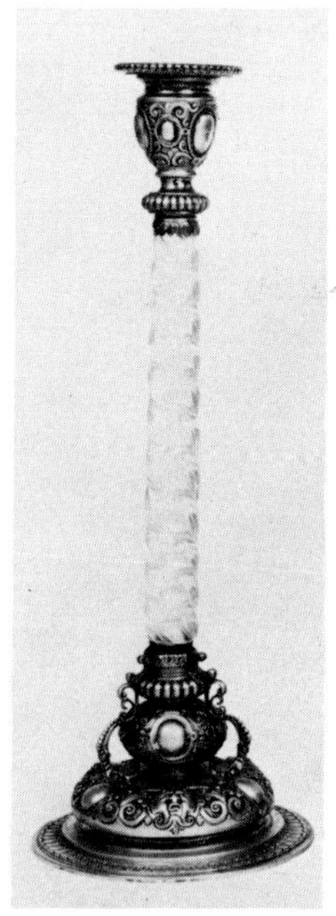

161

161. The unusual rock crystal stems of this candlestick (one of a pair) and the chased silver gilt mounts illustrate the revival of the interest in the Renaissance. Although the height at 12ins. looks impressive, the chasing is not of the highest quality and the overall design is weak.
c.1860 *Pair £1,500 — £2,250*

162. On the whole there were very few new designs forthcoming in candlesticks in the latter half of the 19th century. Many of them were based on earlier styles. This example with the maker's mark of Robert Garrard is cast in mid-18th century style and is of very good quality. A pair weigh 72oz., which is perhaps 50% more than the originals.
c.1875 *Pair £6,500 — £9,500*

163. Small candlesticks like this example, which is only 6ins. high, are based on late 17th century German and Dutch originals. They are die-stamped and loaded and of mediocre quality.
c.1885 *Set of four £2,000 — £3,000*

164. Yet another copy of an 18th century style, the originals would be c.1775. Again die stamped, seamed and loaded.
c.1890 *Pair £1,200 — £2,000*

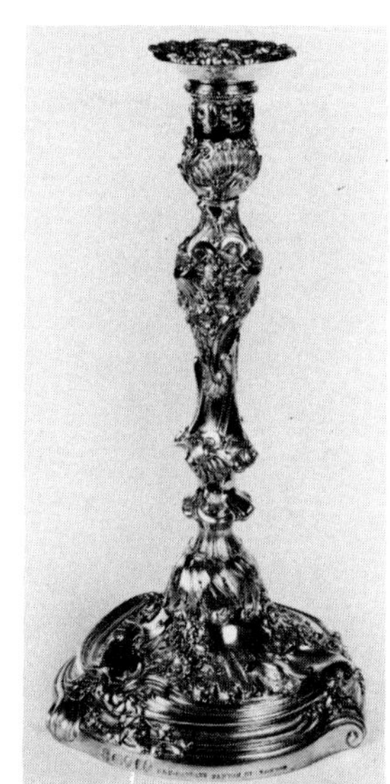

162

163

164

165. The oval base and lyre shaped stem of this candlestick is unusual but is copied from a George III design of c.1795. Sometimes originals are found in Sheffield plate, but at any date this design is comparatively rare.
c.1895 *Pair £1,200 — £2,000*

166. In the late Victorian and Edwardian periods a number of replicas of early examples were made, and it seems that the popularity of the candlestick returned temporarily. This oval based example (11ins.) is in the style of the 1790s and is loaded, as are the majority of these late candlesticks.
c.1900 *Pair £1,000 — £1,500*

167. A much smaller candlestick (6½ins.) in the style of the 1770s and 1780s, probably used on the desk or dressing table. This size is fairly popular as they go very well on a small dining table.
c.1910 *Pair £600 — £1,000*

168. Produced by James Dixon and Sons of Sheffield, candlesticks like this copy of an Arts and Crafts Movement design were mass-produced, but they will not command a price necessarily any higher than other loaded candlesticks despite their attractiveness.
c.1915 *£1,000 — £1,500*

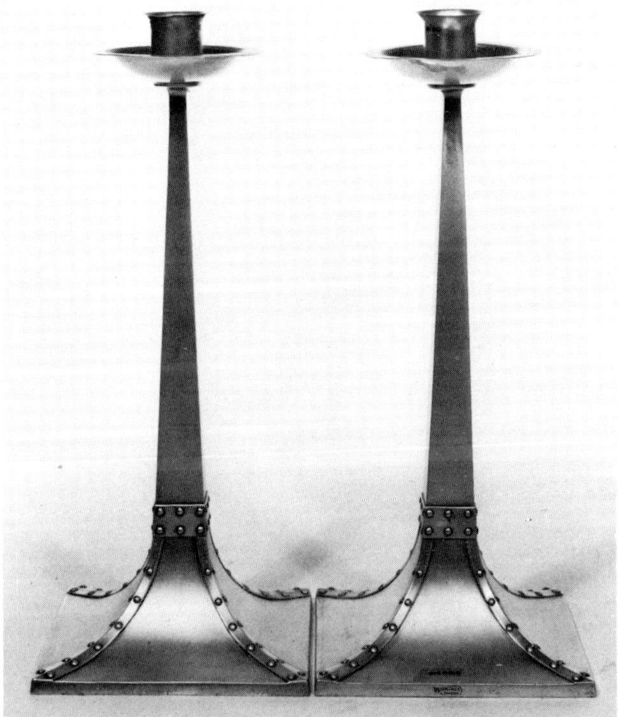

168

165

166

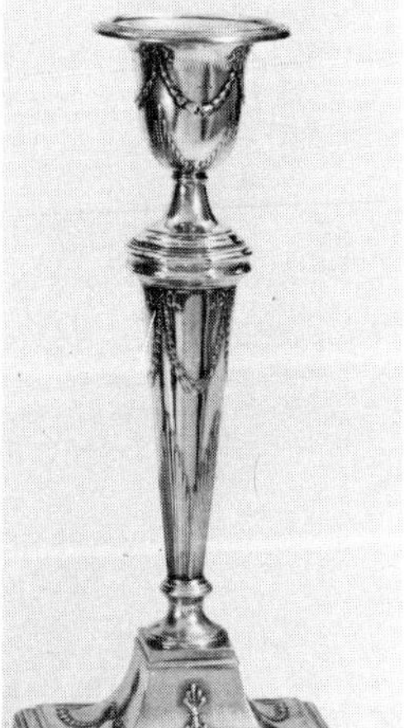

167

Candelabra

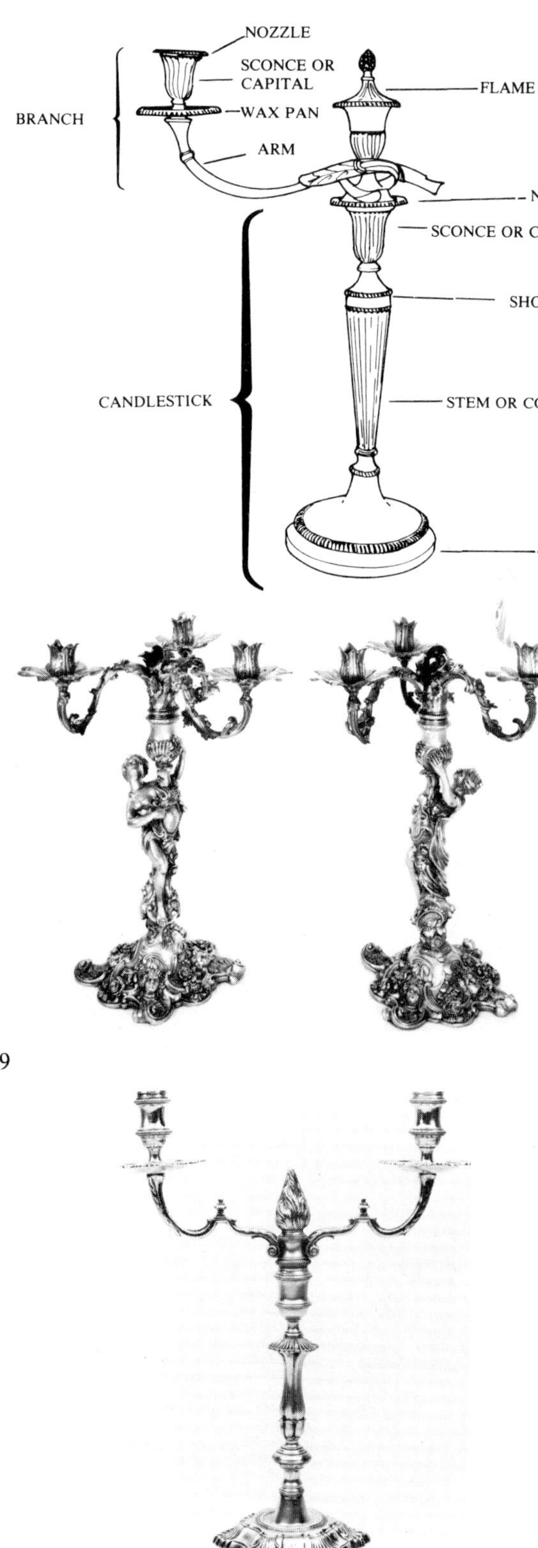

169

170

Although according to contemporary records candelabra existed in the seventeenth century and earlier, hardly any have survived dating before the mid-18th century. The bases normally all follow the form of contemporary candelsticks, which then have two, three or more light branches made with a bezel so that they fit into the candlestick sconce. They are comparatively rare and command prices up to three or more times that of a pair of candlesticks without branches. The drawing on the left shows the names given to the different parts of candlesticks and candelabra.

Hallmarks: the bases are marked in the same way as candlesticks (see Introduction, **Candlesticks,** p. 49). The branches should be fully marked, and this will usually be on the bezel. Sometimes sconces and drip pans unscrew, as well as the nozzles and flame finials being detachable. All these parts should be marked with at least the lion passant, and better still the maker's mark as well. After 1784 the monarch's head duty mark should appear. In the 19th century the nozzles usually will also have a date letter.

Condition: the same comments apply as for candlesticks (see p. 49). The branches should be examined for any repaired breaks or any damage.

Fakes: again, see **Candlesticks.** Because of the rarity of candelabra, branches are occasionally faked and put on to candlesticks, and this is usually done by removing the bezel of a candlestick nozzle and soldering it on to the base of a newly made branch. It is important to heed the statements about hallmarks on other parts of the branch, as stated above.

169. A pair of three light candelabra by Frederick Kandler, finely cast and chased in rococo manner. Very few candelabra pre-1770 have survived and certainly far fewer were made than pairs of candlesticks. Those that do survive are not always properly marked on the branches and it is often debatable whether they are original or not.
c.1745 *£60,000 — £120,000*

170. One of a pair of two light candelabra, the popular shell based candlestick with branches made to fit. The sconces on the branches will usually unscrew and the drip pans will be separate. There should be a lion passant mark on all these and a more complete set of marks on the central sleeve.
c.1760 *Pair £12,500 — £20,000*

171. A three light candelabrum extension to a loaded candlestick in Adam taste. The slender arms are not strong and will occasionally be found distorted or repaired. The sconces on this type do not usually unscrew. All the parts of the branch, except the detachable nozzle, will be soldered together and should therefore be marked on the sleeve and detachable nozzles.
c.1775 *Pair candelabra £8,000 — £12,000*
Pair candlesticks £2,750 — £4,000

172. Cast candlesticks with two light candelabrum branch. The design of the branch does not follow that of the candlestick as well as in the preceding example. The scrolling arms are rather weak for the design of the candlestick.
c.1775 *Pair candelabra £12,500 — £20,000*
Pair candlesticks £5,500 — £9,500

173. A circular based set of candlesticks and candelabra, the two light branches hardly following the design of the candlesticks at all. Be certain that they belong. If by a different maker and/or of a different date, the value will be greatly reduced.
c.1780 *Pair candelabra £12,500 — £20,000*
Pair candlesticks £5,000 — £8,500

174. A candelabrum by John Schofield. The branches have sconces matching the sconce on the candlestick, although of slightly smaller scale. They should be hallmarked on nozzles, sconces and drip pans, which unscrew, as well as the sleeve, which fits into the candlestick. A popular type, although this example is, perhaps, not quite bold enough.
c.1790 *Pair £17,500 — £27,500*

174

173

171

172

175

175. A heavier, larger and better example, usable as either two or three light, the central sconce having a removable flame finial. The base is engraved with contemporary initials below ducal coronet.
c.1800 *Pair £30,000 — £50,000*

176. Another of large size with fine acanthus leaf decoration. This example is made by Richard Cooke in the 'Schofield' manner.
c.1800 *Pair £35,000 — £60,000*

177. One of a pair displaying ancient Egyptian decoration made popular by the discoveries of archeologists at this time. Unusual designs can demand unusual prices! There is, however, a limited number of interested buyers for the majority of these pieces.
c.1805 *Pair £25,000 — £37,500*

178. Loaded circular based candlesticks with gadroon borders. The three light candelabrum branch has plain scroll arms and detachable central pineapple finial which can be used to convert to two light branches. The bases are engraved with contemporary armorials.
c.1810 *Pair candelabra £8,000 — £12,000*
Pair candlesticks £2,500 — £3,500

176

177

178

179. One of a superb, large and heavy pair of four light candelabra by Paul Storr. The branches will be cast in four separate sections with the central column being one, and the three arms being the others. The sconces, drip pans and nozzles are also made separately. They weigh in excess of 300oz. and will be found with hallmarks on every piece.
c.1815 *Pair £70,000 — £110,000*

180. Sheffield made candelabrum with loaded candlesticks, the branches chased with scrolling foliage. The drip pans are now made into a decorative feature, and will be soldered to the arms with the sconces. The nozzles of course remain detachable.
c.1820 *Pair candelabra £7,500 — £10,000*
Pair candlesticks £2,000 — £3,000

181. A four light candelabrum in rococo manner with entwined eagle stem. Extremely heavy. All parts are cast, the sconces and drip pans unscrewing and with detachable central eagle finial and nozzles. Worthy of the designs and craftsmanship of Paul de Lamerie, but made seven decades after his death.
c.1820 *Pair £30,000 — £50,000*

182. Another example in rococo manner with female bust terminals. Not as heavy or fine, but still very desirable and consequently expensive.
c.1825 *Pair £25,000 — £35,000*

183. An impressive nine light candelabrum from Garrards, all cast and chased and weighing a whacking 300oz. and almost 3ft. high. They are based on the early 18th century French designs incorporating strapwork and masks, a style which dominated European silversmiths' work to a remarkable degree until 1730.
c.1860 *Single £10,000 — £15,000*
Pair £30,000 — £50,000

183

182

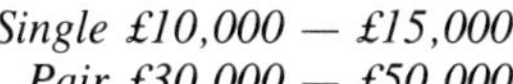

179

180

181

184. One of a pair of late Victorian candelabra in George III style with Adam features of rams' masks and urns. Very few pairs of candelabra are found between the late Georgian and late Victorian eras. As with silver candlesticks they were relegated to the second division by the introduction of lamps and other methods of lighting. Silver plated examples are, however, common at this period.
c.1875 *Pair £6,000 — £10,000*

185. This candelabrum, again in early 18th century taste, is rather bottom heavy and the branches look a little spidery. It is however silver gilt and of good quality. It has the maker's mark of Hunt and Roskell, successors to Storr and Mortimer. All this will add up to a high price for a pair, which will weigh some 220oz.
c.1880 *Single £6,000 — £10,000*
Pair £17,500 — £30,000

186. An individual design, but not well balanced and not of the high quality of the preceding examples. One of a pair made for Mappin and Webb, the candelabra are not entirely cast, but are mainly die stamped and loaded. When the branches are of slender gauge it is comparatively easy for them to become bent through mishandling.
c.1900 *Pair £4,000 — £6,000*

187. One of a pair of three light candelabra by Omar Ramsden with fixed candle branches. An individual design which will command a much higher price than contemporary mass-produced examples.
c.1910 *Pair £20,000 — £35,000*

188. One of an unusual pair of small candelabra, designed by A.E. Harvey. He perhaps got the idea from watching children on a seesaw! Only 6½ins. high and weighing a total of 18oz. for the pair.
c.1935 *£900 — £1,800*

184

185

187

188

186

Chamber Candlesticks

Silver chamber candlesticks first made their appearance in the seventeenth century, although examples in this period are now extremely rare. They were certainly made in sets and it is likely that a household would have as many, or more, chamber candlesticks as table candlesticks, although they need not necessarily have been made in silver. Today however the chamber candlestick is more rare than the table candlestick and it is quite likely that, with the advent of oil and gas lamps, many of them were considered to be obsolete and melted down.

The majority have a circular pan of about 4½ins. or slightly more in diameter, which served as a drip tray. This type of candlestick was used for lighting one to bed and therefore, because of the movement and draught, a large drip pan was needed. The earliest examples have straight handles, at first of flattened form, and later of tubular or hollow form. By 1720 this type of handle was superseded by the flying scroll handle or ring handle. This type of handle does however also occur at an earlier date. The earliest types occasionally have pierced sconces which are partly a decorative feature and partly for prizing out the candle stub. Later in the 18th century the form of the sconce is very similar to that on table candlesticks. Some later examples were made to hold glass funnels similar to those on oil lamps.

From the mid-eighteenth century onwards they were nearly all made with companion conical extinguishers, which either slot into the handle or an aperture on the side of the sconce. Those made to have glass funnels would have a long thin handle with ring finger hole so that it could reach right down into the funnel. Also from the mid-eighteenth century the majority had detachable nozzles, and occasionally, from the end of the eighteenth century onwards, they were made with open-work stems to receive snuffers of the scissor type.

Hallmarks: up to 1720 they are often marked on the top side of the pan in a straight or curved line, and after this date, usually on the underside. Matching nozzles and extinguishers should be hallmarked with the lion passant and maker's mark and after 1784 with the monarch's head duty mark. If you find an example without marks on these pieces then the price should be adjusted accordingly (– 10%).

Condition: good examples of chamber candlesticks are greatly outnumbered by those that have survived in poor condition. They are often split, patched or repaired around the borders and handle sockets, which is no doubt the result of the constant wear they must have received from being cleaned every day. No doubt they were also occasionally dropped or damaged whilst making the trip to the bedroom by someone who had finished a good evening's eating and drinking!

Fakes: occasionally the small taperstick of chamber candlestick form, which would have originally have sat on the centre of an inkstand, is sold as a separate item. Whilst this is not actually a fake, one should not be conned into believing that it is a rare miniature. I have seen one or two mid-eighteenth century chamber candlesticks which have been made from small circular epergne dishes by the addition of a sconce and handle. These are not easy to detect, but look for any difference in colour or wear of the silver between pan, sconce and handle.

189

189. A James II example with very basic circular pan, cylindrical sconce and flat handle. Very utilitarian and quite light. Could almost be made from copper! This type is often in rather poor condition as the design is not capable of withstanding the ravages of time.
c.1685 *Normal condition £1,750 — £2,500*
Very good condition £5,000 — £8,000

190

190. A solid example with gadroon border and lobed sconce, fitted at one side with a small loop to take the extinguisher. This was probably added later, as the majority of chamber candlesticks did not have conical extinguishers until the latter half of the 18th century.
c.1700 *£3,500 — £5,500*

191

191. A very solid example, as is most Queen Anne silver, this one engraved with the royal armorials, which will of course add to the value. It sits on three small button feet and has a cast hollow handle, fairly elongated in proportion.
c.1710 *£3,500 — £5,500*

192. A somewhat similar example, but now with rather shorter handle.
c.1720 *£2,500 — £4,000*

193. A plain, circular example with initialled, flying scroll handle, without the button feet of 190-192, but this time on a rim foot.
c.1720 *£1,500 – £2,750*

194. One of a pair, still with the plain circular pans, engraved with contemporary earl's crest, which is a nice additional feature. Again with flying scroll handles, which have now become the norm, and campana shaped sconces.
c.1735 *Pair £5,000 — £7,500*

192

194

193

195. An unusual rococo chamber candlestick, chased and modelled with a cherub holding a foliate sconce. Exceptional design and therefore of high value.
c.1740 *£8,000+*

196. One of a pair of chamber candlesticks with conical extinguishers, the vase shaped sconces now with detachable nozzles and the simple circular pans with reeded borders. Look for repairs at the handles and where the sconces are soldered on. As with other silver of this period, the thinness of the metal made possible by new manufacturing processes means they have a shorter life than earlier examples.
c.1780 *Pair £3,250 — £4,250*

197. A similar pair, but with beaded borders. Note the handles and extinguishers have some damage; the finial on one extinguisher is broken off completely. This could reduce the price of the pair by half compared with good examples.
c.1780 *Pair (in good condition) £3,250 — £4,250*

195

196

197

198. A chamber candlestick with both conical extinguisher and a pair of snuffers. It is very rare to find snuffers with a chamber candlestick, although one will often find examples with open-work stems to receive these.
c.1790 *£1,500 — £2,750*

199. One of a pair with gadroon shell and foliate borders and open-work stems, but no snuffers and engraved with a fine contemporary armorial. The extravagances of the Regency period were reflected in the production of heavier quality silver, and therefore examples from this period are usually found in better condition than Adam examples.
c.1815 *Pair £3,250 — £4,750*

200. One of a set of four with octafoil pans, again with open-work stems, but no snuffers.
c.1825 *Set of four £5,000 — £7,000*
Pair £2,250 — £3,250

201. An example with shaped circular and fluted pan, almost looking like an early 18th century strawberry dish. Look for splits in the flutes near the rim.
c.1840 *£750 — £1,250*

198

199

200

201

202. One of a Victorian pair in late Georgian style of very simple design with gadroon borders.
c.1850 *Pair £1,500 — £2,500*

203. An un usual chamber candlestick formed from silver modelled shells, not particularly attractive, but quite rare.
c.1850 *£1,000 — £1,500*

203

202

Snuffers & Stands

Snuffers, which are of scissor form, were used for trimming wicks which had not burnt down with the candles. There are only a very few snuffers in existence prior to 1700 and, by the early nineteenth century, the innovation of the more refined candles on which the wick burnt down with the candle meant that they were no longer needed. They all have a chamber between the handle and the point, which cuts and traps the unwanted wick. Some types have an inset of steel, as silver cannot easily be given a lasting sharp edge. Late eighteenth century types have a spring and guillotine action so that as the scissors are closed, the guillotine on spring lifts from the centre of the chamber and snaps down at the final closing of the scissors.

Hallmarks: both stands and snuffers should be fully hallmarked, although they rarely bear the same maker's mark as they were made by different specialist makers.

Condition: the handles of the snuffers should be examined for any breaks and repairs. Some later examples have often lost their three button feet, and occasionally the tips are bent or broken. Snuffers' trays should be examined for erased crests or armorials and any splits at the borders, handles or feet.

Fakes: I have never come across a pair of snuffers which has been faked. Snuffers' trays are sometimes found with added handles or feet, and occasionally converted into toast racks or small inkstands. See also under **Miscellaneous, Spoon Trays** (p. 356).

204

204. One of the earliest hallmarked pair of snuffers and tray in existence, the tray made from sheet silver and embossed and chased with foliage in typical Caroline style. The armorials on the tray are slightly dubious as they are engraved in a different style to those on the snuffers and, as is quite often the case, these two pieces may have been married later, and the engraver has matched the coat of arms. Snuffers and trays are usually made by different specialist makers so that, although the hallmarks may be for the same year, the maker's marks are likely to be different.

c.1675 *£17,500 — £25,000*

205. Snuffers and stand with cut corner square base in the style of candlesticks of this period. The container for the snuffers has a hole in the base for the point of the blades to drop through.

c.1700 *£12,000 — £16,000*

206. Another example with circular base otherwise of very similar construction to 205. Usually rather lighter and not so popular.

c.1710 *£9,000 — £15,000*

207. A Queen Anne snuffers' tray which would have had companion snuffers of the same type as 205, 206 and 208. This time however the decoration and style resembles that of a contemporary chamber candlestick rather than a table candlestick. There are four button feet and a baluster side handle. The coat of arms is contemporary, but rather worn.

c.1710 *£3,250 — £5,500*

With snuffers £6,000 — £9,000

205

206

207

208. Another example with diamond cut octagonal base, this time with attractively engraved contemporary armorials, which is an added bonus. The container for the snuffers is slightly shaped to follow the line of the base and the stem. This design is one of the most popular.
c.1720 *£15,000 — £20,000*

209. This illustration produces some evidence that perhaps all snuffers on stands of candlestick base type had their companion candlesticks. These are all made by the same maker, Francis Turner, and are hallmarked 1722. It is interesting to compare proportions and it can be seen that the base of the snuffer stand is somewhat smaller than the candlestick.
1722 *Snuffers and stand £15,000 — £20,000*
The set £27,500 — £40,000

210. A shaped oblong example with flying scroll handle like those found on chamber candlesticks. The main tray is made from one piece of silver with the moulded border wire soldered on, as are the handle and feet.
c.1740 *£1,250 — £2,000*
With snuffers £3,000 — £5,000

211. The snuffers' tray, although remaining comparatively simple, now has a gadroon border, but the snuffers become much more decorative with scroll cut and chased handles. Notice however that this pair is suffering from wear and tear. Its small feet are rather bent and the tip of the scissors looks a bit like Concorde coming in to land.
c.1765 *£2,000 — £3,000*
Snuffers only £500 — £750
Tray only £900 — £1,250

211

210

208

209

212

212. By this date bright-cut engraving was used and the snuffers' trays no longer have feet or handles, in this case just a shell grip at either end. Much less silver is used and therefore if subjected to any great amount of use, they are likely to be in poor condition.

c.1785 *£1,800 — £2,750*
Snuffers only £500 — £750
Tray only £750 — £1,100

213. The elongated shape of the snuffers' tray is delicately treated with bright-cut bands and pierced motifs. One of a pair, with both pairs of snuffers illustrated. They have undoubtedly been together for a long time as they bear the same crest, which is certainly 18th century. The bright-cut decoration does not however match that on the tray.

c.1790 *One pair of snuffers and tray only £1,800 — £2,750*
Snuffers only £500 — £750
Tray only £750 — £1,100

214. An oval snuffers' tray of good quality with bound reeded border and foliate grips. The snuffers are decorated with shells within gadroon borders and, although probably intended to go with the tray, they do not really have any common features of decoration.

c.1810 *£2,250 — £3,250*
Tray only £800 — £1,500
Snuffers only £500 — £750

213

214

Taperesticks and Wax Jacks

Tapersticks, averaging around 5ins. high, are miniature table candlesticks used to hold a wax taper and all the comments made in the introduction to **Candlesticks,** p. 49, apply here as well. They are practically unknown prior to the Queen Anne period, and are in any case much more rare than candlesticks, although they usually appear in singles rather than in pairs. If you do come across a pair they are likely to be almost as heftily priced as a pair of contemporary candlesticks.

Wax jacks appear from c.1775 (see No. 225) and consist of a circular base with thin stem or horizontal bar around which a coil of wax with integral wick is placed. These are occasionally faked by adding a superstructure to a wine funnel stand or some other small dish. They can be difficult to detect as the mark on an original one will only occur on the base. Do however look carefully for any unusual or poor construction.

218

215. A very early example based on the candlestick shape of the period with cast stem and raised base.
c.1685 *£3,000 — £4,750*

216. One of a pair of Queen Anne tapersticks very similar to the design of a candlestick of the same type (see No. 115), the only difference being that the sconce is slightly more elongated and they are, of course, much smaller.
c.1710 *Pair £9,000 — £15,000*

217. An example of the George I period, cast, and the design following that of the equivalent candlestick (see No. 121). Tapersticks of this period are usually about half the height of a candlestick and an eighth to a quarter of the weight.
c.1720 *£2,000 — £3,000*

218. A George I taperstick.
c.1725 *£2,000 — £3,000*

217

215

216

219. A George II example, based on a popular candlestick design.
c.1740 *£1,250 — £2,000*

220. A rare figure taperstick in the form of a harlequin. I do not know of any candlesticks of this design. This type of taperstick was produced over a period of about ten years, mainly by John and William Cafe.
c.1745 *£1,500 — £2,750*

221. Another taperstick with no equivalent candlestick, of a female holding a daisy in one hand and a foliate sconce in the other.
c.1745 *£1,800 — £3,000*

222. The taperstick is again of candlestick form, this time with detachable nozzle.
c.1760 *£1,250 — £2,250*

223. A cast example engraved with a crest at the stem.
c.1770 *£1,250 — £2,000*

219

220

222

221

223

224. One of a pair with lobed and gadroon borders, again cast. The design is not as clear cut as the preceding example.
c.1775 *Pair £3,000 — £4,500*

225. Wax jacks are fairly rare, and although not always as attractive as tapersticks, can command a price equal to, or above, that of tapersticks. The coiled wax is held by a scissor action drip pan. There is also a small chained extinguisher.
c.1780 *£1,500 — £2,250*

226. A loaded, stamped and chased taperstick. As with candlesticks of this type it is made in Sheffield.
c.1820 *£750 — £1,250*

227. Probably the latest date at which you will find an individual taperstick, although they are found on inkstands right up to the end of the 19th century. This example is stamped, again loaded, and has chased decoration.
c.1840 *£400 — £800*

228. There are however a few individually designed tapersticks in existence, such as this example with a figure stem with an outsized wicker basket on his back to form the sconce. Only 3½ins. high, but the unusual design will command a high price.
c.1845 *£1,000 — £2,000*

228

227

224

225

226

Cruets

229

The earliest cruet frames contained three casters and two bottles and are not found before 1700. Occasionally one finds two-bottle frames for oil and vinegar, but later in the eighteenth century the number of receptacles could be as many as eight or ten, and these would have contained a variety of contemporary sauces such as soy, ketchup, tarragon, etc., and may have had little silver labels on the bottles which described the contents.

Hallmarks: the forms vary so much that there are no hard and fast rules, but the main stand should certainly be fully marked, and if the framework and/or the handle detaches, these should also be marked. After 1784 the silver mounts on the cut glass bottles should also be hallmarked, but before this date some are and some are not.

Condition: there are so many areas to examine that it is difficult to list everything, but always remove all the bottles from the stand and look carefully at the stand itself. Then examine each bottle individually. The glass can so often be badly chipped or cracked and sometimes bottles are ground down, stoppers have been damaged, and feet occasionally have had silver rims applied.

Fakes: the most common fake one is likely to come across is a cruet converted from a silver wine coaster, made by adding a handle and four small feet (see 234).

229. A two bottle, oil and vinegar cruet with octagonal bottle holders. The silver bottle mounts are rarely hallmarked at this date. The frame would be marked on the underside.
c.1735 *£8,000 — £12,000*

230

230. A so-called Warwick cruet with three vase-shaped casters and two cut-glass bottles. Note the applied disc on the stand is finely engraved with the same armorials as the casters. Ten years later this oval disc becomes a rococo cartouche as shown on No. 231. The stand should be marked on the underside and on the handle, which screws in (you can just see part of the thread protruding). The lion passant can be seen on the handle.
c.1735 *£9,000 — £15,000*

231. A slightly later but similar example, one of the main differences being the cast rococo cartouche applied to the side of the frame. It is also slightly smaller in size and the quality is inferior, therefore making it lighter perhaps by 10-15oz. The pierced covers are a giveaway as on this set they look obviously less sturdy without the moulded pillars between each panel of chasing. The handle on this type of frame screws into the centre of the base, sometimes with a nut on the underside.
c.1745 *£5,500 — £9,000*

232. Another frame which an enthusiastic 19th century chaser has embellished. Note that the surface is almost completely covered with a tight mass of flowers, leaves and scrolls. The covers have even had small flowers applied later. This later embellishment halves the value.
c.1750 *£3,000 — £4,000*

233. The frame is now smaller in comparison to the casters and bottles, and the handle is not as tall. The overall weight of silver will therefore be less; the casters are very attractively chased with curved fluting which will also act as a strengthener to the design. One bottle is quite a lot shorter than the other — this is not by design but because the top has been damaged and ground down. This could reduce the price by as much as 10%.
c.1760 *£5,000 — £8,000*

233

231

232

234. In the introduction to this section the possibility of a cruet frame being made from a wine coaster by the addition of a handle and feet was discussed. This example is of wine coaster form, but much larger, and the applied feet and handle will bear maker's mark and lion passant. You can also see the same marks on the rim of the base. This particular cruet frame has a silver covered base on which the full set of marks appear. An extra, rather attractive feature is the engraved names on the bottles. The silver casters are now replaced by glass ones with silver tops, and one is pierced, whilst the other is left blind. Ideally the covers to these bottles should be hallmarked, but unfortunately they rarely are. It is however usually possible to tell whether or not they are contemporary by the dull rather than bright colour, as well as chips and sharpness which will be missing on the old.
c.1770 *£1,200 — £2,250*

235. One of a pair of unusual oil and vinegar cruets of quite small size, measuring only some 5 or 6ins. across. They are decorated in Adam style with goats' masks and beaded borders. The lids and rim mounts on the bottles still have a feel of the rococo and are not so formal as the other decoration.
c.1775 *Pair £3,000 — £5,000*

234

236

235

236. This type of oval cruet with pierced and bright-cut decoration was popular for about a ten year period. This example is in particularly poor condition. There are three bottles missing and one of the caster tops has been replaced. The cruet is hallmarked 1788 and bears the maker's mark of Hester Bateman. Although all the defects cannot be seen in the illustration, it is clear that the left hand foot is damaged and repaired and that the hallmarks are somewhat rubbed. A piece in this condition, even though it is by a noted maker, would sell for no more than a quarter to half the price of a very good example.

1788 — *In this condition £450 — £650*
A good example £1,250 — £2,250
A good example by Hester Bateman £2,000 — £3,500

237. An oval cruet with reeded borders and fluted panel feet. The silver mounts on the cut-glass bottles should all be hallmarked. Note that some of the bottles have silver rims applied to the feet which are not contemporary, but have been put there because the feet have become chipped. The upper framework will be bolted to the base underneath the paw feet and there should be hallmarks on both these parts.

c.1790 — *£2,500 — £3,750*

238. These two heavy cruet frames, which were undoubtedly made to go together, are by Paul Storr and incorporate the typical gadroon and foliate motifs used in the Regency period. The supports to the bottle holders are unusually modelled as leopards' heads sitting on top of a leg. The left hand example will have been used for oil, vinegar, mustard and pepper, whilst the right hand one will have contained a variety of more exotic sauces.

c.1810 — *By Paul Storr £15,000 — £25,000*
By another £7,500 — £12,500

239. A pair of functional, oblong cruet frames, more usually found as single examples. The gadroon, shell and foliate motifs are still in evidence.

c.1815 — *Pair £5,000 — £8,000*
Single £2,250 — £3,750

239

238

237

240. A much smaller, square based cruet with oil and vinegar bottles and two mustard pots, again constructed in the same way. The bent lid and chipped bottles will reduce the price.
c.1825 *£1,000 — £1,750*

241. A seven bottle cruet with doyly pierced sides to the frame. Look carefully for any damage to the piercing. The four bottle mounts should be marked.
c.1840 *£1,500 — £2,250*

242. An oblong example with eight bottles, the upper framework bolted to the floral chased base. All component parts should be hallmarked.
c.1850 *£1,500 — £2,500*

243. Another eight bottle example, this time the shaped oblong base engraved with formal foliage. The handle and upper framework are decorated in the neo-Gothic style, a popular mid-Victorian feature.
c.1860 *£1,500 — £2,250*

240

241

242

243

Casters

Casters do not really become common household articles until the late seventeenth century, since when they have been made in varying sizes and designs, usually either for sugar or for pepper. The word 'caster' is self explanatory in that these vessels were used for casting the contents over food. Occasionally one will find it spelt 'castor', which is a survival of the old spelling.

Hallmarks: the majority of casters are hallmarked in a group on the base, although some seventeenth and early eighteenth century examples, and also late eighteenth and early nineteenth century examples, are sometimes marked on the side of the body. Covers should invariably have a maker's mark and lion passant. If this is not visible, then one should be very cautious.

Condition: examine all surfaces for erasure of crests, initials or coats of arms. Where a caster has a foot, look to see that this has not been pushed up into the body by someone banging it down on the table too hard. Often a reinforcing plate will have been applied where this sort of damage has been restored. The pierced covers are particularly vulnerable to damage, and these should also be carefully examined.

Fakes: I illustrate (above right) a large sugar caster which is trying to look like a late seventeenth century example, but it measures nearly 8ins. high, which would be rare as most vary between 3ins. and 6½ins. and the proportions of the body to the cover are wrong for a caster of that date. This piece has hallmarks for Newcastle, 1770, which are perfectly authentic, but the body of the caster has been made from a tankard which has had the handle removed and the sides modified to a straight cylindrical shape. The cover of this piece did not have a mark, but I have seen examples where a fake lion passant has been stamped on the outer edge. The piercing is unlike any existing late seventeenth century example, and the fact that the piece has George III hallmarks should scream of fake straight away. Another type of fake, slightly more difficult to detect, is on casters or peppers purporting to date from between 1780 and 1800, which have square pedestal feet. I have seen examples where hallmarks from a spoon have been let in to one side of the base. Be very cautious if you see one marked in this way.

A Caster made from a tankard dated 1770, which has had the handle removed and the sides modified.

244

244. A fine large caster with unusual ribbed cylindrical body. The cover has a 'bayonet lock' which is typical of this period. The term 'bayonet lock' refers to two lugs on either side of the cover. These slot through the wire at the rim and are then turned to secure the lid. The cover has applied cut card-work, a very popular feature, and the foot is pierced and engraved, giving a delicate effect.
c.1680 *£12,500 — £20,000*

245

245. A plainer caster of the same type but approximately half the size. These are sometimes referred to as lighthouse casters because of their shape. This one again has a bayonet lock cover, the interior of which has been fitted with a sleeve to cover up the majority of the large holes which are impractical for modern day usage. Granulated sugar is comparatively modern. In the 17th and 18th centuries, with crushed loaf sugar, the large holes were necessary.
c.1690 *£4,500 — £6,500*

246. A set of three casters with the typical late 17th century lobing and fluting more commonly found on porringers. As can be seen, there are four hallmarks on the body, and there should be a maker's mark and leopard's head erased on the cover.
c.1700 *Set of three £12,500 — £20,000*

247. Another set of three with very finely pierced covers, displaying vases of flowers and birds below the popular cut card work at the finial. These are heavier than the preceding set because they are from the Queen Anne period when a thicker gauge of silver was used. This was partly because of the need to counteract the less durable Britannia standard enforced at that time..
c.1705 *Set of three £25,000 — £40,000*

247

246

248. The baluster caster now appears. This example has a band of fluting below the girdle, which is not very often found on casters.
c.1705 *£2,750 — £4,500*

249. The most common type of Queen Anne caster. Although Charles Adam almost had a monopoly in making these, this particular set was made by Richard Greene. The covers, still with 'bayonet lock', are usually in two planes of different design, a feature not commonly found at any other period.
c.1705 *Set of three £7,500 — £12,500*

250. A cylindrical caster, no longer with bayonet lock. The cover on this example extends right down to the girdle below the armorial, partly covering the main body. The hallmarks on this type will be found on the part of the body which is under the cover, whilst the cover marks are usually on the outside. Few of this type are extant and one can only assume that the design was impractical; it certainly was more expensive than other designs as additional silver was required.
c.1710 *£3,000 — £5,000*

251. A 'kitchen' pepper, so called because of the scroll handle on the side. The octagonal shape is comparatively rare and much sought after.
c.1710 *£1,500 — £2,500*

251

250

248

249

252

252. A plain, cylindrical kitchen pepper with slip-on low domed cover. Rather more common than the preceding type. They are made from a sheet of silver which is curved round and seamed under the handle. The base and border wires are then added.
c.1720 *£800 — £1,500*

253. A set of three heavy octagonal casters. At approximately 40oz. they are about twice the weight of 254 at 18oz.-25oz. and are made by David Willaume, a maker of good repute. The covers now have a bezel which fits inside the body and this is where you should find the maker's mark and lion passant, the bodies being marked underneath.
c.1720 *Set of three £25,000 — £40,000*

254. Another set of three octagonal casters of the more usual design. Thomas Bamford was one of the main exponents of these. Occasionally you will find examples by him with maker's mark only, which means he has avoided paying duty on the silver, which at 6d. an ounce was worth avoiding.
c.1725 *Set of three £8,000 — £14,000*

253

254

255. A baluster pepper with 'bun' shaped cover. This will be hallmarked on the base and should have a hallmark inside the lid. If the lid is not marked the likelihood is that it is a later replacement. If the lid is marked, it can add 50% to the price. This design is popular with collectors as at 2½ins.-3ins. it is a convenient size for modern day usage.
c.1730 *£550 — £750*

256. A pair of vase shaped casters, the left hand example with 'blind' cover, which was used for dry mustard. The mustard pot as we know it today did not become popular until the last quarter of the 18th century (see **Mustard Pots**, p. 96).
c.1730 *Pair £2,250 — £3,500*
Single £1,200 — £1,800

257. This vase shaped caster by Paul de Lamerie, like the majority of his work, is of very heavy quality. The subject does not allow him to express his craftsmanship other than in the fine piercing of the cover.
c.1735 *£15,000 — £25,000*

258. The baluster caster returns to popularity and these examples have covers typically pierced in alternate panels of diaper and scroll work. A popular type of which the main exponent was the maker Samuel Wood.
c.1745 *Set of three £3,500 — £5,500*

258

257

256

255

259

259. A set of three with chased floral sprays and curved flutes. Casters were rarely decorated in this way but, in this case, the rarity does not add to the value. A lot of the plain casters of this period were chased in the 19th century but, compared with the present examples, the later decorated ones would be more fully covered with flowers and scrolls (see 232). The cover pierced in spiral panels is a new feature which develops at this date.
c.1755 *Set of three £3,000 — £5,000*

260. A set of three baluster examples with similarly pierced covers to No. 259. Note that the right hand example, although having the same design on the cover, is pierced with much smaller holes. It is probable that this was originally a 'blind' caster for dry mustard. The later piercing does not necessarily detract from value. The writhen finials and corded borders are additional decorative features to a plain design.
c.1760 *Set of three £3,500 — £5,500*

261. Vase shaped casters like this did not appear much after 1765, as the baluster examples became more popular.
c.1760 *£500 — £700*

262. An unusual set of three casters in Adam style with rams' masks and husk swags. The left hand example is 'blind' and this is as late as I have seen this feature. They are hallmarked on the foot rim and therefore one should examine carefully as occasionally the marks from a spoon or fork may be let in. Look for a seam on either side of the mark. These examples however are absolutely right.
c.1770 *Set of three £5,000 — £8,500*

260

261

262

263. A typical baluster caster from this period. It has a much taller foot than most of the preceding examples and is almost a cross between a pure baluster and a vase shaped example. The cover is pierced in the most simple fashion with lattice work engraving, and one can see one of the hazards of mass-production; the quality becomes less than perfect as the piercing is not centred in the lattice work anywhere near as well as on No. 261.
c.1785 *£400 — £600*

264. From 1790 onwards silver casters become much smaller and individual examples are not so common. Larger glass casters, forming part of a cruet set in a frame, take over. This small vase shaped caster is no bigger than an egg cup and sometimes one will find an egg cup with a lid made to fit. There should be a mark on the cover; if there is not, leave well alone.
c.1800 *£250 — £425*

265. Another variation of the smaller casters found at this period, in this case presumably made for the officers' mess of the Northampton Militia. The body is almost a pure egg shape.
c.1800 *£400 — £600*

265

264

263

266

266. A pair of owl pepperettes and mustard pot *en suite*. These novelty designs are extremely popular today and are quite often made by Charles and George Fox.
c.1855 *Set of three £3,000 — £5,000*

267. Another novelty pepperette in the form of Mr. Punch with his dog, Toby. Impressively cast and chased and of very good quality, but only 3½ins. in height.
c.1875 *£1,000 — £2,000*

268. These two birds have detachable and pierced heads to form pepperettes and bear the maker's mark of J.B. Hennell, who was responsible for the manufacture of a number of models and novelty pieces at this date.
c.1880 *Pair £1,200 — £2,200*

269. This time a pig is the subject with detachable head and pierced snout.
c.1880 *£800 — £1,400*

267

268

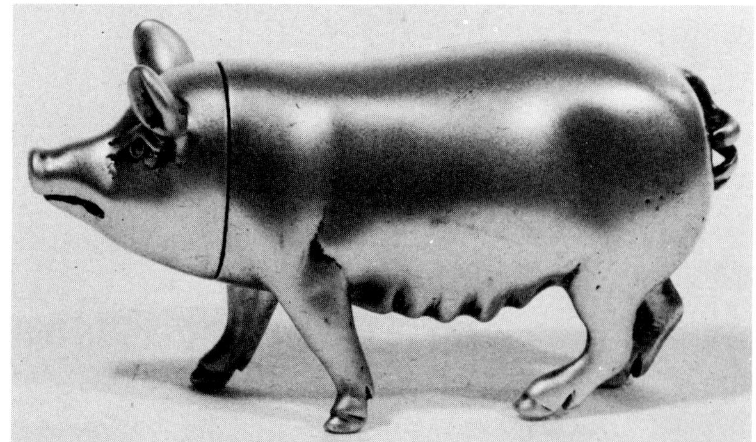

269

270. A pair of hares, rather more cleverly modelled in two differing positions. This is the quality and inspiration one expects from a firm like Hunt and Roskell and the price will be higher than the preceding ones, even though they are later in date and only a little bit heavier.
c.1890 *Pair £1,600 — £3,000*

271. The revival of the use of sugar casters in the late 19th century produced, on the whole, a number of fairly boring designs adapting earlier ideas. This lighthouse shape can also be found with floral and scroll decoration. This example is of particularly large size, measuring 10ins. high, and weighing 19oz.
c.1890 *Per oz. £35 — £50*

272. This rather cumbersome pair of casters is modelled on a mid-18th century Lamerie design. Although a lot of silver is used, the decoration is not of the high quality one would have expected in 1740. They are cast and chased from an original but the treatment of the decoration is very coarse compared with the masterly work of Paul de Lamerie, Paul Crespin and others.
c.1910 *Per oz. £50 — £80*

273. Another sugar caster of mass-produced design with the maker's mark of James Deakin and Sons of Sheffield, but assayed in Chester. A Chester hallmark does not add substantially to the value at this date, although it certainly conjures up a more romantic image than that of Sheffield!
c.1910 *Per oz. £35 — £50*

274. An Edinburgh hallmarked caster decorated with 'odeon' motifs and with a hammer finish. A stark design using graduated stalactites and stalagmites which were influenced by architectural designs of the period.
c.1935 *Per oz. £35 — £50*

270

271

272

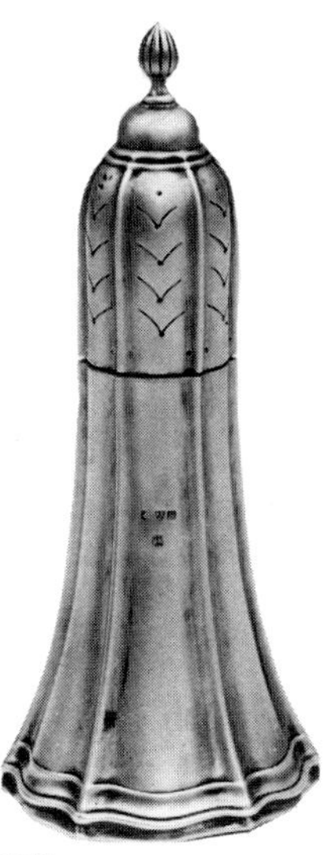
273

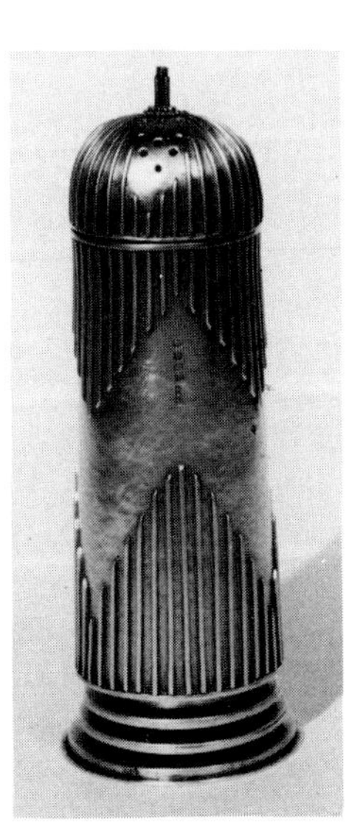
274

Mustard Pots

275

276

277

The mustard pot in the form we know it today did not become common until the late eighteenth century because until that time mustard was used as a spice and applied in dry form. The earliest form of mustard pot is in fact a blind caster, which was used for just that purpose (see **Casters**). Mustard pots usually have glass liners as it is much easier to clean them out than putting mustard straight into a silver pot. Indeed, a great number of mustard pots are either pierced or have openwork bases and can only be used with glass liners. There are some however which do not need liners, and these have gilt interiors.

Hallmarks: mustard pots are marked on either the base or the body with the full set of hallmarks, and on the lid with the maker's mark and lion passant pre-1784, and with the monarch's head as well after this date.

Condition: pierced mustard pots should always be examined for damage to the piercing. Always look for any removed engraving and any worn decoration. Look to see that the handle has not been pulled away and damaged, and especially look at the hinge and thumb piece on the lid, which are susceptible to rough treatment.

Fakes: the most common fakes are those where the hallmark has been let in. This is comparatively easy to do if it is the type where there is an open base with a ridge which supports the blue glass liner. One of the other possible fakes is a conversion from a salt cellar by the addition of a handle and a lid. It should however be possible to detect this by the lack of hallmark on the lid. A number of fakers however caught on to this and put a fake hallmark on the lid, and therefore one should compare the lid marks with the body marks.

275. A drum shaped mustard pot pierced with eccentric Greek key pattern and with a flat lid. Because this is one of the earliest examples you will come across, it has some rarity value.
c.1765 *£700 — £1,200*

276. Another example, this time with blue glass liner, the body pierced with quatrefoils. The 'drum' shape is the predominant shape for the English mustard pot.
c.1770 *£700 — £1,200*

277. By this date the lids on mustard pots are often domed. This example has a waved beaded rim conforming with the waved pierced design of the body (see 311).
c.1780 *£600 — £1,200*

278. An oval mustard pot which is a popular shape. This example has a flat lid again, but because of the shape there is more stress on the hinge, and it is more likely to have been damaged and repaired (see 312).
c.1790 *£600 — £1,200*

279. Another oval example with reeded borders. This type again is popular, and one of the most commonly seen at this date. Sometimes they will have open bases, in which case there will be a blue glass liner. If the base is solid the interior will be gilt.
c.1795 *£600 — £1,000*

280. A vase shaped example echoing the form of some pepperettes of this period. It should have a gilt interior.
c.1800 *£600 — £1,000*

281. A barrel shaped mustard pot, very much in the form of christening mugs of the same period. Be certain that the lid bears the lion passant mark, otherwise it may be a conversion from a mug to a mustard pot.
c.1800 *£600 — £1,200*

281

278

280

279

282. A circular mustard pot with the ever popular gadroon rim.
c.1810 *£450 — £750*

283. A mustard pot of bulbous oblong form, a popular shape at this period for salt cellars and tea sets as well. The attractive engraving makes this example rather better than the norm.
c.1810 *£450 — £700*

284. This is a circular mustard pot based on a popular salt cellar design used from the mid-18th century onwards. Note that this example is well hallmarked on the lid, and in fact is Sheffield made. You will occasionally find salt cellars converted into mustard pots, but usually this is quite clumsily executed, and of course the cover will be unmarked, or have fake marks.
c.1820 *£450 — £650*

285. A circular mustard pot by Paul Storr, almost in the same shape (but not size!) as a teapot of the period.
c.1830 *By Paul Storr £1,500 — £2,250*
By another £450 — £700

282

283

284

285

286. A pierced octagonal mustard pot, partly a revival of the style of the 1760s. It should of course have a blue glass liner.
c.1845 *£450 — £650*

287. A compressed circular mustard pot, like No. 284 based on a popular salt cellar shape. Check the lid for hallmarks. The 19th century silversmiths quite often adapted a piece of old silver. They should have submitted a piece they had altered to the Assay Office for any additions to be hallmarked.
c.1855 *£250 — £400*

288. This is a novelty mustard pot in the form of an owl. The contemporary spoon fits in under the beak and has a mouse terminal (not very clear in the illustration), which the owl appears to be devouring. Unusual items are always very popular. This example has unfortunately lost its original eyes, which have been rather unsympathetically replaced.
c.1855 *This one £650 — £1,000*
In original condition £1,200 — £2,000

289. A foliate and vine decorated mustard pot with the maker's mark of Robert Garrard, typical of the decoration on many pieces at this period, although the grapes are hardly appropriate! A comparatively large example measuring 4¼ins. high and weighing 10oz.
c.1855 *£500 — £800*

289

288

286

287

290

290. Another novelty in the form of Mr. Punch. Even more of a rarity than the owl, No. 288.
c.1855 *£2,250 — £3,500*

291. This is a cylindrical mustard pot chased with the scrolls and flowers so typical of this period. The mustard spoon is unlikely to have been made by the same maker, but may have been with the pot for a long time.
c.1865 *£350 — £550*

292. (left to right) (a) A pair of circular mustard pots with gadroon rims; this is a very popular design used from 1820 onwards. (b) A Slightly taller example of the same type. (c) A plain example.
(a) c.1870 *Pair £600 — £800*
(b) c.1870 *£275 — £425*
(c) c.1870 *£275 — £425*

293. A rather unusual example with flat chased scrolling foliate in Indian taste.
c.1870 *£275 — £425*

291

293

292

294. Another of the unusual novelty designs produced in the Victorian period, this time in the form of a tree trunk with an owl finial. Again fairly large, being 4½ins. high and weighing 7oz.
c.1880 *£2,250 — £3,500*

295. This example is a replica of a George III mustard pot of c.1790, pierced and bright-cut engraved.
c.1890 *£275 — £450*

296. A replica of a mustard pot, c.1770.
c.1890 *£250 — £350*

297. A light die-stamped piece with scrolling foliate decoration made in Birmingham.
c.1900 *£150 — £225*

294

296

295

297

Salt Cellars

298

299

Salt cellars are not commonly found until the eighteenth century in silver, although there are examples in existence earlier than this. The earliest of these were large ceremonial pieces which separated the chief guests from the rest, hence the saying 'sitting above the salt'. The most common type are of compressed circular form with three legs, which were introduced in the 1730s.

Hallmarks: early trencher salts were occasionally marked inside the bowl, and often they are very badly worn through use and cleaning. There are so many different varieties of salts that it is difficult to list all the variations, but in the main the salt cellar will be marked underneath and with circular examples the marks will be scattered. Pierced oval examples will be marked in a straight line on the rim that holds the blue glass liner in place, and boat shaped ones will normally be marked just under the pedestal foot. It is possible that examples will be marked on the side as well, especially after 1790.

Condition: always test the base of the salt cellar to see that it is still sturdy because with excessive cleaning and wear this can often have worn very thin. On those examples with legs look to see that they have not been dented or torn away and patched. On pierced examples look very carefully for any damaged or broken areas.

Fakes: such small pieces are not often faked, but I have come across pierced oval salts which have had the marks let into the rim which holds the blue glass liner. Make sure that there is not a seam at either side of the mark.

300

298. Here is something to start this section which you are unlikely to come across every day. This Elizabethan salt is hallmarked London, 1597, is silver gilt, and in three sections. At this period salt was a rare commodity and a piece of silver like this would only be found on tables in the grandest households.
1597 *£160,000+*

299. This is probably as early as you will find a pair of salt cellars, although earlier examples do exist. This type is referred to as a capstan trencher salt because of its shape. They are usually very light and can consequently be quite worn.
c.1690 *Pair £1,800 — £3,000*

300. A circular trencher salt of better quality and a more popular design than 299. The word 'trencher' was introduced to signify the difference between a low salt compared with the impressive individual standing salts, such as No. 298, which were used up to c.1675.
c.1700 *Pair £2,500 — £3,500*

301

301. One of a set of four circular salts, the heaviest type you will find at this date. They are usually made by Huguenot silversmiths.
c.1700 *Pair £3,000 — £4,000*
Set of four £7,000 — £10,000

302. One of a pair of oval trencher salts. Although engraved with armorials which look contemporary, these have probably been added later. The engraver has made the mistake of being rather too precise in detail for such a small item. One would be unlikely to find armorials on such a small piece at this period; a crest would be more probable.
c.1710 *Pair £2,000 — £3,500*

303. One of a pair of shaped oblong trencher salts with incurved angles. This form is usually quite solid. Other examples without incurved angles tend to be much thinner and lighter.
c.1720 *Pair £2,000 — £3,500*

304. One of a pair of heavy circular cup salts with applied stiff leafage and cast foot. The viscount's coronet and initials are not contemporary; probably added c.1770.
c.1730 *Pair £2,750 — £4,000*

305. These compressed circular salts are a commonly found type but in this case have four trefoil headed feet. One would more usually find three feet at this date as on Nos. 306-308. There are many variations of size and quality in this type and, whilst this example is quite heavy at 3oz.-4oz., the majority weigh between 2oz.-3 oz. and would be half the price.
c.1735 *Pair £850 — £1,500*

302

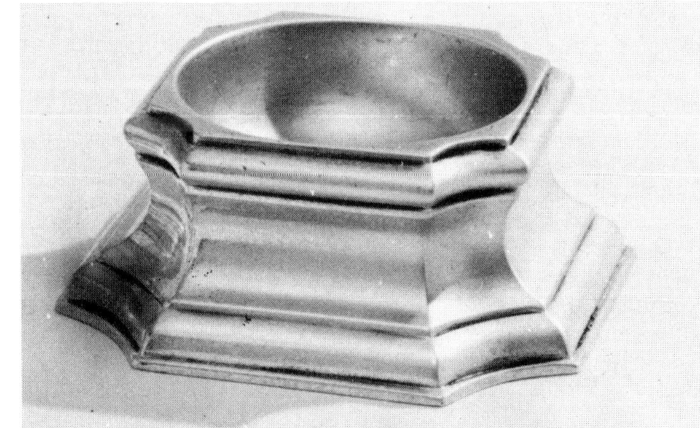

303

304

305

306

306. The lion mask headed paw feet on this compressed circular salt makes all the difference; if it had just plain hoof feet it would be a third of the value. A popular feature is the gadroon rim which will also be found on plainer and lighter examples.
c.1735 *Pair £1,500 — £2,500*

307. (a) (above) One of a pair similar to No. 306, but heavier and with applied floral festoons. (b) (below) This has unusual mask head feet with later chased floral panels between. Salts of this type, if decorated, usually have applied motifs as does (a), so if you come across an 18th century salt on which you can see the decoration on the inside, there is a 90% certainty that it has been added later, and it will at least halve the value.
(a) c.1740 *Pair £1,500 — £2,500*
(b) c.1745 *Pair £450 — £600*

308. A compressed circular salt cellar on three shell headed hoof feet. A very common type, but here with that later chased decoration mentioned in the preceding caption.
c.1745 *Pair £200 — £350*

309. Here is a set of four unusual shaped oval salt cellars, a design used by Edward Wakelin. They are usually very heavy and have a cast foot.
c.1760 *Pair £1,800 — £2,500*
Set of four £4,000 — £6,000

307

308

309

310. These oval examples are of somewhat similar design to No. 309, but with the rams' masks and husk swags applied below beaded rims. The example on the left has a contemporary crest and that on the right two later crests. These are so small that they would not dramatically detract from the value. However, any sign of an erasure or thinness would be a different matter.

c.1775 *Pair £1,800 — £2,500*

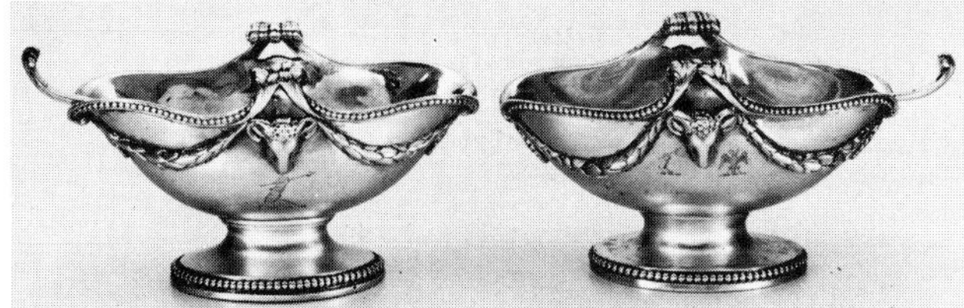

310

311. A matching salt cellar and mustard pot by Hester Bateman with pierced and bright-cut decoration between beaded borders. The salt cellar is a bit worn compared with the mustard pot, which is a definite minus point. The ball-and-claw feet are stamped out and can often be damaged or torn near the body. The base is open with the blue glass liner fitting in and sitting on a small ledge.

c.1780 *Pair salts £1,000 — £1,500*
Mustard pot £1,250 — £2,000
If not by Hester Bateman £600 — £1,000

311

312. A set of four salt cellars by Hester Bateman of shaped oval form, one side centred by an initialled cartouche, the other by a pierced-out star. The small pepperette and mustard pot are by the same maker and have the same type of decoration.

c.1780	*By Hester Bateman*	*If not by Hester Bateman*
Pair salts	*£1,000 — £1,500*	*£550 — £950*
Mustard pot	*£1,250 — £2,000*	*£600 — £1,000*
Pepperette	*£350 — £525*	*£200 — £300*

312

313

313. This compressed oval salt cellar has four shell headed hoof feet. Circular examples of this type with three feet are very common and appear as early as 1740 with plain or gadroon rims, right up until 1785, the later ones having beaded or reeded rims.
c.1780 *Pair £450 — £650*

314. A boat shaped salt cellar on pedestal foot with slight ogee body. Examples with a loop handle at either end are also found at this period and are very popular.
c.1790 *Pair £600 — £900*

315. One of a pair of oval salt cellars with the popular lobed decoration between gadroon borders. Oblong examples with this decoration are also found, sometimes with and sometimes without handles.
c.1800 *Pair £550 — £750*

316. One of a set of six sarcophagus shaped salt cellars. An unusual but rather bland design.
c.1810 *Set of six £3,000 — £4,500*

314

316

315

317. One of another set of six oval salt cellars, this time by Paul Storr. This is one of his most popular designs for salts.
c.1810 *Set of six £7,500 — £12,500*
Pair £2,000 — £3,000

318. A salt cellar on ball feet with gadroon and shell rim. Oblong salts of this design are also found. This example was made in Dublin.
c.1815 *Pair £550 — £750*

319. A set of four Triton salt cellars by Paul Storr. Very heavy, beautifully made and extremely expensive. The only part not cast is the oblong platform.
c.1815 *Set of four £50,000+*

320. This circular, cup-shaped salt is in the style of the 1730s with cast foot and gadroon rim.
c.1820 *Pair £650 — £900*

317

320

318

319

321

321. A pair of salts with mustard pot *en suite*. The open-work bodies are cast and chased in sections and soldered together, the feet then applied. With this sort of design it is often difficult to find the hallmarks, but in this case they are on the feet. The individual spoons are a nice additional feature.
c.1830 *Pair salts £450 — £700*
Mustard pot £500 — £700

322. Two of a set of four pierced octagonal cup shaped salts with blue glass liners, which are unsuccessfully shaped to fit.
c.1840 *Set of four £750 — £1,250*

323. An unusual double salt cellar with the maker's mark of Hunt and Roskell, successors to Storr and Mortimer. The individuality and quality is in the same vein as some of Paul Storr's own creations, and the price will approach the heights of an example by that maker.
c.1845 *£1,500 — £3,250*

324. This set of four octagonal salts with matching mustard pot show Victorian Gothic decoration in a fairly restrained mood. The blue glass liners are shaped to the rims.
c.1850 *Set of four salts £750 — £1,250*

322

323

324

325. A pair of compressed circular salts on lion mask feet in mid-18th century style, but the originals would either be plain or have applied decoration.
c.1850 *Pair £400 — £600*

326. One of another pair in mid-18th century style. The same comments made in caption 325 apply as regards the decoration. As we have already seen in 308, 18th century examples are sometimes decorated later, and can look almost identical to these.
c.1850 *Pair £275 — £450*

327. These could be nothing else but early/mid-Victorian, displaying fussy flowers and having a heavy overall effect.
c.1855 *Pair £400 — £550*

328. One from a set of four hemispherical salt cellars with winged mask and paw feet and decorated with a band of Greek key pattern at the rim, a revival of the influence on design made fashionable by Egyptian campaigns early in the century. These bear the maker's mark of George Angell who was responsible for some good and unusual pieces.
c.1855 *Set of four £750 — £1,250*

328

327

325

326

329. Charles and George Fox produced a number of designs copied from Dutch originals. This salt, one of a pair weighing 39oz., is modelled after an original of Adam van Vianen of Utrecht and stands 8ins. high.
c.1860 *Pair £12,500 — £20,000*

330. A set of six compressed circular salt cellars, again in mid-18th century style, but with beaded borders and bright-cut decoration, a combination not found on this type in the 18th century. The box does not add to their value.
c.1870 *Set of six £1,000 — £1,750*

331. Another example of individual Victorian design with a lion rampant holding the salt dish. The use of the lion, which is here cast and chased, was popular in many designs, and he is more often used than any other animal.
c.1870 *Set of four £15,000 — £25,000*

329

330

331

332. A pair of unusual double salts with figure handles in the form of a Dutch boy and girl. They are parcel gilt which will increase their value by 15 or 20%, even though to some eyes it is somewhat vulgar!
c.1885 *£8,000 — £13,000*

333. An unusual salt cellar design by C.R. Ashbee and probably made by the Guild of Handicraft Limited. Individual designs of this type will command astronomical prices compared with mass-produced salt cellars of more ordinary design. This single example sold at auction in 1979 for £340.
c.1900 *£1,500 — £3,000*

334. This design by Ramsden and Carr is drawn from the 17th century, being a copy of a standing salt. Purely made for presentation and decoration as it stands some 7ins. high.
c.1910 *£1,500 — £3,000*

335. A salt cellar, mustard pot and pepperette of individual design by Omar Ramsden. The hammered finish was a feature he favoured.
c.1920 *Set £2,000 — £3,750*

336. A salt cellar, mustard pot and pepperette by Alwyn Carr, Omar Ramsden's partner.
c.1925 *Set £2,000 — £3,750*

332

333

336

335

334

Dinner Services & Dishes

Cake Baskets

Although these nearly always appear described as 'cake baskets', there is little doubt they were more commonly used for bread and fruit. They are not commonly found until well into the eighteenth century, although seventeenth and a sixteenth century example are known to exist. The early examples tend to have side handles or no handles at all, and it is not until the mid-eighteenth century that the so-called 'swing' handle becomes common. Although the size does not alter dramatically between 1735 and 1850, the earlier examples are usually heavier at around 60oz. in George II period. George III examples of 1760-1800 average 30oz., those between 1800-1840 average 40oz., then gradually shed weight until by 1900 some weigh as little as 15oz.

Hallmarks: cake baskets are hallmarked in different places at different dates. The majority however are marked either on the base, the foot rim or one side, and on pierced examples they can be marked with one mark either side of the handle or with the hallmarks dotted in the piercing, an inch or so apart. The handle, being a separate part, should be hallmarked. However, until the king's head duty mark comes in in 1784 some baskets do not have hallmarks on the handles, although obviously original.

Condition: the main areas to look for are in the piercing and where the handles and feet are applied. Pierced cake baskets are very difficult to repair and usually the repairs stick out like a sore thumb. The base should be tested for any thinness where armorials or inscriptions may have been removed.

Fakes: baskets made from other hallmarked silver will normally have slightly stretched or distorted hallmarks, so beware if the marks are not as you would expect to find them. Make sure also that all the marks are there. If the leopard's head mark is missing it may be that the basket is a conversion of a soup tureen liner.

337

338

337. A fine heavy basket normally between 60 and 80oz. in weight. The base is soldered in as a separate part, the sides being made from sheet and cleverly pierced and chased to look like interwoven basketwork. At this date handles can be either fixed at the ends as in this example, or across the basket like Nos. 338 and 339. There is no rule about this.
c.1735 *£45,000 — £65,000*

338. Another example of the same basic shape showing the interior with superb armorial engraving attributed to Joseph Sympson. The swing handle has caryatid supports for the grip, which is made in two sections, one hollowed, the other flat, and then soldered together. The rim has a satyr's mask at either end, echoing the engraved mask at the base of the armorial.
c.1735 *£45,000 — £65,000*

339. This slightly later type is pierced with the formal geometric designs usually found during this period. Sometimes one will find whole areas broken away. This can happen in one place and someone then has the 'bright idea' of matching up by taking out further sections to make the damage look like original design. Careful examination of the piercing for any repairs is necessary. This example has a fixed handle and an applied rim of cast scrolls and shells. A band of flat chasing can be seen on the base in place of the engraved trellis work.
c.1740 *£20,000 — £35,000*

340. This is a rather more elaborate piece echoing the call of the rococo and displaying a variety of piercing above the cast and applied irregular foot. It still has a band of flat chasing in the base. The handle is now likely to be flat and not 'hollowed'.
c.1745 *£20,000 — £35,000*

341. A more shallow and flared design is now used and the basket is raised on four shell and volute feet. The base is usually only decorated, if at all, by a coat of arms from this date, although some with flat chasing can still be found. Quite often this type is repaired where the feet meet the body. Look carefully for any patches.
c.1750 *£12,500 — £20,000*

342. A rather less elegant basket with lion mask and paw feet. Baskets of this type with four feet nearly always have masks above. They can range from chinamen to female masks variously decorated to display the four elements or seasons. The quality of this example is simpler than 341, but the component parts do not give the same overall pleasing design, and therefore the piece will be less valuable.
c.1755 *£10,000 — £17,500*

342

341

339

340

343

343. A pair of baskets, the feet now interspersed by an open-work apron. The piercing and the rim are now sometimes less intricate as the rococo period is on the wane.
c.1760 *Pair £20,000 — £35,000*
Single £8,000 — £12,000

344. The use of alternate pierced panels bordered by beaded flutes is now common and the foot returns to the design found on the early examples. This basket has Chinese masks on the handle and feet. It was made in the mid-18th century by Robert Calderwood, probably the best and most prolific maker in Dublin.
c.1765 *£7,000 — £9,000*

345. The foot on this example is now of the pierced rim variety, and therefore there is less chance of excessive stress on the body, as found with examples having separate feet. The piercing is simpler.
c.1765 *£6,500 — £8,500*

346. This basket is of quite different construction. It is made from numerous interlocking reeded wires, with a separately made central plate and fixed handle. There is a small insignificant crest at the centre; the appearance would have been enhanced by a full coat of arms.
c.1765 *£6,000 — £8,000*

344

345

346

347. This basket has a rather simpler version of the trellis pattern depicted on No. 345 with a much plainer handle. As with No. 346, it has a separately made base plate which this time has a fine armorial.
c.1765 *£4,500 — £7,500*

348. Another wirework example with applied decoration; the flowers and foliage are stamped and chased and then soldered on to the wire. This type was always marked on the foot rim, as can be seen. The thin wire sides can easily become distorted, and parts of the applied work may be broken off.
c.1760 *£3,500 — £5,500*

349. This has pierced and chased sides with drapery swags, which are susceptible to damage because of the very open piercing. The foliate rim is cast and applied. This type is often marked on the piercing, sometimes with one mark on either side of the handle pivots.
c.1770 *£4,500 — £7,000*

350. Like 346 and 348 this piece has sides made up of wires from a plain base rather than having the fret pierced sides of the other baskets already shown. It is applied with a gadroon rim and a simple rim foot. It has a rather unattractive handle which follows the shape of the ends of the basket so that the handle lies neatly when down.
c.1775 *£3,500 — £5,500*

350

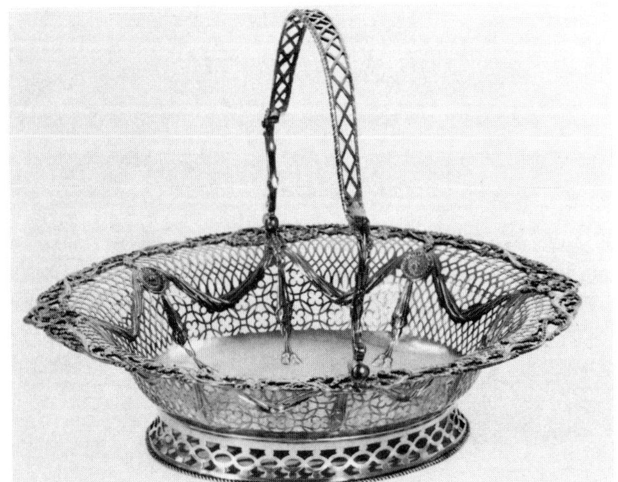

349

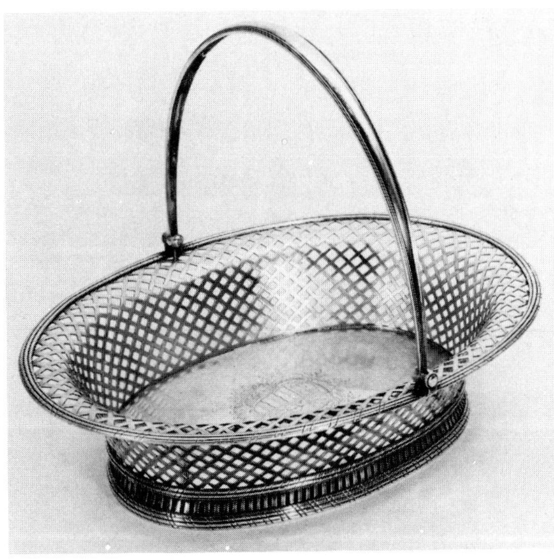

347

348

351. A shallower, more flared and elongated oval example with much less piercing, now incorporating bright-cut engraving. It has a simple, reeded swing handle which would certainly be marked with the lion passant, king's head duty mark and the maker's mark.
c.1785 *£3,500 — £5,000*

352. There is perhaps little to choose between this type and 351, the main difference being a more intricate band of piercing and bright-cut engraving, which adds to the value as long as the bright-cutting is not worn.
c.1785 *£3,500 — £5,000*

353. A slightly deeper example with a heavier foot. The piercing is more formal, giving a much 'stiffer' and slightly less attractive appearance.
c.1790 *£3,500 — £5,000*

354. An unusual wirework type without handle, having twisted wire borders. Baskets without handles are only found occasionally, so the collector should make sure that one has not been removed. These are often termed 'dessert baskets' in catalogue entries.
c.1790 *£3,000 — £4,500*

351

352

353

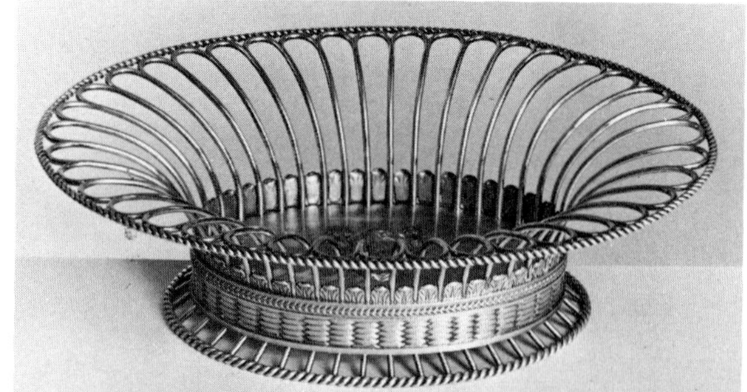
354

355. The oblong shape is found with cake baskets as with many other pieces of domestic silver at this date. This example has an engraved band below the gadroon rim.
c.1805 *£2,000 — £3,000*

356. Another oblong example. By now the bright-cut or wriggle work engraving has gone and lobed or fluted decoration substituted. Still with gadroon border.
c.1810 *£2,000 — £3,000*

357. A pair of escallop baskets, copies of originals made c.1745. The gadrooned border is a giveaway. The earlier original would probably have had a more decorative cast and applied one. Each basket stands on cast dolphin feet.
c.1815 *Pair £20,000 — £30,000*
Single £7,500 — £12,500
Mid-18th century single £15,000 — £25,000
(one is unlikely to find a pair)

358. A heavier example of the same basic shape as 357, the handle being cast with armorial and shells.
c.1815 *£7,500 — £12,500*

358

357

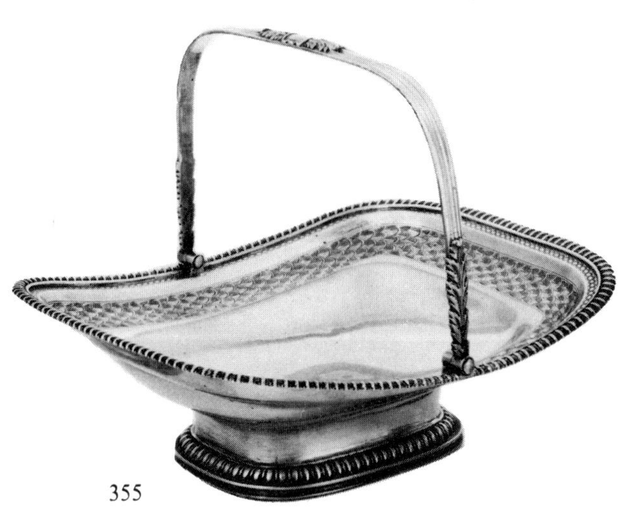
355

356

359

359. A ribbed oval basket with a heavy handle, rim and foot, all of which give a much more solid appearance.
c.1820 *£4,000 — £7,000*
Paul Storr example £12,500 — £18,000

360. A circular example embossed and chased with flowers and foliage in the manner so often attributed to the Victorian era.
c.1825 *£1,500 — £3,000*

361. Another of similar shape, this time with waved rim and flat-chased alternate panels of flowers and diaper. Very simple spreading foot. By this date much less silver is used and quality is generally less good.
c.1840 *£1,250 — £2,750*

362. This basket is slightly shallower and the more deeply waved rim has applied floral and foliate decoration.
c.1850 *£1,250 — £2,750*

360

361

362

363. An oval example in almost 18th century taste. The openwork swing handle is very much like earlier examples. The engraving however is typically Victorian, with floral sprays below engraved arches of formal leafage.
c.1860 *£1,250 — £2,750*

364. The basket-weave design is sturdy and unusual which will probably mean a keener price. The basket is applied at the rim with ears of wheat, and therefore was probably intended for use as a bread basket.
c.1860 *£2,250 — £3,750*

365. This ribbed, circular example has a turned over rim, and a fixed handle springing from the lions' masks, both of which are unusual features. The contrast of flat chased decoration on the basket and relief decoration on the foot gives an added interest.
c.1870 *£1,250 — £2,750*

366. An almost direct copy of baskets made roughly one hundred years earlier. Compare with Nos. 344 and 349.
c.1880 *£1,250 — £2,750*

366

365

363

364

367

367. This is probably more correctly called a fruit bowl. It is silver gilt and was designed by C.R. Ashbee, and made by the Guild of Handicraft Limited. Contemporary designs of originality will always command good prices. Although this only weighs 13oz. it fetched £480 at auction in 1976.
c.1895 *£4,000 — £6,000*

368. This basket made for Mappin and Webb is not of high quality. The decoration is die stamped and the gauge of silver comparatively thin.
c.1895 *£1,000 — £2,000*

369. Yet another period at which mid-18th century design was copied. The quality is just as good as No. 357 and the design is again almost identical. It weighs 70oz.
c.1900 *£5,500 — £8,500*

370. A circular die stamped and chased cake basket reminiscent of a late 17th century floral embossed Caroline design. It stands on spreading foot, but has no handle so should perhaps be called a dessert dish.
c.1900 *£900 — £1,500*

368

369

370

371. The prettily moulded glass dish with floral designs and shaped rim makes up three-quarters of the price of this piece, as without it the article would be useless and it would be difficult to replace. There are only 14oz. of silver and therefore, if comparing the price per ounce, this will seem high, but one cannot ignore the glass.
c.1900 *£900 — £1,500*

372. This type of scroll pierced basket is popular and very decorative. Many examples are based on Dutch originals of the latter half of the 18th century, although this set is of a contemporary design. Total weight 60oz.
c.1905 *Set of three £4,000 — £6,500*

373. This wirework basket from Harrison Bros. and Howson of Sheffield was probably copied directly from one of their early pattern books. The original is likely to have been made in Sheffield plate c.1805.
c.1905 *£750 — £1,250*

374. A mass-produced basket which is die stamped but decorated in the popular art nouveau taste.
c.1910 *£800 — £1,500*

375. This fruit dish is rather unusual in that it is enamelled at the border in greens and browns to give a realistic ivy design. It measures 10½ins. in diameter and weighs 27oz. Dessert dishes of this type, but with more delicately pierced and engraved vine decoration, are more common. They are also very popular.
c.1935 *£900 — £1,600*

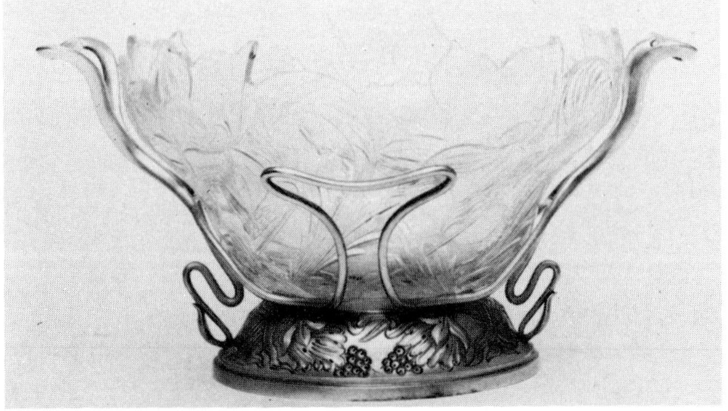
371

372

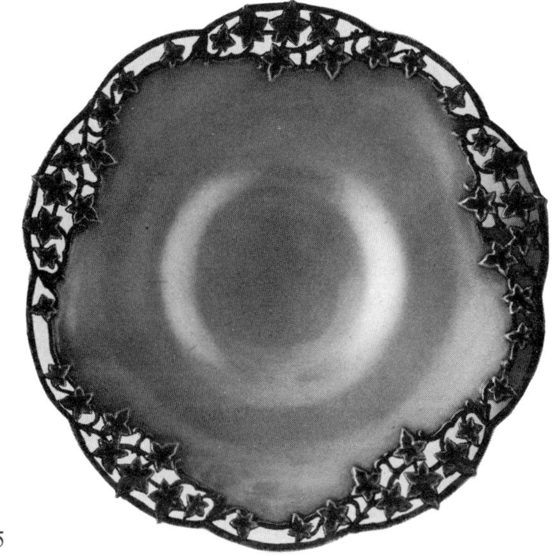
375

374

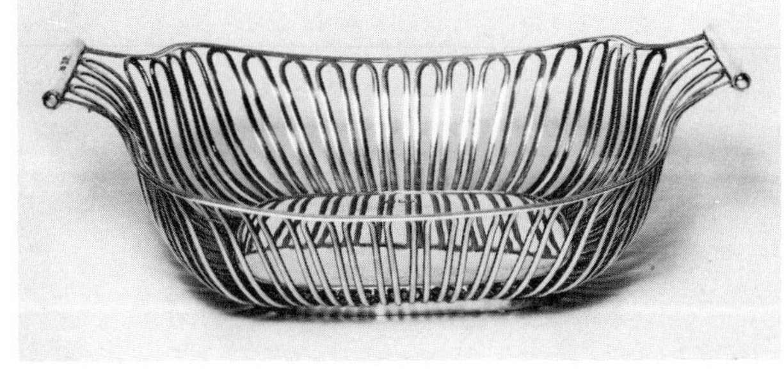
373

Dessert Dishes

Dessert dishes, also known as tazzas or comports, were normally silver gilt. In the last 25 years of the reign of Queen Victoria, sets of, and single dessert dishes were produced whilst the popularity of the cake basket declined. By this date of course mass-production generally meant that quality was sacrificed and less silver was used.

376. A typical example displaying rococo revival decoration. It is often difficult to find the hallmarks on a piece like this as they are usually in the chasing. If you are lucky you may find one being sold as plated!
c.1885 *£1,500 — £2,000*

377. A set of three simpler examples in sizes, echoing 1770s type decoration.
c.1890 *Set £3,750 — £6,000*
Large size, each £1,500 — £2,000
Smaller size, each £1,000 — £1,500

376

377

378. A set of four oval, and one pedestal dish, the bases embossed with various fruits on a matted panel.
c.1890 *Set £6,000 — £8,500*
Individually £900 — £1,600

379. A set of pedestal and oval dishes made from silver gilt, as were most dessert services. This design is usually indicative of greater weight than 378.
c.1890 *Set £6,500 — £9,000*

378

379

Dinner Plates, Meat Dishes & Chargers

This section includes dinner plates, which usually are found in dozens or multiples thereof, with an average weight of 18oz.-23oz. per plate, meat dishes which are normally of oval outline and vary in size, ranging in weight from 20oz.-200oz. plus, and chargers, or sideboard dishes, which are circular and weigh anything from 80oz.-250oz. The uses of dinner plates and meat dishes are obvious. A charger or sideboard dish, however, is likely to have been used for a variety of purposes, from being just purely decorative to being a large serving dish. In the majority of cases these were all made in exactly the same way. Sheet silver is hammered to the shaped design and then has a border wire of gadroon or some other ornament soldered on. It may be assumed that all of these articles were made for comparatively grand households, and it is unusual to come across any that do not bear the coat of arms of a noble or landed family. Soup plates were made in exactly the same style as the corresponding dinner plates, but they are often rather heavier because more silver was required to produce the deeper bowl.

Hallmarks: with the exception of very early examples, these will always be marked underneath the rim between the booge (inner border) and the border wire, in a straight or semi-curved line. If the hallmarks fall very close to the border or in the booge then one should be extremely cautious.

Condition: a number of dinner plates have obviously had a large amount of use and the first place to examine is the centre of the plate where there will almost certainly be knife scratches, which should not necessarily put one off. Test the centre of the plate to see whether the knife scratches of successive generations have been polished out, leaving the area thin. Then look at the borders to see whether any coats of arms or crests have been erased. Tilting the item in the light should show up any indentations or unevenness where this might have occurred.

Fakes: rather than deliberate fakes, there are many plates which have been altered to accommodate the latest fashion, and in these cases one can usually tell by the hallmarks, as they are either stretched, in an unusual place, or partially worn away. For example, the early 18th century plates which were of plain circular design bearing Queen Anne or George I marks, were often reshaped in the 1750s or later, and applied with gadroon borders. Silver soup plates have never been particularly fashionable, and as dinner plates are more popular, being more useful, occasionally one will find that a soup plate has been converted into a dinner plate by hammering out or cutting out the depth of the bowl. This should however be readily discernible as there will be either crease marks or an unnatural seam at the booge.

380

381

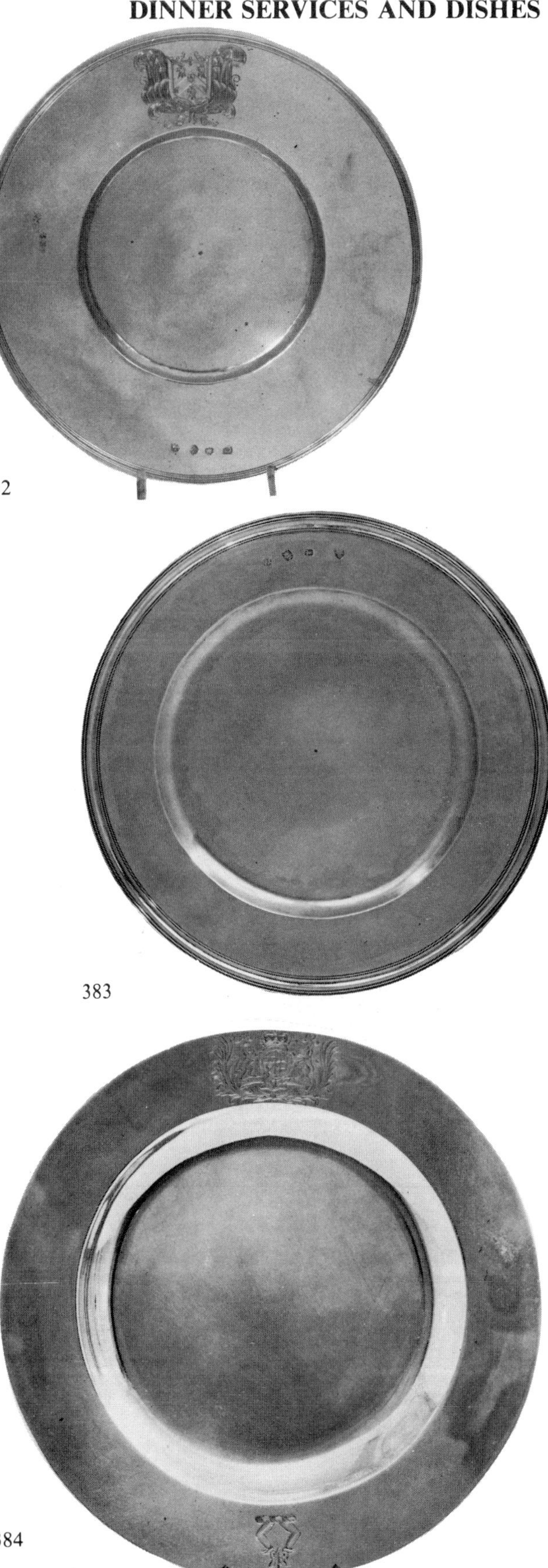

382

383

384

380. In the mid-17th century the plain charger, or sideboard dish, developed from the earlier rosewater dishes, which normally had accompanying ewers. This is probably one of the earliest plain examples, 18ins. in diameter. At this date it will be fairly deep with a well pronounced boss in the centre. The boss is now a decorative feature, which on earlier examples was there so that an accompanying ewer could be placed on the centre.
c.1650 *£40,000 — £75,000*

381. A slightly later charger than 380, this example is much shallower and the border now has reeded moulding, indicating a later date. The boss is less defined.
c.1675 *£40,000 — £75,000*

382. It is highly unlikely that one will find a set of plates dating from this period, but occasionally single examples do appear on the market. They tend to be much lighter and flimsier than their later counterparts and, instead of having an applied border wire, have a chased reeded border. They are comparatively rare and can command up to half the price of a dozen plates of later date. This one has very clear hallmarks on the front of the plate, which is common until the turn of the 17th century.
c.1670 *Single plate £5,500 — £8,500*

383. This dinner plate is slightly larger than 382 at 9ins. diameter as opposed to 8ins. diameter, and has a narrower border, looking very much like the shape of plate we are used to in modern times. The border again is not applied separately, but is hammered into a slightly thicker edge within reeded bands. The pinpoint at the centre of the plate is where the silversmith has placed his compass to make sure that the plate is truly circular.
c.1680 *Single plate £5,000 — £7,000*

384. This is the earliest form of plate that one might find in dozens. This is in fact part of an ambassadorial service which would have been issued on appointment and is engraved with the arms of Queen Anne on one side and the crest of the ambassador on the other. There is no applied border wire on the front of the plate, but a slightly convex moulding at the border on the underside.
c.1710 *Per dozen £95,000+*
Without royal arms £70,000+

385

385. This charger is really a large version of the dinner plates which were made at this period. In comparison with 381 the border is narrower and the centre has no boss. This design was popular between 1700 and 1725. The knife scratches on the centre of the dish are quite deep, but it is preferable to see a piece in this sort of condition than in a highly polished form, which would indicate that all the scratches have been buffed out, with the silver looking almost like new without that nice old patination.
c.1720 *Per oz. £350 — £600*

386. A much grander example than 385 with the contemporary royal armorials at the centre, and probably issued as a piece of ambassadorial plate. The plain gadroon border on this charger is much bolder than the type found on later dinner plates and implies an earlier date.
c.1730 *Per oz. £450 — £750*

387. The border moulding is now on the upper side of the dinner plates which are illustrated here with a larger circular serving dish. All are engraved with the arms of the Earls of Hopetoun.
c.1730 *Per dozen £55,000 — £75,000*
Serving plate, per oz. £350 — £550

388. This is the most common form of dinner plate, together with a soup plate (right). They have applied gadroon borders and were made extensively from 1740 onwards.

Per dozen:	*Dinner Plate*	*Soup plate*
George II	*£12,000 — £20,000*	*£7,000 — £11,000*
George III	*£10,000 — £15,000*	*£6,000 — £9,000*
George IV	*£10,000 — £15,000*	*£6,000 — £9,000*
William IV	*£9,000 — £13,000*	*£6,000 — £9,000*
Early Victorian	*£7,000 — £10,000*	*£5,000 — £7,000*
Late Victorian	*£6,000 — £7,000*	*£4,000 — £5,500*

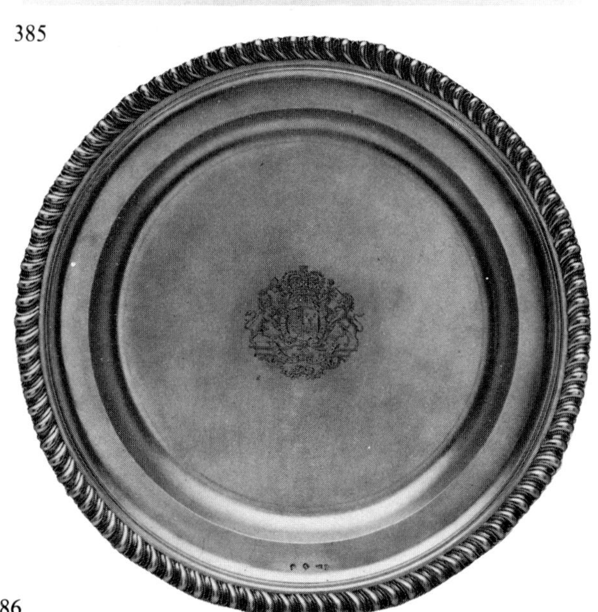

386

387

389. A series of the most common shaped oval meat dishes matching the most popular dinner plates shown in the preceding example.

Per oz. £45 — £80

(Examples over 100oz. usually at lower end of the scale.)

390. A variation of the same type of plate as 388 with leaf mouldings at the shaped points, again made extensively from 1740 onwards. Although slightly more desirable, the prices will be the same as for 388.

391. A shaped oval meat dish about as early as one will find with applied moulded border. Illustrated here with its mazarin (a pierced oval platter used on top of the dish to allow the juices to drain through).

c.1740 *Per oz. £60 — £100*

392. The design of this charger is really Queen Anne and was probably copied from an original model by the silversmith, David Willaume II, whose father was a Huguenot. The centre is engraved with the arms of George Booth, 2nd Earl of Warrington. As a great patron of the arts, his ownership is very likely to indicate fine quality and will add weight to the price. The gadroon border and shell and scroll motifs are all cast and applied.

c.1740 *Per oz. £400 — £650*

388

389

392

391

390

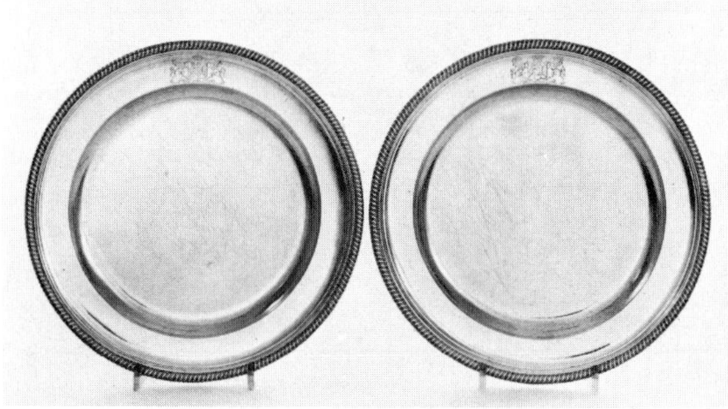

393

393. The plain circular plate with gadroon border was occasionally made from 1780 to 1820 and is not quite as popular as 389 and 390. This is for two reasons: firstly they are difficult to match and secondly they are lighter. The price will not however be very different.
c.1780-1820 *Per dozen £10,000 — £15,000*

394

394. The innovation of the tea tray in the late 18th century seems to have put the sideboard dish into oblivion, although examples of very simple form, like the dinner plate with shaped gadroon borders, are known. However, during the Regency period the intrigue with things antique left the way open for some silversmiths to produce these decorative dishes again. This example is in Caroline taste and was made by William Pitts. There are however a number of fakes of this type of sideboard dish which have been made from meat dishes or have had hallmarks let in, but in nearly all cases the hallmarks are in an unusual position and are either distorted or at an unusual angle.
c.1810 *Per oz. £130 — £175*

395. Of heavier design than 393, these dinner plates, with leaf flanked shell mouldings interrupting the gadroon border, were produced by Paul Storr and other top makers in the Regency period. Three dinner plates are illustrated at the centre, flanked by two slightly larger so-called second course dishes, which are not usually found in sets of more than four, and were presumably used as serving dishes.
c.1815 *Per dozen £12,000 — £18,000*
Set of four serving plates, per oz. £120 — £180
Paul Storr £22,000 — £35,000
Paul Storr, per oz. £180 — £250

395

396. A meat dish with gadroon border interrupted by leaf flanked shell motifs corresponding to the dinner plate shown in the preceding example. Its companion mazarin is more formally pierced than the example shown in 391 with scrolls and foliate motifs.
c.1815 *Per oz. £50 — £85*
Paul Storr £110 — £160

397. The dinner plate in the centre has a bound reeded border with vine motifs at intervals. It is occasionally found and is of the same quality as 395. The two flanking plates show an unusual variation of the plain circular plate with a straight gadroon border outside a beaded band.
Centre, c. 1815 *Per dozen £15,000 — £22,500*
Left and right, c.1800 *Per dozen £13,500 — £21,000*

398. A tree and well meat dish embossed so that the juices are channelled into the well, sometimes called venison dishes and usually very large.
c.1815 *Per oz. £45 — £80*

398

397

396

399

399. Edward Farrell was another maker who was very fond of antique designs and incorporated them in many of his pieces. Like 394, this dish again is in Caroline style, showing the Dutch influence of the auricular or lobate motif at the border and with a well chased plaque of a battle scene at the centre.
c.1820 *Per oz. £120 — £150*

400. A small Victorian christening plate, 5½ins. in diameter. These were usually made as part of a set with knife, fork and spoon and, occasionally, a mug. Sometimes they will be found completely plain and at other times with an engraved scene depicting a nursery rhyme or children's story. This example is unusual in that it is engraved with a scene in the gardens at Windsor Castle and was undoubtedly made as a royal christening present.
c.1850 *Examples with engraved scenes £800 — £1,200*
Plain examples £300 — £400

401. This is a silver electro-type replica of the Shield of the Amazons. The original design was executed by Antoine Vetche about 50 years earlier. Elkington and Co. produced the majority of the silver electro-types, and were commissioned by the Victoria and Albert Museum shortly after the date of this piece to make electro-types of the massive pieces of early English silver in the Kremlin.
c.1870 *Per oz. £45 — £75*

400

401

402. This sideboard dish was made by Gilbert Marks, one of the best chasers of his era. However, I think this particulai example is not of his best quality.
c.1895 *Per oz. £80 — £135*

403. The interest in collecting antiques encouraged a number of manufacturers at the beginning of the 20th century to produce near replicas of older pieces. This charger could at a pinch date from about 1725, but the decoration is a bit too enthusiastic and the original would most probably have had an impressive coat of arms in the centre. The accompanying ewer does not copy an 18th century design, but is of quite a pleasing shape.
c.1900 *Charger, per oz. £55 — £70*
Ewer £2,250 — £3,500

404. A large sideboard dish chased by L. Movio, whose work is comparable with that of Gilbert Marks. The design is not as accomplished as some of the latter's, and in fact the same motifs are here repeated three times.
c.1905 *Per oz. £85 — £150*

404

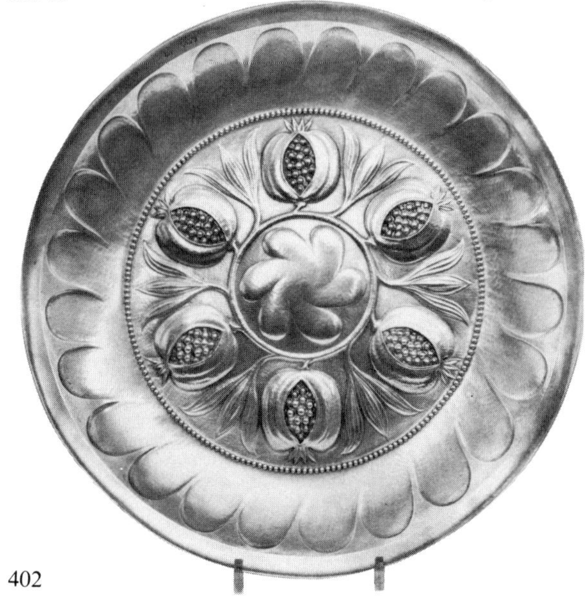

402

403

Dish Crosses & Dish Rings

Dish crosses were a development from the much earlier braziers (which are so rare that they do not fall within the scope of this book) and were used on the sideboard or table with a dish on top. They date from the mid-eighteenth century, but fall from favour once the heater base (occasionally still found with entrée dishes, see 417) was introduced in the late eighteenth century. They have sliding supports so that they can be adjusted to any size of dish, and the burners are occasionally detachable.

Dish rings were the Irish equivalent of the English dish crosses but without burners, and have occasionally been mis-named potato rings. This seems to have developed from the late 19th century myth that they were all used with a napkin or glass bowl in the centre. There are, in fact, eighteenth century examples known with wooden bowls, but there is no evidence to support the 'potato' theory. Few, if any, dish rings were made between 1790-1890 and therefore none are illustrated.

406

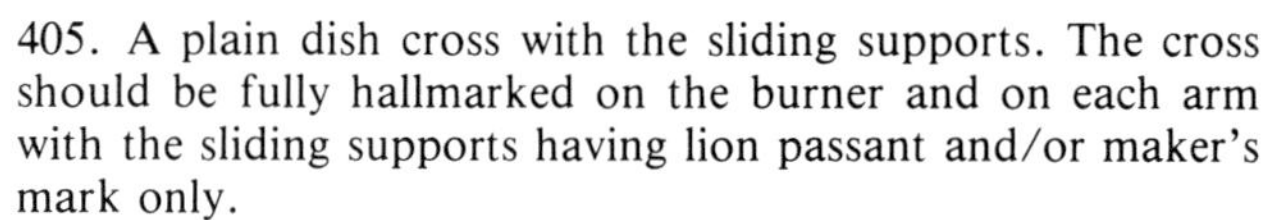

405. A plain dish cross with the sliding supports. The cross should be fully hallmarked on the burner and on each arm with the sliding supports having lion passant and/or maker's mark only.
c.1760 *£1,500 — £2,500*

406. An Irish dish ring of the most typical form with pierced and chased birds and animals amongst scrolling flowers and other motifs. These are usually marked around the bottom rim, but always examine carefully. They were made in large numbers in the late 19th century and many of them had Georgian marks let in, so look out for any unnatural seams.
c.1770 *£3,250 — £4,500*

405

407. This later dish cross has beaded borders (also found with gadroon borders) which indicate the date, but is of very similar form to 405 and should be marked in the same way.
c.1780 *£1,500 — £2,500*

408. Two late 19th century/early 20th century dish rings, often fitted with blue glass liners, and occasionally called potato rings (see Introduction).
1890-1910 *Left £750 — £1,250*
Right £600 — £900

409. Another replica of an Irish dish ring made by West and Sons of Dublin. Collecting antique silver became popular in the late 19th century and there was a reaction against some of the pretty Victorian designs by reverting to making replicas of earlier pieces.
c.1920 *£750 — £1,250*

409

408

407

Entrée Dishes

The entrée dish has many forms and was undoubtedly used for a variety of different dishes. The earliest examples, if they can be described as entrée dishes, do not have covers. The most traditional form is the plain oblong shape with a cover of matching depth and form, but slightly smaller, so that it fits inside the rim of the base. Entrée dishes and covers were invariably numbered so that base 1 would fit lid 1, base 2 with lid 2, and so on. From the late eighteenth century onwards they were found made with accompanying heater bases, which were the same shape and were used with a spirit lamp, charcoal or hot iron, or hot water. They were invariably made in Sheffield plate, although silver examples are known. A single dish usually is worth only a third of the price of a pair.

Hallmarks: they are usually fully marked in a straight line on lid and base, either below the rim on one side or on one of the ends. Only occasionally will they be marked underneath the base. Detachable finials should have the maker's mark and lion passant and after 1784 the monarch's head duty mark.

Condition: always examine the sides for any erased coats of arms or crests. Look at the corners for any splits or bad dents. Examine the borders to see that they are not worn away and have no splits or holes, and examine the finials and finial locking plates.

Fakes: entrée dishes are not commonly faked. However, you may find that an early example has been up-dated by the addition of a more ornate border or floral chasing. This is, of course, not desirable and can halve the price.

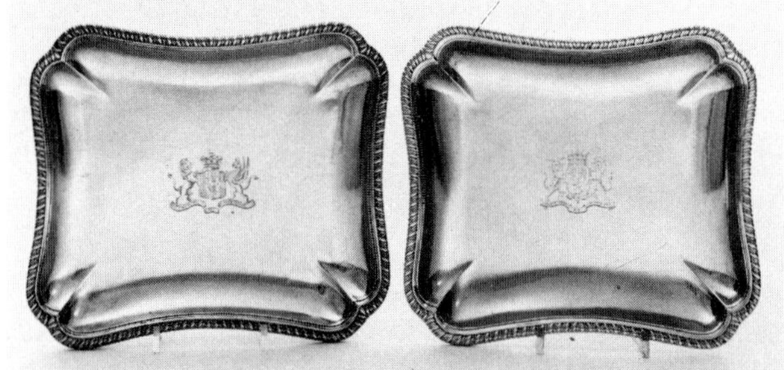

410

411

410. This is one of the earliest forms of entrée dish, called 'cushion shape' for obvious reasons, frequently found without a cover, but occasionally with a domed plated cover. With these early examples armorials were engraved in the centre, a fairly pointless exercise as they could not be seen when the dishes were full.
c.1760 *Pair £4,000 — £6,000*

411. This ribbed circular vegetable dish or entrée dish is of similar quality to the first example, and again the armorials are in the centre of the dish. The gadroon border is a feature found on the majority of entrée dishes.
c.1760 *Pair £4,000 — £6,000*

412. This example is not really an entrée dish but has been included for the purpose of comparison. A shaped oval meat dish and domed cover has been placed on a Sheffield plate heater base.
c.1770 *Pair £6,000 — £9,000*

413. This oval example is not of very heavy gauge, which is the case with all entrée dishes with hinged handles. Not a particularly popular type because they are light and frequently in rather poor condition. From this date it is usual to have a cover.
c.1775 *Pair £3,000 — £4,750*

414. Another oval entrée dish with a cover which doubles as a second dish; instead of a central finial it has two side handles. Again this is of thinner gauge than the following examples. This one has a reeded border typical of the 1790s.
c.1790 *Single £2,250 — £3,250*

415. This cushion shaped entrée dish, with high domed cover, has a beaded border found in the last twenty years of the 18th century. The domed cover has an unusual earl's coronet finial which gives extra character and value.
c.1790 *Pair £5,500 — £8,500*

412

415

414

413

416

416. The octagonal entrée dish was popular over the next decade, both with reeded border as shown here, and with gadroon border. This example has a family crest as the finial, but there is no sign of engraved armorials. It is most likely that these have been removed at some later date as it seems most improbable that a silversmith went to the trouble of casting a family crest finial at great expense without engraving a full coat of arms on the body.
c.1795 *Pair £5,500 — £8,500*

417. This is the classic entrée dish of plain oblong form with gadroon borders and reeded and foliate ring finial, which locks into position in a tongue and groove mechanism. This one has a heater base, normally made in Sheffield plate; perhaps one in a hundred was made in silver. They work on the principle of insulation with hot water or heating by an iron core previously placed in a fire.
c.1810 *Pair £4,500 — £7,000*
(Add £500 for heater bases)

418. Oblong entrée dishes like this example, with a higher domed cover than is usual, are quite popular. The band of lobes above the rim gives the effect of the lid not being quite as high as it actually is.
c.1810 *Pair £6,000 — £9,000*

417

418

419. Occasionally the shape of the entrée dish reverts back to the cushion shaped examples of the 1760s, but they normally come with domed covers, and this example has a very finely modelled crest finial which is also engraved above the coat of arms.
c.1815 *Pair £6,000 — £9,000*
If by Paul Storr £13,500 — £20,000

420. Circular entrée or vegetable dishes were also produced at this time and this example has very similar mouldings to 419, but is on a Sheffield plated heater base with lion mask handles. Circular dishes are not always as popular as the oblong ones, in the same way that circular soup tureens are not as popular as oval ones.
c.1815 *Pair £6,000 — £9,000*

421. Another circular example, this time of much plainer form and consequently a good deal lighter in weight.
c.1815 *Pair £3,500 — £5,000*

422. The plain oblong entrée dish with gadroon borders was popular during the first 35 years of the 19th century, and here is yet another pair showing one of them standing on its Sheffield plated heater base. The boldly modelled shell and foliate feet on the heater base both indicate a late George III or George IV date.
c.1820 *Pair £4,000 — £6,000*
(Add £500 for heater bases)

419

422

421

420

423

423. A slightly more elaborate oblong dish using the leaf flanked shell motif to break up the straightforward gadroon border. The lion mask and acanthus leaf finial is typical of Paul Storr, and other craftsmen, who supplied Rundell, Bridge and Rundell, the royal silversmiths.
c.1820 *Pair £5,000 — £7,500*
By Paul Storr £12,500 — £16,000

424

424. A rather more elaborate version of 423 with heavily modelled shell grips. It is also heavier and this will be reflected in the price. Again probably made by Paul Storr for Rundell, Bridge and Rundell.
c.1825 *Pair £5,500 — £8,000*
By Paul Storr £13,000 — £18,000

425

425. Here is a pair of shaped oval entrée dishes on Sheffield plated heater bases. The entwined foliate finials are a feature which becomes fairly popular from this period onwards. The right hand dish is shown with the contemporary coat of arms, the left hand with a crest within garter motto, which is probably later.
c.1830 *Pair £4,500 — £7,000*
(Add £500 for heater bases)

426. A pair of shaped circular dishes with shell grips and entwined foliate and branch finials. It was often a common procedure to engrave armorials on one side of the lid, and the crest on the other.
c.1835 *Pair £4,500 — £7,000*

426

427. Another pair with ribbed circular bodies and lids. Although the borders and finials are somewhat fussy, the overall effect is slightly more restrained.
c.1835 *Pair £5,000 — £7,500*

428. An oval entrée dish, rather plainer than the preceding example. There are not that many Victorian examples in existence, presumably because the Potteries were by then producing complete porcelain dinner services which were more practical than silver.
c.1845 *Pair £4,000 — £6,000*

429. From the 1830s onwards there was a great vogue for naturalistic motifs, and often entrée dishes were made with finials in the form of various vegetables as in these examples.
c.1855 *Pair £4,500 — £6,500*

427

428

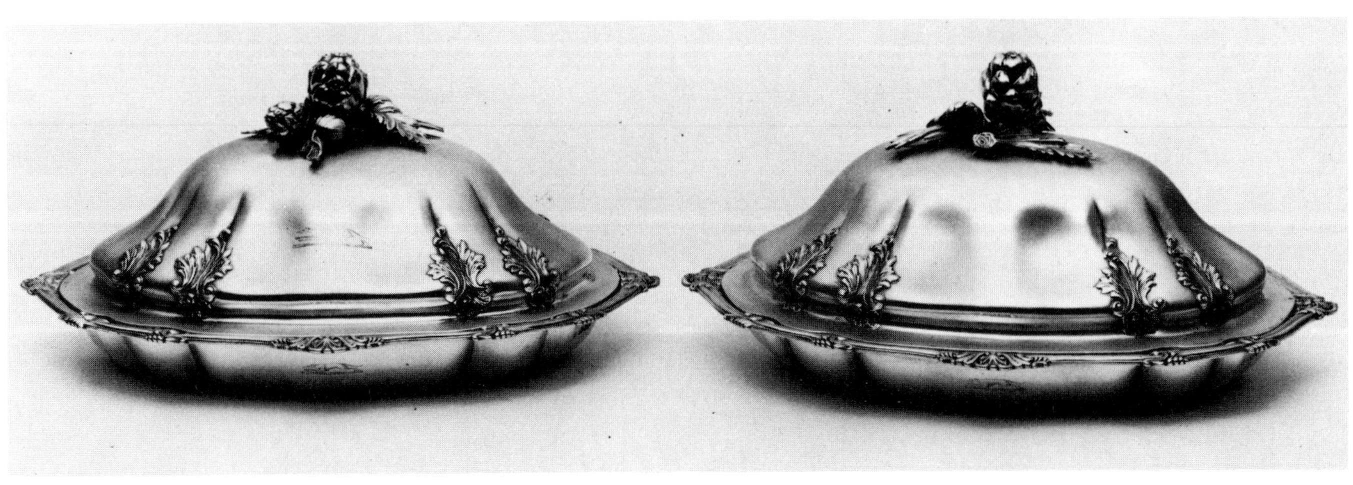

429

430

430. The form of the majority of entrée dishes did not alter much throughout the 19th century. This one still follows the shape used c.1815. There are comparatively few Victorian examples, with most echoing earlier designs.
c.1855 *Per oz. £35 — £55*
1900 and later, per oz. £25 — £35

431

431. These rather extraordinary egg shaped vessels were introduced at this date and are always called breakfast dishes as presumably they were placed on the sideboard containing bacon, kippers or other breakfast fare. An example like this with engraved fern motifs is the most popular.
c.1870 *(Usually found singly) £2,000 — £3,250*

432. A pair of breakfast dishes in the same form as 431. One can see from this illustration how the lid is on a swivel hinge and, when opened, rests right underneath the base. They should all have pierced liners.
c.1880 *Pair £4,000 — £6,500*

432

Sauce Boats

The sauce boat was first introduced into English silver in the reign of George I. The earliest examples are of the double lipped variety, one at either end, and with two scroll handles, one on either side. By 1725 the single lip boat on collet foot was introduced, and by 1740 nearly all examples had three individual supports. These are the three basic variations of the one theme which recur at different periods. They are nearly always oval, only occasionally octagonal or circular, and the earliest examples are shallower and wider. These are not gravy boats, as anyone who has tried using them for this purpose will tell you. Silver conducts heat and you would be likely to have a nasty scald the minute you picked up one filled with gravy. They were therefore used for cold sauces. Prices are given per pair; single examples will normally be 30% to 35% of that price.

Hallmarks: the majority of sauce boats will be marked underneath in a straight line. Occasionally in the 1770s and later they may be marked under the lip, and a few examples with a collet foot are found marked on the foot itself.

Condition: it is fair to say that normally the earliest sauce boats, if they have survived at all, are in fairly good condition, unless they have had armorials removed. Once the three-legged type was introduced there was more likelihood of damage as there are more stress points. Look to see if the feet have been pushed in. This is an area where the bodies can easily split, and sometimes you will find large patches where they have been restored. The sort that have rims not reinforced with an applied border are susceptible to splitting near the rim, and therefore should be examined carefully for a blob of solder where a split has been repaired. The handles, which are in the main cast and applied, are also susceptible to some stress, and should be examined at the joins to see that there is no excessive soldering or repair.

Fakes: sauce boats are not commonly faked, but you will find some early examples are 'duty dodgers' (see p. 256). As with other silver which is on a pedestal foot, I have seen sauce boats which have had marks from a spoon let in on the foot rim, but apart from these examples most other fakes should be apparent after studying this section.

433. A pair of the double lipped sauce boats mentioned in the introduction. Although they are attractive to the collector, they appear impractical as the rims are shaped in such a way that the contents would overflow if filled above a certain level. This type is usually of good heavy quality and here you can see a fine contemporary coat of arms. However, being raised from sheet, it is possible that there may be some weak spots if they are not of thick gauge. Test carefully with thumb and forefinger any area which you may suspect.
c.1725 *Pair £25,000+*

433

434

434. Here is an example of the earliest single lipped sauce boat on a similar oval foot to 433. The engraved armorials displayed on the right hand example are later, and the engraver has made the mistake of using a style fashionable in the William III/Queen Anne period. Notice at the lower terminal to the handle there is an applied oval which is probably an afterthought when it was found the body was not strong enough to take the handle.
c.1730 *Pair £15,000 — £20,000*

435

435. This is the earliest of the three legged examples which are not commonly found until after 1740. This pair is rather unusually attractively engraved below the shaped rim and there is a well engraved cartouche on both sides, one with the crest, the other with the armorials. The hoof foot, occasionally found at this early date, is more common on the flimsier sauce boats made around 1780.
c.1735 *Pair £12,000 — £16,000*

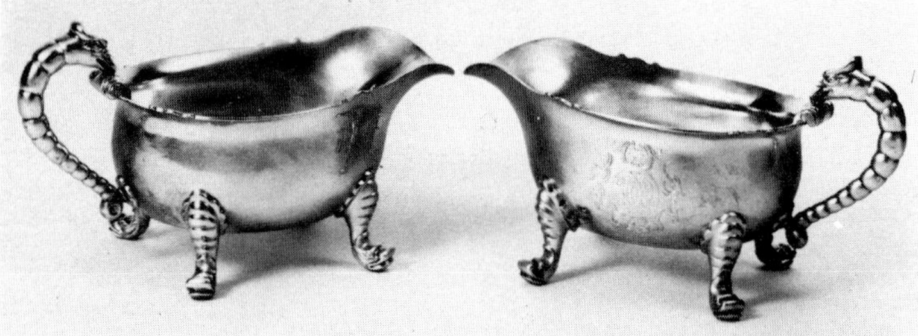

436

436. These are still comparatively shallow and have knuckled feet and handles. The four feet as seen in this pair are rather unusual. The more complex mouldings will mean a heavier quality sauce boat. The plain rims have only a small amount of shaping just above where each foot is applied.
c.1740 *Pair £12,000 — £16,000*

437. The shell shape was occasionally used in the design of sauce boats. This one is out of the ordinary and of good quality; therefore the price will be competitive whereas a single sauce boat is usually worth a lot less than half the price of a pair. This also has an unusual bird's head handle and lion mask and paw feet.
c.1740 *Single £4,500 — £7,500*

437

438. Sauce boats with ornamental handles can turn an ordinary item into the sort of collectors' piece that will command a high price. The flying dolphin gives a completely different appearance to the plain basic shape. Imagine them with ordinary double scroll handles and the price will be halved. The shell feet are used quite a lot with sauce boats. The sauce ladles illustrated were obviously not intended to go with these boats, as they are much too large. They do however date from the same period, the earliest at which one will find ladles.
c.1745 *Pair £12,000 — £18,000*

439. The applied lion mask and paw feet, cartouche and floral swag decoration is worthy of that used by Paul de Lamerie, and again turn a simple shape into a good quality item. The leaf cap, double scroll handle will be found on a large proportion of sauce boats between 1745 and 1765.
c.1745 *Pair £12,000 — £18,000*
If by Paul de Lamerie £85,000+

440. The majority of sauce boats from this date take on the traditional shape and this example has the combination of leaf capped flying scroll handles with gadroon borders. There are so many combinations of the simple themes that it is not possible to illustrate one example of each, but one can compare by mixing and matching. As there are a great many more sauce boats extant from this date onwards, the price comes right down.
c.1750 *Pair £4,000 — £6,500*

441. The shaped rim without any applied border is often susceptible to damage, and the flying scroll handle, whilst giving a more delicate overall effect, can often be strained at the junctions. The likelihood of damage or repair is so high that one rarely sees a perfect pair. This is the lightest and most straightforward design imaginable, and not particularly popular.
c.1750 *Pair £3,000 — £5,000*

438

439

440

441

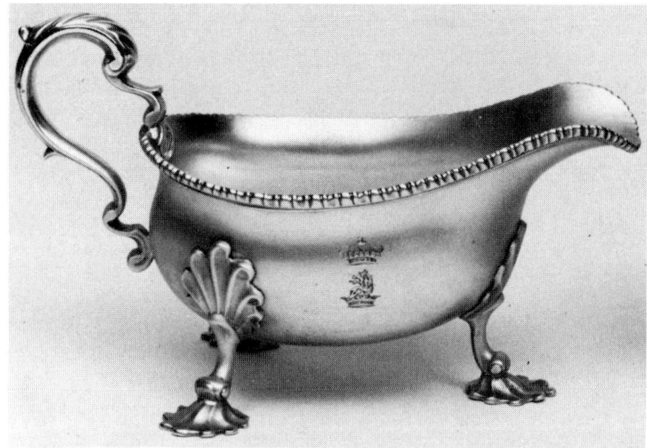
442

443

444

442. Another example from a very straightforward pair but this time without the flying scroll handle and with very boldly modelled shell feet. It looks and is more solid, but look out for thin patches where engraving has been removed.
c.1755 *Pair £4,000 — £6,500*

443. After a period of twenty or so years, the collet or pedestal foot is re-introduced. The handle and border mounts are of traditional shape, whilst the body becomes deeper. This type is occasionally hallmarked under the lip or by the handle although this one is in fact marked underneath.
c.1760 *Pair £5,500 — £8,000*

444. Double lipped sauce boats were occasionally produced later than the 1720s and 1730s but they were nearly always of very individual design (and price!). This example has a heavy cast foot and the side ring handles of earlier examples are replaced by open-work scroll grips. They are more likely to have been used with a ladle rather than for pouring.
c.1760 *Pair £11,500 — £17,500*

445. This very popular type is usually of thick gauge with cast foot and is rarely found in poor condition because of this. The reeded loop handle is much more simple and more practical.
c.1765 *Pair £6,000 — £9,000*

445

446. This is a traditional Irish type with shallow flutes and beads below the punched rim. They are nearly always of very thin gauge and quite often have been repaired, especially around the rim and at the handle junctions. The hoof feet return and are much thinner than on earlier sauce boats and often susceptible to cracking.
c.1770 *Pair £3,000 — £4,500*

447. By this date the sauce tureen was much in evidence and therefore fewer sauce boats were produced. These are of thin gauge again, and have the same sort of punched rim as 446. Notice how some of the legs are bent and, as with the last example they were not made to withstand any rough handling.
c.1780 *Pair £2,500 — £4,000*

448. One of a very bland pair with a delicate band of bright-cut engraving around the foot. The beaded borders will suggest the date. Still of comparatively light gauge and with a larger expanse of body, where one might find weak spots. A few pairs like this by Hester Bateman exist.
c.1790 *Pair £3,000 — £5,000*
If by Hester Bateman £5,500 — £9,000

448

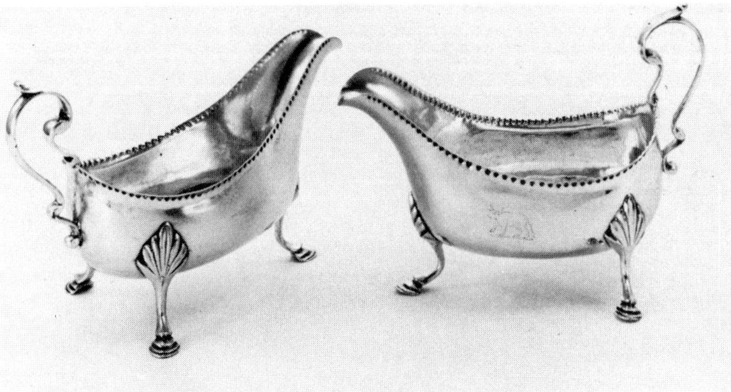
447

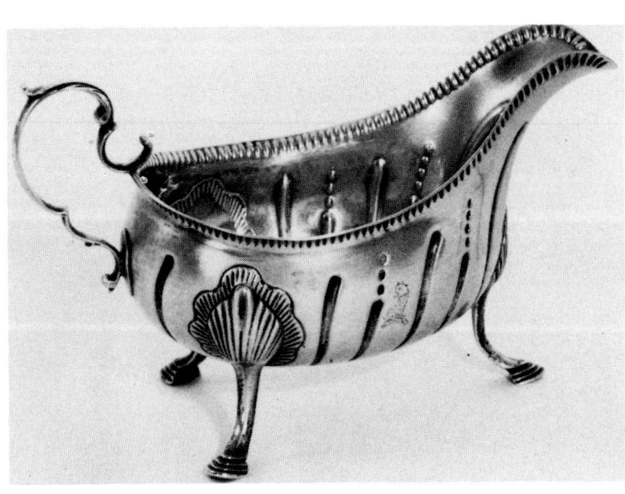
446

449

449. This massive pair of boats made by Paul Storr are the complete antithesis of 448. The Regency period prompted a reaction against the more delicate Adam style, and Paul Storr has here used a mid-18th century design and given it his own interpretation. There is a small amount of flat chasing but the main decoration is all cast and applied.
c.1810 *By Paul Storr, pair £50,000+*

450

450. Another very fine and heavy pair, this time made by Robert Garrard and mainly cast. They are also based on an earlier design of the rococo period by Nicholas Sprimont. The ribbed shell-like body has a detachable liner which makes cleaning easier.
c.1820 *Pair £45,000+*

451

451. A pair of deep boats in early George III style, but with chased acanthus leafage and unusual pierced out feet. This makes them a lot lighter than 452.
c.1825 *Pair £6,500 — £9,500*

452. One from another heavy pair by Robert Garrard. The asymmetrical design indicates a later date, although the handle is still very formal. The armorials, with a crest above without any attempt to enclose it in the cartouche, is also a 19th century innovation.
c.1835 *Pair £8,000 — £13,500*

453. Robert Garrard again has used a similar mount here on the border, whilst embellishing the bodies with dragon-like creatures and using flying scroll handles. Although not made by Paul Storr, the quality is worthy of him!
c.1840 *Pair £10,000 — £14,000*

454. A Victorian copy of a mid-18th century sauce boat, again with flying scroll handle. The silversmith has used sturdy hoof feet but the handle is rather thin, and as you can see, somewhat bent downwards. Look carefully to see that they are not cracked or repaired.
c.1850 *Pair £1,750 — £2,750*

455. Very few new designs of sauce boat were produced from the mid-19th century onwards. Most examples are based on 18th century originals. This pair is copied from a design of c.1735 and is of good heavy quality weighing 34oz. Many copies, however, are extremely flimsy and have not withstood the ravages of time very well.
c.1930 *Pair £1,750 — £3,000*

452

453

454

455

Sauce Tureens

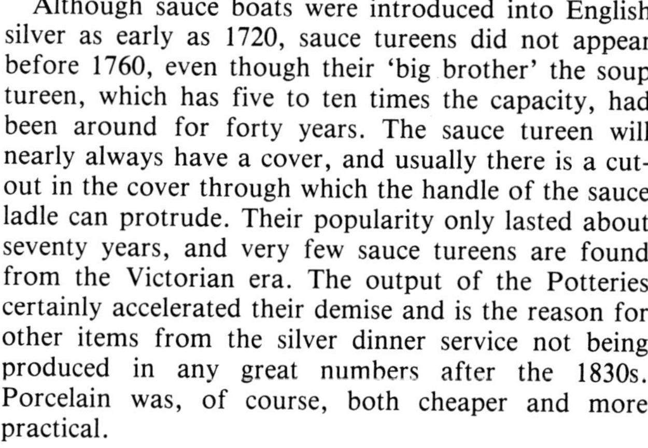

Although sauce boats were introduced into English silver as early as 1720, sauce tureens did not appear before 1760, even though their 'big brother' the soup tureen, which has five to ten times the capacity, had been around for forty years. The sauce tureen will nearly always have a cover, and usually there is a cut-out in the cover through which the handle of the sauce ladle can protrude. Their popularity only lasted about seventy years, and very few sauce tureens are found from the Victorian era. The output of the Potteries certainly accelerated their demise and is the reason for other items from the silver dinner service not being produced in any great numbers after the 1830s. Porcelain was, of course, both cheaper and more practical.

Hallmarks: the main body of the tureen should be fully marked and the lids will also be fully marked or may have maker's mark and lion passant only before 1784, and king's head, lion passant, date letter and maker's mark after 1784. The marks appear in the same position as on soup tureens, that is, either underneath, or in the case of those on a pedestal foot, around the rim of the foot, and occasionally on the body.

Condition: the same comments apply as for soup tureens (see page 154), the main areas to look being on either side where crests or armorials may have been removed.

Fakes: again similar to soup tureens (see page 154). On examples with a pedestal foot look very carefully in case the marks have been let in from a spoon and, if the marks are at all irregular or stretched, be cautious in case it is a conversion from another piece of silver.

456

457

456. An unusual set of four sauce tureens and stands, one of the few types I have seen without covers, made by Thomas Heming, the royal silversmith of the day. Extremely good quality, although not perhaps the most elegant of designs. The stands are like miniature meat dishes and should be fully marked.
c.1765 *Set of four £12,500 — £17,500*

457. One of a pair of shaped oval sauce tureens, a miniature replica of soup tureens of the same period. The pomegranate finial is a popular feature on this type, and is cast and applied, as are the feet.
c.1765 *Pair £5,500 — £8,500*

458. A pair of very heavy quality tureens with covers, stands and their original ladles. They are decorated with almost every conceivable Adam motif, applied goats' masks, swags, Vitruvian scrolls etc. These are again by Thomas Heming and weigh well in excess of 100oz. for the pair. Their individuality will demand a high price.
c.1770 *Pair £25,000 — £35,000*

459. The boat shaped sauce tureen, like the soup tureen, was introduced at about this time and remained popular over the next 25 years. This example has a rather unusual cone finial as well as the applied swags which commend it, although, because it is a single example, the price will be less than half a pair. The foot is cast and applied in a lap joint method to a collar which has already been soldered to the base of the body, as can be seen by the seam on the illustration. This seam would not normally be so noticeable but the camera never lies and the application of dulling spray shows up blemishes.
c.1775 *Pair £4,500 — £7,000*

460. A rather plainer example of the same type with slightly higher lid. The seam where the foot is applied can again be seen and, as the marks are likely to be on the foot, the collector must be sure the body has not been rebuilt.
c.1775 *Single £1,500 — £2,000*
Pair £4,500 — £7,000

460

459

458

461

461. This tureen is even more simplified and has the beaded borders popular around the 1780s. One can quite clearly see on the right of the lid the cut-out for the sauce ladle. The marks around the rim of the base should be carefully examined as this is the place where marks would be let in. the fact that the main marks are all the right way up is a good sign and there is no seam either side of the marks.
c.1780 *Pair £4,500 — £7,000*

462. One of a pair, somewhat lower and more solid than the examples which follow, and with reeded borders. If anything, this is a more popular type than preceding examples because of the smoothness of line and extra weight.
c.1785 *Pair £4,500 — £7,000*

463. An example of the most traditional boat shape, a little lighter than 462, and with simple ring finials to the domed lid. It has very attractive armorials within a drapery cartouche, which gives it more character than if it had been left plain.
c.1790 *Pair £4,500 — £7,000*

464. This slightly later type can be identified by the square pedestal base rather than the oval bases of the earlier ones. The gadroon border is also an indication of slightly later date.
c.1800 *Pair £4,500 — £7,000*

462

463

464

465. A more dumpy version, again on a square pedestal foot, and with additional lobed decoration to the cover. The shape is sliding towards the oblong form which was very popular from 1805 to 1820.
c.1805 *Pair £4,500 — £7,000*

466. One of a pair of oblong tureens following more the line of entrée dishes rather than soup tureens, and with goat's head and drop ring handles as opposed to the more common lion's mask handles. The finials on this type of sauce tureen are often detachable with a thread on the base of the bud, and a nut to hold the finial in place.
c.1805 *Pair £4,000 — £6,000*

467. One of a very heavy pair of oval tureens by Paul Storr. Few other makers would have produced this quality of tureen. The lion mask terminals to the handles are a feature often used by him and he has made the finials in the form of the crest of the landed gentleman who ordered them.
c.1810 *Pair £15,000 — £22,500+*

467

466

465

468

468. One of a pair of circular tureens in the same vein, but not as heavy nor as heavily decorated. As with soup tureens, circular sauce tureens are slightly less popular.
c.1810 *Pair £5,000 — £8,000*
If by Paul Storr £12,000 — £16,000+

469. The very basic design of this oblong tureen and the simply engraved armorial without cartouche is typical of many items of domestic silver made during the first twenty years of the 19th century. These designs were produced with the middle class buyer in mind and therefore the cost has been cut — for the Austin Princess owner as opposed to the man with a Jaguar or better!
c.1815 *Pair £4,000 — £6,000*

470. Another pair of oval tureens, very similar in design to soup tureens of the same period.
c.1815 *Pair £4,500 — £7,000*

469

470

471. One of a pair of oblong sauce tureens with floral and foliate chasing, not of the highest quality. The slender supports with paw feet are also not a great feat of craftsmanship.
c.1820 *Pair £4,000 — £6,000*

472. One of a set of four tureens of dumpy proportions, rather unusually engraved with a crest only within an elaborate cartouche. The finials are in the form of earl's coronets. Although the crest is contemporary, one would normally expect a full coat of arms and, if you find a crest only in a cartouche, check carefully that it has not been engraved later, and that the original arms have not been removed.
c.1825 *Set of four £12,000 — £16,000*
Pair £4,500 — £7,000

473. Sauce tureens were not produced in any quantity much later than this date until the turn of the century when a number of reproductions were made. These examples have die stamped and applied borders and feet and are ribbed to give strength to the body. Made in Sheffield for John Watson and Son, and weighing 54oz. for a pair.
c.1840 *Pair £4,500 — £7,000*

471

472

Soup Tureens

One of the earliest known English soup tureens is one by Paul de Lamerie in the collection of the Duke of Bedford, which is hallmarked 1723. There are quite a number of George II examples, but the soup tureen did not become really common until the reign of George III. The majority of them are oval and this is the most popular form. Oblong and circular examples, although more rare, do not command such high prices. The bodies are usually raised from one piece with border wires, handles and feet cast and applied. The covers are almost invariably domed and have central handles which are fixed by a nut and bolt. They occasionally have detachable liners, which in the case of a very ornate example would have been more than welcome to the person who had to clean out the contents. The liners are not always made in silver, but quite often in Sheffield plate.

Hallmarks: until 1784 the bases and lids should be fully hallmarked but often the detachable handles on the lids are not marked. From 1784 the bases will still be fully hallmarked, but it is acceptable for lids to have maker's mark, monarch's head and lion passant only and normally the handles on the lids will bear these same marks. If there is a stand for the tureen this should be fully marked with the possible omission of the town mark.

474

Condition: the most likely area for damage on a tureen is where the coat of arms or crest has been removed and left the body thin. Because on the whole these tureens are made from one piece, the bodies will not stand having the coats of arms erased more than once, unless of very heavy gauge. If you test the body with your thumb and it is thin, then steer well clear. If it is not thin, breathe on the piece to make sure that a patch has not been inserted. Always examine the area on the body where the feet are applied as these have often been knocked up and again there may be patches.

Fakes: there are very few convincing fakes of soup tureens. The most common type is made from a liner (see above) with feet and handles added and a lid made for it. However, a liner would not be fully hallmarked. The town mark at least would have been omitted. Therefore, if this is missing, you can be fairly confident that it is a fake. Other fakes include examples with a let-in mark, particularly on a tureen with a pedestal foot, as these are marked right on the edge of the foot and so marks from a spoon can easily be inserted. There are also tureens with fake marks — be cautious of anything that is stylistically out of period.

474. To start off with the best here is a shaped oval tureen by Paul de Lamerie. As always the care he has taken with the decoration gives it an almost life-like effect.
c.1740 *£120,000+*

475. When you compare this example with 474, you can see just what a master Lamerie was. Here Thomas Williamson of Dublin has used the same stylistic formula, but the lion masks, although individually quite well modelled, do not tie in with the applied cartouche, the border, or the flat chased cover. It is a much more stilted creation.
c.1745 *£20,000 — £30,000*

475

476. Here is an example of one of the most popularly produced mid-18th century tureens which has fairly basic decoration, apart from the finely cast pomegranate finial. The gadroon borders are in evidence as ever and, although the amount of work put in is less than on 475, the effect is more pleasing and the price not dissimilar.
c.1755 *£17,500 — £27,500*

477. Another example with vegetable finial, but this time decorated with fan lobing.
c.1765 *£15,000 — £22,000*

478. From this date until the end of the century few tureens are found on four feet. The majority have a pedestal foot and the so-called 'boat' shaped body is used extensively. This fine example by Louise Courtauld and George Cowles displays some of those typical Adam motifs. The fluted stand is separate.
c.1765 *With stand £15,000 — £27,500*

479. Frederick Kandler, among others, produced a number of small shaped circular tureens, of which this is one. They are neither particularly beautiful, heavy or popular.
c.1770 *£8,000 — £12,500*

479

478

476

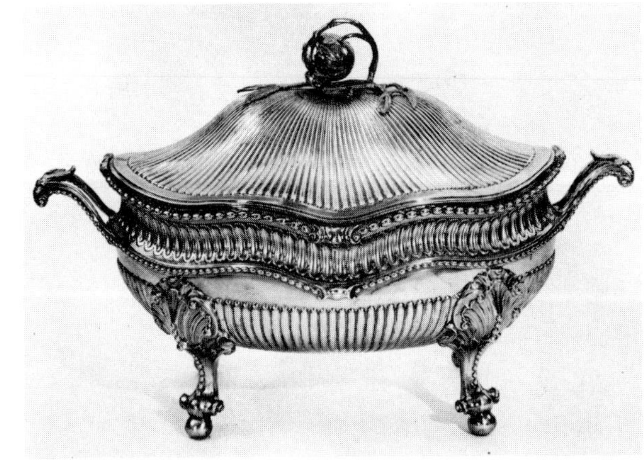

477

480

480. A very plain oval tureen which was quite common, and comes in slightly varying forms. This is the type on which to look out for let in marks around the rim of the foot (see the introduction to this section). Always breathe over the area of the foot wire to make sure there is not more than one seam. The finials on this and the following two examples are often soldered on, rather than bolted.
c.1785 *£9,500 — £15,000*

481. To my mind a much less attractive example of the boat shaped tureen. It is most likely that a coat of arms has been removed from the body, especially as the cover is engraved with two crests. A piece of silver as large as this would be unlikely to have a crest only.
c.1790 *£8,000 — £12,500*

482. An Irish boat shaped tureen, chased with bands of shallow fluting. It is interesting to note that although the armorials are contemporary, they are stylistically out of period because they were either copied from an earlier piece of silver belonging to the same owner, or the engraver was not conversant with the latest fashion.
c.1790 *£8,500 — £14,000*

483. An elaborate example of the boat shaped soup tureen made as a specific presentation piece. The crest finial is an unusual feature on a soup tureen, and is more commonly found on sauce tureens and entrée dishes. Made by John Schofield, and of very good quality.
c.1800 *£15,000 — £22,500*

481

482

483

484. A lobed, oblong soup tureen. This type of decoration was common to many pieces at this date. A more practical than beautiful example in a style which has never been particularly popular and can therefore be bought quite reasonably.
c.1805 *£7,500 — £12,500*

485. A massive soup tureen on a stand by Paul Storr, displaying the sort of features for which he is famous. Bold lion masks decorating the handles and the use of shells and acanthus leafage are typical. The stand is attached by a nut applied to a screw thread soldered to the bottom of each foot.
c.1810 *£50,000+*

486. Almost a replica of a mid-18th century example, but distinguishable as late George III by having a taller overall appearance as well as gadroon and shell borders, and a lobed band, which you would not find on a George II example.
c.1815 *£12,500 — £17,500*

487. This is a less impressive tureen of the same basic shape, which is lighter in weight because the applied decoration is not so bold. The contemporary armorials are a real asset to the design.
c.1815 *£10,000 — £15,000*

484

485

487

486

488. Although apparently similar to 487, this is a much smaller tureen with 'size 17' feet! The only good point is that it is certainly very solid and has therefore remained in pretty good condition.
c.1820 *£8,000 — £12,000*

489. Again a circular example, but with finely cast and modelled dolphin supports, made by John Bridge for the royal silversmiths, Rundell, Bridge and Rundell, and engraved with the royal armorials. Although of similar quality to a piece by Paul de Lamerie (see 474), the composition is not as effective. It is unlikely to be admired by everyone and therefore it might be difficult to sell at the sort of price the workmanship deserves.
c.1825 *£20,000 — £30,000*

490. A shaped oval tureen made in Sheffield with well chased foliate mounts. The gauge of silver was reduced to the minimum acceptable level by the Sheffield manufacturers so that they could offer more competitive prices. The London trade had been so long established that it took Sheffield (assay office established 1773) many years to make any real inroads into their market.
c.1830 *£9,000 — £14,000*

491. Another Sheffield example with a presentation inscription. This does not add to the value unless of particular historical significance. A coat of arms is more acceptable as it is less obviously personal. This tureen is fitted by nuts and bolts to a shaped oblong stand, the proportions of which are not entirely fitting.
c.1835 *£12,500 — £17,500*

488

489

490

491

492. There are few Victorian soup tureens, and those that do exist are usually much lighter and with less ornate mounts than earlier examples. The porcelain soup tureen was much more popular during this period.
c.1850 *£7,500 — £10,000*

493. This tureen draws its inspiration from a mid-18th century original. One might even think from the illustration that it had been made by Thomas Heming in 1760. One giveaway however is the coat of arms which is engraved in a mid-19th century style.
c.1860 *£7,500 — £10,000*

494. A very cumbersome looking tureen with plain gadroon mounts and a rather oddly bulging cover. The engraved armorials are attractive with a drapery mantling which is unusual at this date.
c.1870 *£6,000 — £8,000*

495. A replica of a late 18th century soup tureen in a design which was also used to copy the smaller sauce tureens at this date. This example weighs 54oz. and measures 16½ins. over the handles.
c.1910 *£2,200 — £3,500*
i.e. £42 — £65 per oz.

495

494

492

493

Strawberry Dishes

The name strawberry dish is now commonly given to circular dishes with fluted sides and scalloped rims. They were undoubtedly used for many purposes and some old inventories refer to dishes of this type as 'salad dishes'. They usually measure 7 to 9ins. in diameter, although included in this section are some smaller dishes between 4ins. and 6ins. in diameter, some of which would have been used individually, while others may originally have been *en suite* with an epergne.

Hallmarks: they are usually marked on the base in a line following the curve of the sides, or just below the rim at one point in a straight line.

Condition: strawberry dishes date from the first half of the eighteenth century and as they are generally of a reasonable gauge, if they have survived at all, their condition is quite good. The obvious places to look, however, are for splits in the ribbing or at the rim, and for any weakness in the centre where armorials may have been removed.

Fakes: a number of strawberry dishes have been made from hammering up a dinner plate, but in doing this the hallmarks usually become distorted or are at such a peculiar angle that one can judge something is wrong. They are also likely to be fairly flimsy around the sides if they have been hammered up.

496

496. A very attractive pair of strawberry dishes of typical form, but given a special touch by the finely engraved armorials. The sides are about as deep as they come.
c.1715 *Pair £12,500 — £17,500*

497. A smaller, shallower example with many more ribs to the sides, which is indicative of the later date.
c.1725 *£5,000 — £7,000*

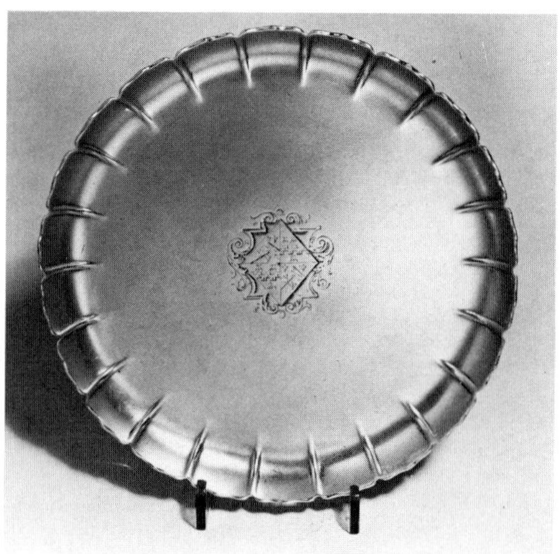

497

498. This small, plain circular dish with slightly raised sides may have been intended as a tea or coffee pot stand. It has no feet but sits on a flat base. The crest and cartouche are probably fifteen or twenty years later as they are obviously rococo in style.
Hallmarked 1723 *£1,750 — £2,750*

499. An unusual strawberry dish which has no ribbing and perhaps is less attractive, the only slight saving grace being the coat of arms.
c.1730 *£5,000 — £7,000*

500. A small dish of strawberry dish form, originally made to go with, or on, an epergne: you may occasionally find signs on the centre underneath where a screw thread has been removed and there may also be four small panel feet. The flutes are finely flat chased and engraved with demi-figures and diaper work, but the centre is engraved with a later coat of arms. The engraver has got the right style, but it is very unlikely that an epergne dish would be engraved with anything more than a crest. He has not been able to capture the boldness, as has the engraver of the dish No. 501.
c.1730 *£2,250 — £3,500*

501. The very fine engraving immediately tells one that this has come from a top workshop; it is in fact by Paul de Lamerie, although other makers like Augustin Courtauld or Paul Crespin might have produced a similar item. The ribbing to the sides does not run through to the base like some of the previous examples, and the base is slightly sunken.
c.1735 *By Paul de Lamerie £22,500 — £35,000*
By another, £7,500 — £10,000

501

500

498

499

502

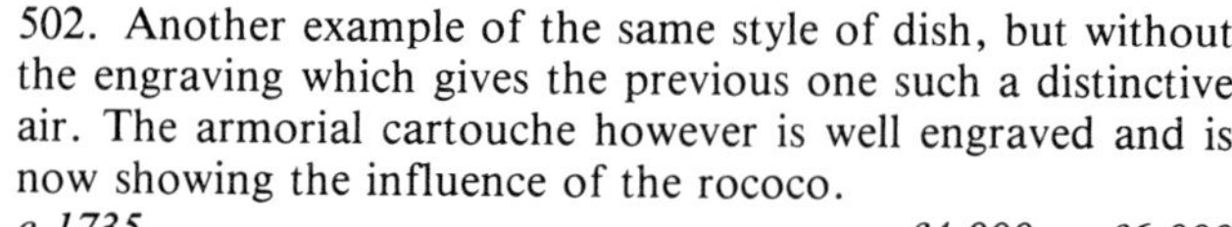

502. Another example of the same style of dish, but without the engraving which gives the previous one such a distinctive air. The armorial cartouche however is well engraved and is now showing the influence of the rococo.
c.1735 *£4,000 — £6,000*

503. A miniature example only 4ins. in diameter which may have been used as a spoon tray. This type has been called a 'patty tin', and it is of convenient size to be used as a bon-bon dish.
c.1740 *£900 — £1,350*

504. Two matching dishes which are similar in style to the preceding, but which unfortunately have been engraved with a coat of arms at a later date. If a previous coat of arms had been removed, there would certainly be some thinness at the centre which could reduce the price by a half. A later coat of arms on its own and, as in this case, not unattractive, would perhaps only reduce the price by 20 or 25%.
c.1745 *Left £2,250 — £3,500*
Right £3,000 — £4,500

505. The rim is turned over instead of being purely vertical and is a feature found on these later examples. The engraved decoration again gives a distinctive appearance and certainly adds 40 or 50% to the value.
c.1745 *£6,000 — £9,000*

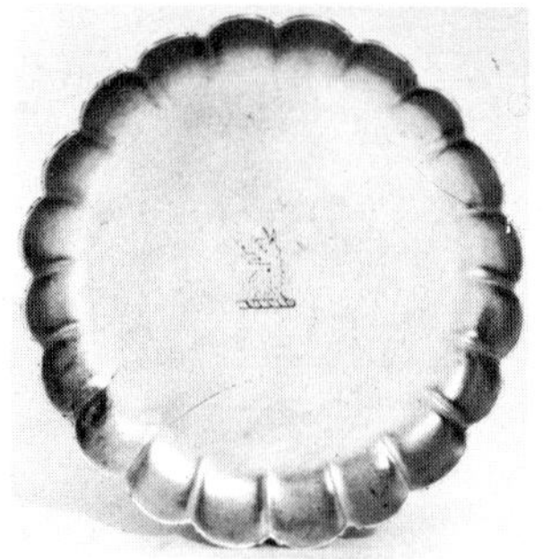

503

505

504

Drinking Vessels

Beakers

Beakers are usually made in three parts, the sides being made from sheet which is hammered into the round and then seamed vertically, and the base and foot wire applied separately. The form of the beaker varies very little from the seventeenth to the nineteenth centuries, but what slight variations there are will be sufficient to give an approximate date when appraising any example.

Hallmarks: normally in a group on the base until late eighteenth century, after which they are usually marked in a line near the lip.

Condition: examine the whole surface for any weak points and/or removed engraving. Look at the rim for any splits.

Fakes: by virtue of the construction of early beakers, it is possible to use the hallmarked base and make a new body. It can be extremely difficult to detect this. If in any doubt about a piece, leave well alone and try always to buy from reputable sources.

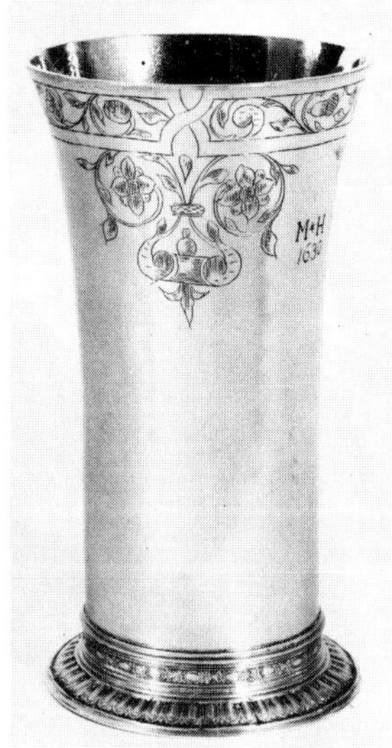

506

506. An early 17th century example, approximately 6ins. high, with the typically hatched scrolling foliage and flowers used from the Elizabethan period up to about 1620. This example has been initialled and dated 1630, about 25 years after it was originally made, but so unobtrusively as not to alter the value. The foot is decorated with stamped ornamentation typical of this period.
c.1605 *£20,000 — £30,000*

507

507. Two mid-17th century examples, again with the hatched decoration, but no longer with the same detail found in the earlier part of the century. Beakers now tend to be 3 to 4ins. high, and the foot wires are usually very plain, as shown here.
c.1650 *Left £3,500 — £5,500*
Right £2,500 — £4,500

508. A Charles II example with embossed flower heads and leafage, a popular Stuart motif.
c.1680 *£2,500 — £4,500*

508

509. A small beaker with cover, hallmarked 1708. Very plain apart from cut card work on the cover. Beakers are comparatively rare at this period but this is not necessarily an indication of high value.
1708 *£2,000 — £3,000*

510. Another Queen Anne example, this one made in Dublin. Note how the repaired split in the body shows up in the photograph. This would not be so noticeable in real life if the piece was 'showroom clean', but would show up if one breathed upon it. A repair like this obviously detracts from value by perhaps 20%.
c.1710 *As shown £2,000 — £3,000*

511. A George II example with contemporary coat of arms. Beakers are now occasionally found in pairs, and of course value is substantially increased per unit.
c.1730 *Single £1,500 — £2,500*
Pair £4,500 — £7,500

512. A George III example with contemporary armorials, the body now tending to become rather more slender with a slightly bolder foot.
c.1770 *Single £1,250 — £1,750*
Pair £3,500 — £5,000

509

510

512

511

513. A double beaker in the form of a barrel. These were made between 1765 and 1800 and are comparatively rare. The earlier examples would be marked on the bases rather than the sides as here. They are quite likely to have gilt interiors.
c.1795 *£2,750 — £4,000*

514. Beakers at any date are comparatively rare, but during the 19th century there are so many small mugs and goblets that it seems few beakers were made. This example is from Hunt and Roskell and hallmarked 1874. The appropriate decoration is hop vine on a matted ground.
1874 *£750 — £1,250*

515. Occasionally in fitted dressing cases there is to be found one or two beakers (toothmugs!). One cologne bottle is shown inside a beaker in the illustration, and this is how it would have been arranged in the rosewood fitted case. These are silver gilt and attractively engraved. The monogram is typical of the style of engraving of the period.
c.1880 *One beaker £600 — £800*
The set, with bottles £1,750 — £2,500

513

514

515

Travelling Beaker Sets

516

517

These are occasionally found from the late seventeenth century onwards and are sometimes referred to as 'camp canteens'. Some have become split up over the years, so any of the items shown in the three examples shown here could be found individually. They are very often incompletely hallmarked, with some of the early examples bearing a maker's mark only. The beaker itself should bear a full set of hallmarks, whilst the other components will often only have maker's mark and lion passant. They were all made with leather or shagreen covered wood cases which follow the shape of the beaker.

516. A late 17th century example with knife, fork, spoon and double spice box, originally probably contained in a fitted leather or shagreen covered case. The handles of the implements all unscrew so that they would fit inside the beaker. The engraving is after designs by Simon Gribelin and therefore gives this set added interest.
c.1690 *£15,000 — £20,000*

517. A travelling beaker set with all the accoutrements fitted inside the beaker. There is a wooden block which has holes for each implement. This set is engraved with the monogram of Queen Charlotte, and this association would add substantially to the value.
c.1790 *£6,000 — £9,000*

518. Another example showing the fitments, this time including a vase shaped spice container which doubles as a corkscrew.
c.1800 *£5,000 — £7,500*

518

Cups & Porringers
(with and without covers)

I have included in this section all two-handled vessels which will incorporate porringers. You will sometimes come across the term 'caudle cup', which is not used very often today, porringer being the more common word. It is debatable in fact whether there is a difference between the usage of the two names; it has been suggested that a porringer is straight sided, whereas a caudle cup is bulbous or baluster. In the main these cups were undoubtedly ornamental, but the word porringer is a derivation of porridge, and caudle was a type of broth given to women convalescent after childbirth; whether the majority of the earlier examples were actually used for these purposes is difficult to say. Certainly from the eighteenth century porringers and later cups and covers were only used as centrepieces or ornaments.

Hallmarks: cups will be marked either on the base in a scattered group, or on the body near the lip and to the side of one handle in a straight line. If there is a cover this will be fully marked, with few exceptions, right into the second quarter of the eighteenth century. After this it is possible to find the maker's mark and lion passant only, and once the monarch's head duty mark is introduced, this should also be included on the cover.

Condition: always examine both sides to see if any engraving has been removed and if there are any thin spots. With the early porringers, look for any holes in the chasing which may still be there, or may have been repaired with solder. It is a good idea to hold the piece up to the light and examine the inside. Always examine around the handles to see that they have not been strained or pulled away and later repaired or altered. If the piece has a foot, make sure that this is not splitting away at the seam, and has not been bashed up into the body. If there is a cover look at the finial as this will occasionally have been repaired or split around its base; look too at both the rim of the cover and the rim of the cup for any splits.

Fakes: fakes will usually involve either let in marks or adaptations and substantial alterations to the original form of the piece. Always try to guess the date of an item before examining the hallmarks. The illustrations below show a two-handled porringer and a detail of the base. Stylistically it appears to be from the 1680s, but the hallmarks tell us that the date is apparently 1724. Further examination however shows us that there is a lot of solder flooded around the edge of the plain area which comprises the foot. The marks have undoubtedly been let is and were perhaps taken from some other piece which was badly damaged. It is difficult to say exactly when this was made, but it is most likely to have been within the last hundred years when silver has been avidly collected. Duty dodging (see p. 256) resulted in another type of common fake in cups and covers, but as long as one is satisfied that the marks are compatible with the style, there should be little problem. It is always nice to be able to see the impression of the hallmarks coming through on the inside of the base.

A porringer (left) whose style appears to be that of the 1680s. In the detail of its base (right) the hallmarks show a date of 1724. Probably, however, it was made within the last 100 years.

519

519. A very early porringer. These rather unusual squat cups are not generally found in any great number before the Restoration. This example has flat chased flower heads and leafage, which developed from pounced decoration and are typical of the late Charles I period.
c.1640 *£15,000 — £25,000*

520. A smaller porringer with the more austere decoration one associates with the Commonwealth period. The matted roundels and punch work have an attractive naïvety. The scroll handles are cast, but not particularly well finished off. The piece is however very desirable in spite of its crudeness.
c.1650 *£7,500 — £12,500*

521. This is the earliest type of Restoration porringer with the lid somewhat clumsily fitting over the upper rim. The ring finial on this example is unusual and one would more often find a capstan shaped finial, which doubles as a small foot if the the lid is taken off and used upside down as a saucer. The bold flowers, including daffodils and poppies were a very popular embellishment.
c.1660 *£10,000 — £15,000*

522. The chasing on this porringer shows a stag amongst flowers. After the Restoration lions, unicorns and dragons, all symbolic beasts with royal associations, were also popular for decoration. The caryatid scroll handles are another feature commonly used, and were usually cast and chased. This example rather unusually has a slightly spreading foot, which one does not normally find after the Restoration.
c.1665 *£5,000 — £7,500*

520

521

522

523. Another example with those daffodils and poppies, but noticeably later in date because of the higher body and lid, which has a rim and bezel to fit inside the cup. Note also that there is no separate foot but a bossed out plain base;
c.1670 *£7,500 — £12,500*

524. Small porringers without covers, measuring only 2 or 3ins. in height, were also fairly popular. The decoration is more often chased or pounced rather than chased in high relief. The handles are occasionally simplified just to pure silver wire, as on this example.
c.1670 *£2,250 — £3,750*

525. After the bold Stuart flowers came the vogue for more restrained acanthus and palm leafage decorating the lower half of the body. This one has an applied cast foot which is common to the larger porringers at this date. Scroll handles now generally become much more simple and have only small tongues or occasionally beaded rat-tails for decoration.
c.1680 *£15,000 — £20,000*

526. A smaller example of the same type, but note that there is no applied foot. The base is slightly hammered out with a small plain band before the decoration starts. The engraved crest is later in date, probably mid-18th century.
c.1680 *£2,500 — £3,750*

526

525

523

524

527

527. At this time cut card work, indicative of heavy quality, was introduced as a popular form of decoration. This porringer has a simple band of applied leaf motifs around the base, whilst it is otherwise very plain and solid, relieved only by the contemporary widow's armorials.
c.1680 *£4,500 — £7,500*

528. A porringer with chinoiserie decoration, typical of the period. The scroll handles have beaded rat-tails as a further embellishment.
c.1685 *£40,000 — £75,000*

529. From the reign of William and Mary through to Queen Anne, the curved lobes and flutes, as seen on the lower body of this porringer, were a popular form of decoration. This is perhaps one of the most common types of all with, in this case, a scale and acanthus cartouche. These are usually comparatively light in weight.
c.1700 *£1,500 — £2,800*

530. A larger covered example with the same type of decoration, but in this case no chased cartouche. Still of comparatively thin gauge, but not so common as 529 which is much smaller and would never have had a cover.
c.1700 *£7,000 — £10,000*

528

529

530

531. This is a very fine cup with applied cut card work, which is usually indicative of heavy quality. The contemporary coat of arms is also typical of the period in that the cartouche is engraved in more detail than the armorials. At this date there was not a universal understanding of how to engrave the different tinctures, and so only the main charges are engraved with some shading, in this instance six amulets or rings on the left (male) side of the shield, and three dogs' heads on the right (female) side.
c.1700 *£27,500 — £40,000*

532. A very plain example that would be extremely boring without the contemporary coat of arms, which gives the piece what little character it has. The thin solid scroll handles will not appear much later than this.
c.1705 *£5,000 — £8,000*

533. The shallow fluting on this cup is not only a form of decoration, but also gives more rigidity to the piece, thus enabling the gauge of silver to be reduced. The scroll handles are made in two halves and soldered together, so there will be an airhole at the heel.
c.1705 *£6,000 — £9,000*

533

532

531

534

534. This is a Dublin made example displaying similar decoration to 533. The armorials are not of the latest fashion, and could in fact have been copied from a design twenty years earlier in date. This is not unusual on a piece made outside London.

c.1705 *£3,000 — £4,000*

535. A pair of cups and covers of very simple but solid design with the applied girdle which becomes a common feature over the next twenty to thirty years. The engravers' art is becoming more developed and this fine earl's coat of arms is the saving grace on these cups and prevents them from being totally boring.

c.1710 *Pair £15,000 — £25,000*

536. A superlative example of applied strapwork, which like cut card work, is indicative of heavy quality and was a Huguenot innovation. This example by David Willaume, which weighs in excess of 150oz. as opposed to the more normal 60-80oz., is probably as good a cup as one will find at this date.

c.1715 *£30,000 — £45,000*

537. A cup of 60-80oz. and about 12ins. high, with applied strapwork, this time incorporating classical portrait busts and rather more ornate decoration than the preceding example. Again of very heavy quality, and with a more involved coat of arms. The double scroll handles are cast in two halves.

c.1730 *£12,500 — £20,000*

535

536

537

538. This simple type of two handled cup was produced with very little variation from 1725 to 1765. This one is in fact hallmarked 1736 and has that typical applied girdle. It is much smaller than the preceding examples, measuring only about 5 or 6ins. high.
c.1736 *£1,000 — £1,750*

539. A fine cup and cover made at the height of the rococo movement, with asymmetrical applied strapwork, bordered by scale work chasing. The applied cartouche is also a feature frequently used at this date. Even from the illustration you can see that this is in excellent condition with decoration as crisp as you could hope for; all the same look out for any cracks or flaws in the applied cast work.
c.1740 *£12,500 — £20,000*

540. An example with contemporary flat chased decoration, without any applied work apart from the girdle. It is not as pleasing as 539 because the decoration is rather insignificant and not in sympathy with the size of the cup. A much less important piece that might look better without the chasing. The fact that the handles are more ornate than on a plain cup gives an assurance that the decoration is not later.
c.1745 *£6,000 — £9,000*

540

538

539

541

541. The chasing on this example is in slightly higher relief than the preceding cup, and is very reminiscent of that used on sets of tea caddies made by Samuel Taylor. The chased cartouche is again a common feature. Although the handles are similar to those found on plain cups this does not necessarily indicate later chasing. The decoration is quite restrained, whereas a 19th century chaser would have covered the whole surface with flowers and scrolls.
c.1745 *£4,000 — £6,000*

542. Pairs of two handled cups, similar in size to 538, were very popular in Ireland in the 18th century. These were made by Robert Calderwood of Dublin, who is a sought-after maker, and have the benefit of an attractively engraved coat of arms. The leaf capped double scroll handles indicate a later date than 538.
c.1750 *Pair £2,250 — £3,500*

543. A fine cup with applied and chased decoration of grape vines, which is undoubtedly contemporary. This very pleasing example was made by John Swift.
c.1755 *£12,500 — £20,000*

544. Another example displaying grape vine decoration, this one made by Thomas Heming, and with serpents entwined around the handles. Although not as fine as the John Swift cup, it is a very good piece.
c.1760 *£10,000 — £17,500*

542

543

544

545. This is after a design by William Kent of 1735, the original example being made in gold. The majority of decoration is cast and applied. Again of very heavy quality. The existence of the original design will add weight to the price.
c.1760 *£14,000 — £22,000*

546. These two cups were made by Samuel Johns of Limerick, and are similar in design to 538, made in 1736, but with a much higher foot. The price would be little more than half if they were London marked pieces.
c.1760 *Right £1,750 — £2,750*
Left £1,250 — £2,000

547. This cup is after an Adam design for Lord Dundas, and several variations of the theme were produced, mainly for Richmond and Doncaster Races. The majority are silver gilt, and the same plaques of horses and jockeys are cast and applied, although the cups differ.
c.1765 *£25,000 — £40,000*

548. A Dublin made, silver gilt cup and cover, with chased stiff leafage. The attractively engraved coat of arms is stylistically typical of this period.
c.1775 *£8,000 — £12,000*

548

547

545

546

549

549. This is a more typical vase shaped cup found at this period. It tapers more steeply to the junction of the foot, while the cover is more peaked and again has that stiff leafage. The Prince of Wales' plumes could indicate a Royal presentation and any hint of its recipient will push up the price.
c.1780 *£8,000 — £12,000*

550. A very fine example in silver gilt by Hester Bateman (her mark can add 50%-100% to the price). Being just ten years later than the previous example, it is even taller and thinner.
c.1790 *By Hester Bateman £14,000 — £22,000*

551. Another Dublin made cup (see 542) of a type that is often found in pairs. Examples are only 5½ to 7ins. high and are less expensive than earlier pairs. The price, however, depends a great deal on whether or not they are attractively engraved.
c.1790 *Pair £1,100 — £1,600*

552. Here is a cup executed by Paul Storr from a design by John Flaxman, R.A. The combination of a famous designer and a top maker can send the price through the ceiling. Flaxman and others produced many designs based on classical and biblical stories and events, and adapted from pieces which were discovered by archeologists. This is silver gilt, very heavy and 14¼ins. high.
c.1810 *£70,000+*

550

551

552

553. The campana shape was very popular between 1815 and 1840 for presentation cups. This example is in fact a silver gilt racing trophy.
c.1820 *£7,500 — £11,000*

554. Matthew Boulton is the most renowned of Birmingham silversmiths; the fact that an assay office was established there was in large part due to him. Here is a racing trophy made by him illustrating a variety of fine decoration which is superb when examined band by band, but the overall effect is cluttered. Nonetheless a fine piece of silver.
c.1820 *£6,000 — £9,000*

555. An early Victorian cup and cover with a higher foot than one finds on early 19th century cups, and a flower finial, a popular late feature.
c.1850 *£3,000 — £4,500*

556. The Victorian period was rife with people presenting cups, as well as other items of silver, for all manner of events from agricultural or horticultural prizes, to racing or sailing trophies, and this example is for the Great National Brass Band Contest! It is often possible to find in the Public Records Office contemporary accounts of a presentation, and any historical association can add to the value.
c.1860 *£750 — £1,250*

556

553

554

555

557. A large presentation trophy cup and cover. The adventurous waisted design is on slender pedestal foot with applied scroll brackets. Pieces of this nature are not particularly popular unless their design is attractive or there is some interesting historical association. This one weighs just over 100oz.
c.1865 *£3,000 — £5,000*

558. A cup and cover in Gothic taste with enamelled royal armorials. Again a Trophy cup weighing 80oz.
c.1885 *£2,500 — £4,000*

559. This is a direct copy of an 18th century design from c.1765 but more massive than the original is likely to have been. This example weighs 105oz.
c.1900 *£2,500 — £4,000*

557

558

559

560. This attractive small silver gilt cup and cover is again likely to have been made as a presentation piece and is engraved with the arms of a baron. It weighs only 12oz. but because it is so attractive, will fetch a much higher price per ounce than some of the massive examples already seen.
c.1900 *£400 — £600*

561. Many cups were made in this very simple design as presentation pieces. They are mass-produced with spun bodies and applied handles and feet. If there is no sign of an inscription, it will have almost certainly been erased. Value will be closely related to silver content.
c.1905 *Per oz. £8 — £15*

562. Heavy silver gilt cups of this individual type and design will only occasionally command a high price as they have very specific appeal. This one weighs 180oz. but has unusual sea-horse handles and tower stem, both relating to the chased city armorials.
c.1910 *£4,500 — £7,000*

562

560

561

Goblets

Wine goblets in English silver from 1600 onwards were fairly common until the latter part of the century when the popularity of glass pushed them into comparative obscurity until a century later. Churches, however, would always have had metal for communion vessels and there are goblets made for this purpose dating from between 1680 and 1760. Mugs were also popular throughout the eighteenth century and perhaps contributed to the disappearance of goblets. From 1760 onwards, the advent of new silversmithing techniques gave a lift to production because of competitive pricing, and goblets became more commonplace until 1820 when the popularity seems to wane again.

Hallmarks: in the seventeenth century, goblets should be marked on the foot with a lion passant, and on the bowl with the full complement of marks, although this is not always the case. If there is no mark on the foot, make absolutely sure that it has not been restored or replaced. Eighteenth century examples can be marked with the full set of marks on the bowl or on the foot. The marks will usually be in a curve following the line of the foot, or in a straight line around the bowl.

Condition: examine the rim for any splits or repaired splits, and the bowl for any weak spots where engraving may have been removed. Look at the base of the bowl for any reinforcement and bad dents where the foot may have been pushed upwards into it. If there is any decoration make sure it is contemporary — if it is later the price can be halved.

Fakes: one of the most common types of fake is where a mark from a spoon or fork has been let in to the foot rim. Careful examination should reveal a seam at either side of the mark and, if the hallmarks are at all distorted or placed differently to the options discussed above, then beware.

563

563. Most parish churches in existence at this date would have had a chalice very similar to the illustrated example. The cover doubles as a paten. The engraved arabesques are the most common type of decoration, and usually the foot wire will have stamped ornament of tongue and dart. The decoration on the cover is not clearly visible, but again a much used form is 'hit and miss', which basically consists of parallel lines of spaced dashes.
c.1570 *£7,000 — £10,000*

564. A James I wine cup with flat chased or pounced decoration of grape vine, very often found in silver gilt. The foot rim has similar stamped ornament to 563, but the stem now is very different in that it is slender and cast in two halves. This type is obviously secular and is generally more sought after than the communion chalice.
c.1610 *£17,500 — £30,000*

565. From this date plain wine goblets are found and usually have a slightly tapering bowl, cast baluster stem and spreading foot. They are always marked in an almost straight line just below the rim and should have the lion passant on the underside of the foot. Look out for repairs at the base of the bowl. Occasionally the foot may have come off and a reinforcing patch applied.
c.1630 *£7,500 — £12,500*

566. This type of wine goblet was probably made as a communion vessel and is made at the same period as the preceding example. It should again be hallmarked in the same way. If it bears any religious inscription or device the value is not enhanced. Occasionally sunbursts are engraved with 'IHS' at the centre and this reduces the value by about 50%; understandably collectors are not keen to have a sacred vessel.
c.1650 *£5,000 — £8,000*

567. At this time small wine goblets about 4 or 5ins. in height are found with matted or sometimes a shallow embossed decoration as shown in the two illustrated here. These are not common but when they are offered for sale are comparatively highly priced for their size. Quite often they are pricked with contemporary initials and sometimes a date.
c.1650 *£4,000 — £6,000*

567

564

565

566

568

568. In the 17th century travellers and merchants brought back to this country coconuts, exotic shells and rare birds' eggs, which were given silver mounts. This is an example of how a coconut was used to form the bowl of a wine goblet. These very often only have a maker's mark or perhaps no mark at all. They are rarely found with a full set of hallmarks. 17th century examples like this one normally had the rim mount joined to the foot mount by three equally spaced vertical straps. This example has typical hatched leafage at the borders, common during the reign of Charles II. Soon after this date the vogue for mounting coconuts died out for a time, and it is not until the reign of George III that examples are again found. At that date the coconut is often completely lined in silver and the foot and rim mounts are extremely plain and do not have any vertical straps.
c.1680 *Maker's mark only £1,500 — £2,500*
Add 75% if hallmarked
Deduct 30% if no mark at all

569

569. A small Charles II wine goblet with very severe beaker shaped bowl and simple trumpet foot, the only decoration being a corded wire around the base of the bowl. From this date until the reign of George III wine goblets become rarities although obviously a certain number of chalices were made.
c.1680 *£4,000 — £6,000*

570. Wine goblets are now reintroduced as a piece of domestic silver. Bowls are usually fairly thin and one should look for repaired splits around the lip. At this date one would expect to find hallmarks either near the rim or on the edge of the foot. If on the latter look carefully to see whether the marks have been let in from a spoon handle. If they have been, a small seam will be found on either side of the marks, maybe an inch or two away from the nearest mark.
c.1765 *Single £600 — £800*
Pair £1,500 — £2,750

571. Goblets become rather more elegant now with more vase shaped bowls and higher slender stems. This example has a beaded foot wire and is most likely to be marked underneath the foot. The armorial is a welcome bonus to an otherwise rather plain piece.
c.1780 *£700 — £900*

570 571

572. The base of the bowl and the stem merge at this date and give a simpler line. Bright-cut engraving is also popular now and if it is crisp and not worn, can add up to 100% to the value in comparison with a plain example. It is also quite common to find the bowls with gilt interiors, which was used because gold does not stain as easily as silver.
c.1790 *£750 — £1,500*

573. One of a pair of wine goblets with chased stiff leafage at the base of the bowls. This type of goblet will be heavier than the plain or bright-cut engraved examples because of the extra thickness of silver necessary for chasing.
c.1790 *Single £700 — £900*
Pair £2,000 — £3,750

574. An example with Greek key type motifs at the borders, a popular feature at this period, which was also used as ornamentation on teapots, milk jugs and other domestic silver. The scrolling initials are probably contemporary and do not particularly add or subtract from the basic value. This is an even sturdier example than 573 — silver from 1800-1820 is often heavier and more solidly designed than the Adam silver of the preceding 25 years.
c.1800 *£600 — £900*

575. A rather more squat example with octagonal foot and a band of wriggle engraved fruit and nuts at the rim. The crest would probably add slightly to the value as it is less obviously personal than, for example, the initials on 574.
c.1800 *£600 — £900*

576. A pair of very plain design with the rather dumpy proportions often found after the turn of the century, perhaps a reaction to the sophisticated and elegant line of the Adam period. The engraving is the only thing that gives a hint of interest.
c.1805 *Single £600 — £800*
Pair £1,400 — £2,500

576

575

572

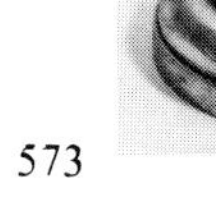

573

574

577

577. One of a pair of campana shaped wine goblets with applied vine motifs with the mark of Paul Storr for Rundell, Bridge and Rundell, the royal silversmiths of the day. This was not however an exclusive Paul Storr design and can be found by other makers. This looks, and indeed is heavier than the other examples shown so far. The weight is characteristic of the majority of silver with the maker's mark of Paul Storr. Note Rundells' Latin inscription on the foot.
c.1815 *Single £2,000 — £3,500*
Pair £7,500 — £10,000

578. A rarity, just for fun! A coronation souvenir of George IV, the wooden goblet with applied silver mounts and a shield engraved with the royal armorials. It is unlikely that this type of goblet would have been made in the numbers produced for 20th century coronations and celebrations, and therefore has rarity value.
c.1820 *£1,750 — £3,000*

579. As with most things Victorian, the decoration is more involved. This goblet is chased with a hunting scene and is of campana shape and has a slightly higher domed foot than earlier examples.
c.1840 *£500 — £750*

580. An attractively engraved small goblet, perhaps intended as a christening cup because of its smaller size. The only lozenge left vacant would have been for a crest or initials. Look carefully to see that nothing has been removed.
c.1850 *£500 — £750*

578

579

580

581. Four different wine goblets of the mid-Victorian period showing some of the typical decoration used. These were often inscribed as presentation pieces and have since been erased, almost certainly leaving the body weak, particularly as they were not in any case of very heavy gauge.
1870 and 1880s *Each £250 — £400*

582. This is a replica of a wager or marriage cup, based on a 17th century design. Quite a number of these copies were made in Germany and imported into England. They are fairly popular as ornamental items, but traditionally they were used by filling up the skirt and the small goblet held above the head, which pivots on two pins near the rim. Then either one person drank the contents of both without spilling, or husband and wife drank from the piece at the same time, again hopefully without spilling!
c.1880 *£650 — £1,000*

583. This was probably meant as just an ornamental vase rather than a goblet and is based on a Pompeiian original. The body is cast and chased and has an inner sleeve. It measures some 4 or 5ins. high.
c.1890 *£400 — £600*

584. Three wine goblets by Omar Ramsden and a pair on the right by Ramsden and Carr, made between 1915 and 1930, and showing their very individual designs with that typical hammered finish to the bowls.
1915-1930 *Each £500 — £800*

584

583

581

582

Mugs

During the nineteenth century it became a popular fashion to give a mug as a christening present, but seventeenth and eighteenth century examples were certainly used for alcoholic beverages. The term 'mug' is traditionally used for a single-handled, lidless drinking vessel. They are nearly all either of pint or half pint capacity, and like tankards, they are raised from sheet silver in one piece with no seams, and then the spreading foot and handle are soldered on. A half pint example is worth 60% of a pint mug in comparable condition. The cylindrical examples at the end of the eighteenth century are usually hammered into the round from sheet and seamed under the handle. The popularity of mugs stretches over the same period as that of tankards, that is, from the late seventeenth to the late eighteenth century, and it is possible to trace the stylistic changes within the period.

Hallmarks: mugs are normally marked on the base until the 1770s, after which it was more common for them to be marked on the side, near the handle. There are, however, exceptions to this rule as some are marked on the body in the early eighteenth century, and some are marked underneath in the late eighteenth century. Occasionally a mug might be hallmarked on the body and have the maker's mark on the base.

Condition: the mug, in the same way as the tankard, has often been subjected to a hard life, and should be examined carefully. Always test the front to see whether any weak spots are apparent where engraving has been removed and make sure there are no patches. Look at the handle junction to see whether they have been split, damaged or repaired, and look at the foot to see that it has not been bashed up into the body.

Fakes: mugs were also, like tankards, candidates for the 19th century chaser, and one should be dubious of any example which is decorated. I illustrate an example, c.1770, which has been decorated in the 19th century. Whilst some people prefer these more ornate pieces, to the collector this one is a non-starter, and the value is about half that of a good example in original condition. The other common alteration to a mug is the conversion to a milk jug, and the small octagonal christening mug as shown here hallmarked 1846 has had a lip added some 50 years or so later. This constitutes an illegal alteration to the piece and unless the spout is officially hallmarked, it is not legally saleable in this country, and indeed, neither is it particularly desirable.

An 18th century mug decorated by a 19th century chaser.

A Christening mug, hallmarked 1846, converted into a milk jug by the addition of a lip.

585. This is the earliest type of mug you are likely to come across. Mugs are very rarely found as early as tankards. The body is raised from sheet with applied heavy foot wire and simple strap handle with a beaded rat-tail. The reeded neck is incised and not applied.
c.1680 *Pint £2,000 — £3,000*

586. A similar example with chinoiserie engraving which adds substantially to the value.
c.1685 *Pint £6,000 — £9,000*

587. A bulbous example with chased lobes and flutes as found on tankards of the same period. The handle is a cast solid type, not hollow like those found on tankards. These are not found as frequently as the type shown in 585 and therefore have some rarity value. They also tend to be slightly heavier.
c.1695 *Pint £2,500 — £4,000*

588. A tapered cylindrical example with reeded band near to the neck and the hollow scroll handle with beaded rat-tail. Mugs from now on tend to follow the line of tankards. This type is invariably marked on the body (see 589).
c.1700 *Pint £2,000 — £3,000*

588

587

585

586

589

589. A similar but plainer example engraved with the royal arms, A.R. for Anna Regina, which adds to the value. Any historical interest other than the age of the piece itself is an added selling point and therefore puts up the price. The hallmarks can be seen on the body of the mug.
c.1705 *Pint £2,750 — £4,500*

590. A typically Scottish mug called a 'thistle' cup because of its shape. The lobes are applied and not embossed from the inside. The girdle, the foot and the handle are also applied. Always examine these areas for any poor original workmanship or later repairs.
c.1700 *Half pint £3,250 — £5,000*

591. A plainer example of the same basic shape. Pairs are occasionally found and this increases the value. The price would be lower than for 590 because the design is not as adventurous.
c.1700 *Half pint, single £2,250 — £4,000*
Half pint, pair £6,000 — £10,000

592. A tot cup or small mug, perhaps used as a stirrup cup before setting off at the hunt (see p. 193). Stirrup cups in silver did not become really popular until the reign of George III. This example has a cast spreading foot and applied wire at the rim.
c.1715 *£1,500 — £2,500*

590

591

592

593. A tapered mug with double scroll handle which is cast in two halves and then soldered together. The base is slightly tucked in above the cast and applied spreading foot.
c.1720 *Pint £1,500 — £2,750*

594. A pair of mugs with double scroll handles, again cast in two halves, with small tongue on the top scroll. Although the shape is basically the same as tankards at this date, they differ by not having an applied girdle and by having cast handles. Inexplicably pairs of mid-18th century mugs tend to sell for half as much again as two single examples. Supply and demand? It is difficult to find pairs.
c.1740 *Pint, single £1,200 — £1,800*
Pair £3,000 — £5,000

595. Mugs have now become slightly taller and more baluster in shape. This pair of mugs still has a double scroll handle cast in two halves, the upper scroll now with leaf capping. The engraved crest is Scottish because it has a banner above with motto; crests in English heraldry are rarely found with mottoes at this date.
c.1760 *Pint, single £900 — £1,500*
Pair £2,750 — £4,500

596. An unusual barrel shaped example with matted alternate panels to simulate the staves of a barrel. The reeded loop handle is also an unusual feature. This mug is somewhat larger than the preceding examples.
c.1775 *Quart £2,000 — £3,000*

596

595

593

594

597

597. A tapered cylindrical mug, very similar to tankards of the period in both design and size, but with a tongue on top of the scroll handle. If there is no tongue, look carefully to see that a hinge and lid have not been removed. Mugs are usually smaller than their contemporary tankards.
c.1790 *Quart £1,500 — £2,250*

598. With the start of the 19th century the pint mug and tankard become less common, the only mugs frequently found being small christening cups. This shows two tapered cylindrical mugs with reeded bands. This type of mug was popular from the late 1790s up until 1820 as a christening present. The example on the left is 1816 and that on the right 1814, both with a London hallmark. Very simply made with a seam which can be seen running down under the handle terminals.
c.1815 *Either example, half pint £350 — £550*

599. A George IV christening or child's mug of baluster shape with the rather indifferent chasing which is common at this date. Look for any lead solder or other repairs in the chasing. Some of the marks are slightly rubbed, but still legible and acceptable.
1822 *£400 — £600*

600. A campana shaped example with scrolling foliate handle and curved ribs interspersed by applied flower heads. Look carefully at the foot to see there are no splits and that it is not bashed up into the body.
c.1835 *£400 — £600*

601. This rare silver electrotype cup in ancient Greek taste was manufactured by Elkington and Co. in Britannia standard silver. It is only some 4½ins. high, but weighs a whacking 16oz., rather than the more usual 7-8oz. It is the only time I have come across the Britannia mark on a Birmingham made piece.
c.1845 *£750 — £1,250*

598

599

600

601

602. A panelled christening mug decorated with children in various pursuits. Anything slightly unusual will command a high price if in good condition. The base on this example is rather unhappy however and would mitigate against a very high price.
c.1850 *£750 — £1,200*

603. Two floral embossed christening mugs typical of the period, each with very small double scroll handles. Look out for erased inscriptions.
c.1855 *Each £300 — £500*

604. A more unusual silver gilt christening mug with the maker's mark of Francis Higgins, with the winged cupid handle and foot cast and the decoration to the body chased.
c.1865 *£600 — £1,200*

605. Two mugs of very similar shape, one displaying floral engraving within strapwork cartouches and with mask terminated handle, and the other with bands of foliage and matting within beaded surrounds. This type of mug is the most common in the mid-Victorian era. The decoration will vary but the basic shape stays the same.
c.1870 *£250 — £450*

605

605

604

602

603

606. A larger mug, 6½ins. high and weighing 12oz. It was probably made as a presentation piece.
c.1870 *Pint £500 — £900*

607. A christening set in a case. These sets were usually in silver gilt. This was highly impracticable and therefore they are nearly always in good condition and very collectable.
c.1870 *£1,500 — £3,000*

608. A christening mug, again bright-cut engraved with ferns and a butterfly so popular at this period. The ball feet and simple loop handle may be practical, but are certainly not beautiful.
c.1875 *£400 — £600*

609. An unusual mug in the style of the Arts and Crafts Movement made for Liberty and Co. Limited. The naïve 'antique' decoration commands a high price nowadays as long as the piece is from a recognisable stable. This example is inset with cabochons at the rim, and is only some 3¼ins. high.
c.1900 *£1,200 — £2,000*

606

607

609

608

Stirrup Cups

The name 'stirrup cup' derives from having a cup whilst one's feet were in the stirrups. It was filled with a drink such as mulled wine and served to the huntsman when already mounted. Various designs of fox masks examples are known. The earlier they are, the less realistically modelled they seem to be. Some of them have inscriptions around the neck, such as 'Tally Ho!' or 'Success to Fox Hunting'. I have also illustrated in this section some rarer types.

Hallmarks: occasionally one comes across examples which are unmarked but generally they should be hallmarked somewhere around the neck in a straight line.

Condition: defects in condition should be easily visible on such a small object. Hold it up to the light and look for any holes. Look to see that any texturing or decoration is not too worn and that there are no bad splits in the ears, or around the rim.

Fakes: some fakes are known where a mask stirrup cup has been made and had marks from a spoon let into the rim mount. Look for any unusually placed seams and make sure that it is in the period style that coincides with the marks.

610

610. Mask stirrup cups were first introduced in the early 1760s and usually took the form of a fox's head. At this date they are usually chased in two halves and soldered together. These early examples are usually much flatter than real life, with bared teeth.
c.1760-1775 *£4,000 — £6,000*

611

611. A hare's head example, extremely rare, made in the late 18th century, and again like the early fox masks, rather unrealistically modelled.
Late 18th century *£6,000 — £9,000*

612

612. From the late 1790s onwards the fox's mask was rather more realistically modelled. The great exponent of this was the firm of Phipps and Robinson.
c.1800 *The larger £4,000 — £6,000*
The smaller £3,000 — £5,000

613. Another hare's head example from the early 19th century. As with the fox head examples, the modelling has improved.
Early 19th century £6,000 — £9,000

614. A stag's head example with very clear hallmarks for London, 1847. Some artistic licence has been used with the antlers to make a handle. This is a rare type and therefore should command a higher price than one from the same period.
1847 £6,000 — £9,000

615. A fox mask stirrup cup with suspension ring. The modelling and tooling of the face are even more realistic than on earlier examples. Very often the later in date the heavier in quality.
c.1850 £2,750 — £4,500

616. This fox mask is of the same heavy quality (24oz.) but does not look quite as docile as the preceding examples.
c.1885 £4,000 — £6,000
20th century example
(unlikely to be as heavy, perhaps 12oz.) £1,500 — £2,500

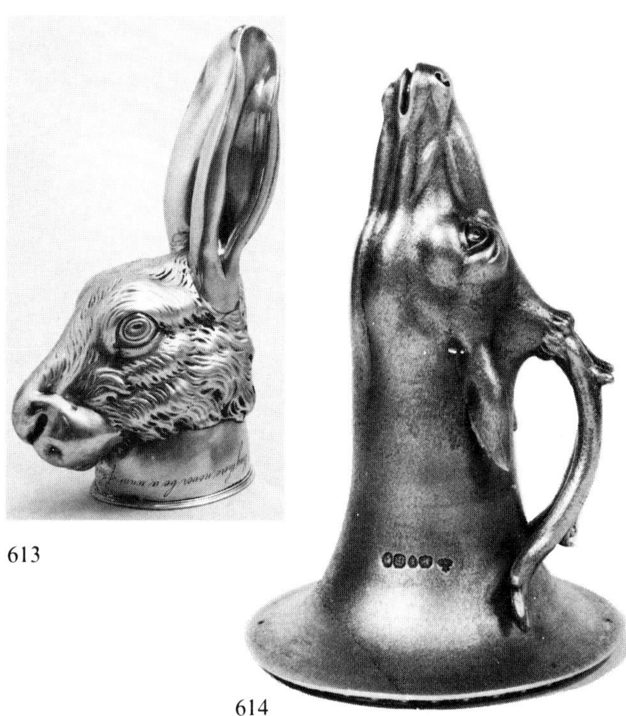

613

614

615 616

Tankards

The tankard has been popular with collectors for a long time and although unlikely to be used for its original purpose today, it makes a nice centrepiece for a small table. From the late seventeenth century to the late eighteenth century a great number of tankards were made, but outside this period very few seem to exist. It is possible to trace the stylistic changes within this period, as you will see, but later and earlier examples are so few that there is no set form. Tankards are very often of quart capacity, usually much bigger than mugs, which were on the whole of pint or half pint capacity. The name is traditionally used for a single handled drinking vessel with a lid.

Hallmarks: London marked tankards should all have a full set of marks on both lid and base, and up to the George I period the handles should bear a maker's mark. This occasionally differs from the maker's mark on the body of the tankard as there were specialist handle makers. Some provincial tankards will be found without hallmarks on the lid, or perhaps just a lion passant and/or maker's mark.

Condition: the tankard was obviously susceptible to great wear and should be examined very carefully. There may be splits or repairs around the lid and occasionally the flat lids of the late seventeenth century and early eighteenth century are later domed in the George I period to accommodate the latest fashion. Always look at the rim for any splits, especially near the handles. The barrel should be examined for any weak spots and for any erased engraving.

Fakes: the majority of tankards were not decorated, although you will see one or two examples on the following pages which are exceptions. The tankard was obviously considered vulgar in the Victorian period and a number have been converted to jugs by the addition of a spout and/or embossed and chased with flowers and scrolls so that they are more ornamental. Illustration (a) is of a tankard of about 1780 which has been chased in this way, and has also had a later coat of arms engraved. This will halve the value. Illustration (b) is of a Commonwealth tankard with good marks for 1652. The decoration has again been added probably about 180 years later. This would now probably sell for a third of the value of a good example. (c) is of a late George III tankard/jug which is in fact authentic and in its original form. Compare it with the similar style tankard (No. 641) later in the section and you will see that the main difference is that the lid is domed. You would be well advised to avoid any jug that looks vaguely like a tankard unless the price is right.

(a)

(b)

(c)

617

618

617. This is probably the forerunner of the tankard and is in fact a German pottery baluster vessel, sometimes known as 'tiger ware' because of the speckled glaze, with Elizabethan silver mounts. The foot and lid are nearly always embossed and chased with fruit and foliage. The rim mount can be engraved, as here, or embossed. These vessels date between 1550 and 1610.

c.1590 — *£25,000 — £40,000*

Without hallmark £10,000 — £15,000

618. This rare type of tankard was found in the late Elizabethan and early James I periods and would more usually be found with engraved formal foliage. The border ornament stamped from a repeating die is typical of this period and is not found on latcr tankards.

c.1610 — *£40,000 — £60,000*

619. This is the earliest date at which the familiar basic tankard shape occurs. Although the quality would usually be rather good and heavy, the whole thing is very simple and austere and, without any armorial, looks rather dull. The thumb pieces are very plain but a more elaborate design develops later in the century. The scroll handle however remains in this form on the majority of tankards right into the 18th century.

c.1640 — *£20,000 — £30,000*

620. Although this is the most commonly found 16th century tankard, they are not often discovered in good condition. The lid now has a single step to it and the borders are reeded. The armorial engraving with scrolling foliate mantling is typical, as is the twin cusp thumb piece. The handles on tankards are made in two parts, a curved undersection and a flat outside section. These are soldered together and applied to the tankard. During this process the air inside the handle expands and so there has to be an outlet for this, usually a small hole or slit in the bottom terminal. People have often thought that this slit was in fact a whistle to call for more ale!

c.1675 — *£10,000 — £17,000*

619

620

621. This type of tankard was perfected by John Plummer, a York silversmith, from a design imported from Scandinavia, where pomegranate feet and thumb pieces were common. Occasionally similar tankards were made by other York and Newcastle makers. The engraving is particularly fine and adds substantially to the value. The handle however has been subject to some clumsy repair and this will obviously detract from the value by perhaps 10-15% but careful restoration would eliminate this.
c.1675 *£20,000 — £30,000*

622. An unusual example which you are unlikely to come across, but we can all live in hope! Tankards were rarely decorated to such an extent. This particular example is made by Jacob Bodendick, who was an ex-patriot German where highly decorated tankards were fairly common at this date. This example is absolutely right and has not been decorated at a later date. If you find one with decoration, try to imagine what it would have look like if it had been plain, if you then think it is the same basic shape as one of the plain tankards on these pages — beware!
c.1675 *£30,000 — £50,000*

623. A cylindrical tankard with acanthus and laurel leaf embossing to the lower body, which again is 'right'. The engraved armorial with plumage springing from vases is also typical of this date. The thumb piece is of entwined scrolling foliage, but the twin dolphin type as seen on 624 is more typical.
c.1680 *£12,000 — £18,000*

624. A plainer example than 623, but with cut card decoration (which adds to the value) around the leaf capped handle. The lid has a twin dolphin thumb piece. 'Triad' initials are often found at this date and are usually those of husband and wife, the upper initial being the surname, e.g. this tankard could have been made for 'William and Freda Aldridge'.
c.1680 *£9,000 — £15,000*

624

623

621

622

625

625. Another example showing acanthus embossing. The barrel however is a rare quatrefoil shape, the lid and foot conforming in outline.
c.1680 *£20,000 — £30,000*

626. A tankard with chinoiserie decoration which was popular over about a ten year period. It is however rarely found and adds considerably to the value if the condition is good and the decoration not worn. The handle is still of the same scroll type. This thumb piece is usually termed a corkscrew thumb piece. The cover has two steps, a development from about 1675 onwards.
c.1685 *£35,000 — £50,000*

627. An example without decoration other than the armorial, which is in fact a (merry?) widow's coat of arms! (The lozenge-shaped shield denotes a widow.) The majority of tankards are of quart capacity, and this is no exception.
c.1690 *£10,000 — £15,000*

628. A tankard displaying chased alternate lobes and flutes. Occasionally tankards have had this decoration added later, but when this is so, the decoration is often more prolific and covers more of the surface area. It is nearly always the case that the heel of the tankard handles touch the table, if it does not, a rim foot may have been added.
c.1690 *£10,000 — £14,000*

626

627

628

629. A Queen Anne example. The foot is now slightly bigger and domed outward and the thumb piece is simplified to the foliate volute type. The engraved armorials are perhaps slightly old fashioned as the 'foliate mantling' cartouche had all but died out by 1700.
c.1705 *£8,000 — £12,000*

630. This example has a lion thumb piece which was occasionally used from 1690 up to 1720, and adds to the value. Applied girdles around the body are now fairly commonplace and handles occasionally have a reversed small scroll section near the heel. The contemporary armorial is more simple than some of the late 17th century engraving.
c.1710 *£12,000 — £18,000*

631. This type of tankard enjoyed a fairly long reign with only minor variations. Lids become slightly domed and careful examination should be made if there is a dome in the lid earlier than this date as occasionally 17th century examples are re-fashioned. Thumb pieces again slightly more simple.
1710-1730 *£5,000 — £8,000*

632. The body is now slightly tucked at the base with an applied foot spreading further. The cover is slightly more domed and with an extra ridge. The engraving of armorials is rather more adventurous and occasionally incorporates masks or figures and animals.
c.1725 *£4,000 — £6,000*

632

629

631

630

633. This is a Scottish example with a finial in the centre of the lid, a feature which is rarely found on London examples. There are however a few Newcastle tankards known with this type of finial. The thumb piece is also not of a type found in London at this date.
c.1725 *£5,000 — £8,000*

634. A Newcastle example of c.1740 with leaf cap scroll handle, more typically found on mugs. Note the absence of a thumb piece. Very fine rococo armorial.
c.1740 *£5,000 — £8,000*

635. An example showing the applied girdle and with openwork 'chair back' thumb piece. The lid no longer has a shaped peak.
c.1735 *£3,500 — £6,000*

636. A slightly plainer example with a similar thumb piece to 635. Double scroll handles are now common.
c.1740 *£3,500 — £6,000*

633

634

636

635

637. A tapered cylindrical example, again with similar thumb piece; the double scroll handle has a heart shaped terminal. A rather unusual girdle is used here with corded motif, rather than the more commonly found reeded type already shown.
c.1745 *£3,000 — £4,750*

638. Another baluster tankard with volute thumb piece and slightly higher domed cover.
c.1760 *£3,000 — £5,000*

639. An unusual example displaying the familiar Adam motifs of rams' masks and swags, also with applied bands of acanthus foliage and reeded loop handle. Tankards with contemporary decoration are rare, whilst later decorated examples are plentiful.
c.1775 *£5,000 — £8,000*

640. A tapered cylindrical example, having a comparatively simple skirt foot with open-work chair back thumb piece to the domed lid. The later the tankard the more slender and taller it becomes in both plain and cylindrical examples, and baluster ones up to 1800.
c.1780 *£3,000 — £4,750*

640

639

637

638

641

641. A cylindrical example with reeded hoops almost imitating a barrel. The squared off scroll handle is typical and note the much simplified hinge made by pinning two lugs on either side of the handle. Erect open-work thumb piece. This type is not as popular as earlier examples because of its rather severe lines.
c.1795 *£2,250 — £3,500*

642. Tankards were not generally made in the 19th century but here is an example which was presumably commissioned for a sporting man and whilst the shape is 18th century, the decoration is Victorian. Also, if you compare it with some of the earlier ones, you will see that the handle on this one differs in that it is more tubular and has a leaf capped upper scroll, more in the style of a mug handle.
c.1850 *£1,750 — £3,000*

643. Other 19th century tankards fall into two categories. They are either replicas of earlier examples, or made as large trophies. This one is based on the 17th century Norwegian original and is 11½ins. high. Quite probably used as a biscuit barrel or simply an ornament.
c.1860 *£2,750 — £4,000*

642

643

644. This is a large horse racing trophy appropriately chased and applied with horses and on massive lobed base and bun feet. It weighs 130oz. and was made for R. and S. Garrard and Co.
c.1860 *£6,000 — £10,000*

645. Again a purely ornamental piece made by Charles and George Fox and weighing 90oz. It is obviously heavy to lift, even when empty, and therefore should perhaps be called a centrepiece rather than a tankard.
c.1865 *£4,500 — £8,000*

646. Another presentation piece of more usable size, weighing 27oz. and a combination of Danish and English 17th century design.
c.1870 *£1,500 — £2,000*

647. The London City Companies often commission replicas of some of their earlier tankards or other early pieces to present to members of the Company. This is a 37oz. copy of the Clothworkers' Company 'Burton' Tankard. The original dates from the late 17th century.
Hallmarked 1937 *£1,500 — £2,000*

647

646

644

645

Tumbler Cups

Tumbler cups were made from the mid-seventeenth century, throughout the eighteenth century and occasionally later. These are very plain, small bowl shaped drinking vessels and are hammered up from sheet silver of thick gauge, the sides becoming thinner towards the top, leaving a greater weight at the rounded base. When they are knocked onto their sides they will automatically right themselves — hence their name. Seventeenth century examples are usually shallower and wider than those made in the eighteenth century, but the basic shape does not really alter over a century and a half.

Set of four tumbler cups with extremely convincing fake hallmarks for 1698.

Hallmarks: tumbler cups can bc hallmarked either on the base or on the sides, or even sometimes with hallmarks on the side and the maker's mark on the base.

Fakes: very few tumbler cups are faked. However, a set of four is illustrated (above left) with extremely good fake hallmarks for 1698. These were only detected because (a) the fake marks are a well known series and have a specialist spoon maker's mark, and (b) the very obvious hammer marks which would normally on the originals have been smoothed down to a plain surface. It was also somewhat suspicious that this was a set of four, when no other set had ever been recorded.

648

648. A 17th century example, which as you can see, is slightly wider than it is tall. A number of provincial makers produced tumbler cups of this type, including those in York, Newcastle, Hull and Norwich. Provincial examples command a higher price than the equivalent London made tumbler cups, but it is difficult to be precise about the differential. Norwich and York are the most popular.

17th century	*London example £1,250 — £2,000*

649

649. A pair of tumbler cups, hallmarked 1721, one showing the hallmarks, the maker's mark being on the base, and the other displaying a crest in a cartouche headed by a baron's coronet.

1721	*Single £1,000 — £1,500*
	Pair £2,500 — £4,000

650

650. Two George II examples, both with Latin inscriptions; and with initials on the smaller one.

	George II	*George III*
Large	*£750 — £1,250*	*£600 — £900*
Small	*£500 — £750*	*£400 — £600*

Egg Cruets

The egg cruet frame was first introduced in the eighteenth century and provided the silversmith with an excuse to make something slightly different. The egg cups nearly always have gilt interiors, otherwise the frame is made entirely of silver gilt as the gilding does not suffer from egg yolk stains or tarnish like silver. They are not considered particularly beautiful or useful today. The size varies to accommodate four or more egg cups in a frame, and the cruet includes spoons and an occasional salt cellar.

Hallmarks: they should be marked on all detachable parts. If the spoons are original they will not necessarily be by the same maker as the rest of the frame as spoons were made by specialist makers. Frequently however they have been replaced by teaspoons of assorted dates and makers and this obviously reduces the value.

Condition: the majority of frames are of fairly flimsy manufacture and they should be carefully examined for any reinforcements or repairs. Egg cups are unlikely to have any hidden damage as they are such small items, and any repair should be easy to see.

Fakes: I have never come across a fake egg cruet frame, and in my opinion these items are so hideous that I cannot imagine why anyone should want to produce a fake!

651. A six cup frame with a salt cellar at the centre. The spoons are not original. They are teaspoons and not egg spoons and so the value is reduced overall compared with 652.
c.1790 *£1,250 — £2,000*

652. Another example from the same period, this time with proper egg spoons. These have certainly been with the frame for over 150 years as all the pieces bear the same crest and motto, which date from the early Victorian period.
c.1790 *£1,250 — £2,000*

653. A six cup frame with gadroon borders, so often used at this period. The spoons are missing. The frame is of the heavier quality one would expect to find during the Regency period.
c.1810 *£1,500 — £2,500*

651

652

653

654

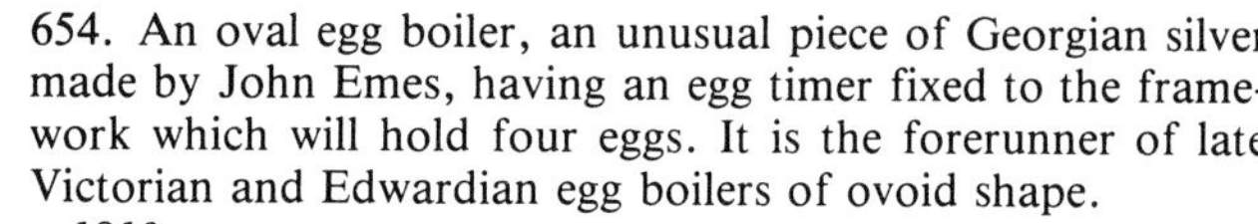

654. An oval egg boiler, an unusual piece of Georgian silver made by John Emes, having an egg timer fixed to the framework which will hold four eggs. It is the forerunner of late Victorian and Edwardian egg boilers of ovoid shape.
c.1810 *£1,800 — £2,750*

655. An early Victorian wirework frame of small cake basket form with only four cups. At least on this example some thought has been put into the design, and it is not purely functional.
c.1850 *£1,250 — £2,000*

656. There are few egg cruets in existence and the majority of mid- to late 19th century examples are replicas of earlier Georgian designs. This is in the style of c.1800, but is of a slightly heavier quality than the original would have been. As it is also only 100 years old, it is likely to be in a rather better condition.
c.1875 *£1,250 — £2,000*

655

656

Epergnes & Centrepieces

The epergne, or centrepiece, was introduced into English silver in the mid-eighteenth century. Eighteenth century examples consist of a large central basket which is flanked by smaller dishes or baskets, the earliest type having four small dishes, and by the Adam period six or more. They are nearly always fairly elaborate and were presumably used for holding fruit and petit fours. At the beginning of the nineteenth century the use of glass dishes on a silver framework became popular and was taken up in various forms by the Victorians. For the amount of work and craftsmanship involved they do not command high prices because one needs a very large table to put one on. They may be from twenty to thirty inches across and weigh up to about 150oz. It is also, of course, a very laborious task to clean them.

Hallmarks: all detachable parts of the epergne should be marked. The large central basket (which is usually detachable) and the four-legged stand should both have a full set of hallmarks, whilst the branches and dishes (which are detachable) should at least have the maker's mark and lion passant. After 1784 the monarch's head duty mark should also be included on these, and in the nineteenth century a date letter as well.

Condition: it is very important to look for any damage to the piercing, for splits or breaks at the rims to the baskets, and for repairs to the scroll arms. They probably need more careful examination than any other item discussed in this book because there are so many vulnerable parts.

Fakes: I do not know of any fakes but see 663.

657

658

657. This is the earliest type that one is likely to come across with a pierced central dish. The four small flanking dishes are a type which can be given an added sconce and handle to make them into a fake chamber candlestick (see p. 71). The openwork apron between the four main supports is cast and applied. It is very susceptible to damage as pieces can be broken off whilst cleaning if handled roughly.
c.1750 *£17,500 — £30,000*

658. An even more elaborate example. This time, instead of having four dishes, it has four small sweetmeat baskets which are pierced with a similar design to the central basket. They also have swing handles so that they can be used individually without the main body of the piece. Sometimes small baskets of this type appear on the market and are sold as sweetmeat baskets. They will however only have maker's mark and lion passant and should be priced at much less than a contemporary sweetmeat basket.
c.1760 *£15,000 — £25,000*

659

659. Once into the George III period epergnes usually have six or more side baskets and dishes. This elaborate example is decorated with vine motifs and has four small baskets with swing handles and, rather unusually, four glass dishes with silver mounts. It is quite possible that the silver mounts on the glass dishes will not be marked.
c.1760 *£15,000 — £27,500*

660. Ten years later the cast and applied decoration disappears and most of the effect is given by the shaped panels of piercing to the baskets. This very leggy example is unusual in having only four baskets.
c.1770 *£10,000 — £15,000*

661. The use of bright-cut engraving and less intricate piercing is now apparent, and there is a rather more airy and light appearance to the whole thing. The engraved armorials on a piece of this type do not necessarily contribute to the value as they have a lot of other decoration with which to compete. On this type always look for any breaks in the applied hanging swags, and adjust the price if there are any bad repairs.
c.1790 *£15,000 — £25,000*

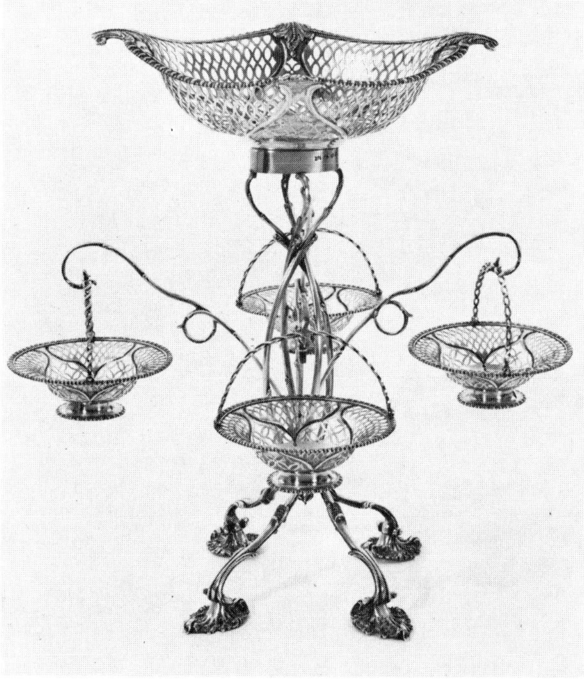

660

661

662. A slightly more elaborate version of the same type of epergne, the central basket this time, however, has two loop handles.
c.1790 *£15,000 — £25,000*

663. Here is a curious centrepiece. If one compares it with the preceding example, it can be seen that the central basket and four smaller dishes are of a very similar nature, if one ignores all the applied grapevines. A silversmith in the 1830s has used a mid-George III epergne and re-created a centrepiece of even more flamboyant style. Apart from the baskets, the only other part which remains roughly in its original state, is the oval base, though this has had goat's mask feet applied to it. The cherubs and the female figures all date from the 1830s, and as long as all the additions have been hallmarked, it is legally saleable. Not a piece to buy, unless you fall in love with it, as its resale potential will not be great.
£7,000 — £10,000

664. This example is made by Matthew Boulton of Birmingham and has a silver framework used with glass dishes. The branches are all detachable, as are the glass dishes. If any of these dishes are damaged or broken the value will be drastically reduced. A number of this type were made in Sheffield plate and command about one fifth the price of a silver example. They sometimes appear without their glass dishes, which may reduce the value to less than one tenth.
c.1810 *£9,000 — £15,000*

665. Occasionally centrepieces combine a candelabrum with a central dish. This example has six candle branches and a glass dish for the ornamental fruit or flowers. This combination became popular in the Victorian period. A lot more silver was used and the extra weight will mean extra cost. The candle branches should be marked as mentioned in the introduction, and, as on candelabra, the detachable sconces and nozzles should also bear marks. This one is of particularly fine quality, if a little fussy, and is another masterpiece by Paul Storr. The weight is three or four times that of earlier examples.
c.1815 *£30,000 — £50,000*

665

664

662

663

666

666. A combination of central dish and candle branches is used here again, but in true Victorian taste they are more fussily decorated with grapevine and the stem is applied with three classical female figures. Messrs. Barnard of London and Elkington of Birmingham were possibly the most prolific makers of these large centrepieces. The latter also produced great numbers of them in silver plate. The designs vary tremendously, some having various animals such as stags, goats or horses, whilst others have either male or female figures, and perhaps more commonly, sickly little cherubs.
c.1850 *£8,000 — £14,000*

667. This is a much more modest centrepiece for a smaller table, and could have been made either for use on its own, or there may have been two or four all matching, which would have flanked a centrepiece similar to 666. This measures only about 12ins. high, whereas the previous piece is two and a half times that size.
c.1860 *£1,000 — £2,000*

668. Another centrepiece of similar proportions, this time with four cast seahorses applied to the base.
c.1870 *£1,000 — £2,000*

667

668

669. A more massive centrepiece with four classical female figures supporting the central dish and two sweet little cherubs holding up the side dishes.
c.1870 *Per oz. £40 — £60*

670. The combination of flower vases and fruit dishes was another popular Victorian innovation and this example, whilst having a comparatively plain silver stand, has attractively etched glass rather than cut glass. A great deal of value is placed on having all the original dishes and vases.
c.1880 *£2,250 — £3,750*

671. Here is a pair of silver gilt dessert stands which could quite happily be used individually today in the centre of a small table. Most of the decoration to the bases is cast and applied, whilst the dishes are pierced and chased.
c.1880 *£2,250 — £3,750*

671

670

669

672. A shaped oval epergne in art nouveau taste, manufactured by Elkington and Co. of Birmingham and with cut glass dishes. It is 28ins. wide, but weighs only 46oz. (of silver).
c.1905 *£2,000 — £3,000*

673. A centrepiece entirely in silver with ribbed and shaped detachable bowls. It is 20ins. wide and weighs 56oz.
c.1910 *£2,500 — £3,500*

674. A much larger centrepiece with attractive piercing to the borders. Although weighing 200oz. and nearly 3ft. high, the open-work airy design makes it appear much lighter.
c.1920 *£6,000 — £9,000*

672

673

674

Inkstands

The inkstand was not a common feature of household silver until the eighteenth century. Some seventeenth century examples exist, but these are really so rare that they are outside the scope of this book. The main requirement was to have a container for ink and a container for the sand or pounce, which was used for drying the ink rather than the blotting paper we know today. There would also be space to put the quills. In addition there may be a taper stick to hold a small candle for melting the sealing wax, and perhaps a container for wafers which were also used as seals. A number of the early eighteenth century inkstands also have bells to call the servant so that the letter may be despatched.

Hallmarks: all the parts of the inkstand should be marked, the main stand itself bearing the full set of hallmarks and the detachable parts with the maker's mark and the standard mark, i.e. the lion passant.

Condition: examine the stand for additions or repairs to the feet and body. Make sure that crests or armorials are contemporary, that no later chasing has occurred, and that there are no additions to the original form. If any of the removable parts are not hallmarked, careful examination should reveal whether these have been replaced. Comparison of the colour and tone of the silver and the form of construction should make this apparent.

Fakes: the most likely fakes are those where a small oblong dish or tray (particularly late eighteenth century snuffer trays) has had inkwells added to it, and a lack of matching hallmarks would normally point to this.

675

675. A George I inkstand with oblong base incurved at the angles. The raised sides are engraved with leafage which is probably a later embellishment. The armorials however are contemporary and occur twice on the stand. The inkwell, pounce pot and bell are merely engraved with a crest.
c.1715 *£20,000 — £30,000*

676

676. A similar example but rather plainer and with royal armorials, which add to the value. This was perhaps issued to an ambassador or government minister and if any known historical association exists, this would also increase the price. The plain curved feet are typical of the period and may also be found on salvers.
c.1720 *£20,000 — £30,000*

677

677. A rather more elaborate George II example, displaying the free design of the rococo period with gadrooned border and shell feet. There are pen depressions on either side of the fittings and one should always examine these to make sure that they have not been added later. The bell has none of the gadrooning shown on the inkpot and pounce pot and is engraved with a different crest. Without even examining the hallmarks, this would indicate that it is a later replacement or at least not originally with the inkstand.
c.1740 *£7,000 — £10,000*
With the right bell £10,000 — £15,000

678

678. A simple oblong example, this time without a bell but with a wafer pot and just one pen depression below the raised border. It has a crest in a rococo cartouche on the opposite side. A very simple and functional piece with no great artistic merit.
c.1740 *£6,000 — £8,000*

679

679. A shaped oblong example, this time displaying more adventurous craftsmanship with scroll and shell borders, again with just one pen depression, and instead of a wafer pot, a quill holder. The claw-and-ball feet are a feature also found on salvers of this period.
c.1745 *£6,000 — £8,000*

680. An oblong example, this time with central taperstick flanked by the pounce pot and inkwell. The bold gadroon and shell borders give a very solid appearance, and indeed this is a good example.
c.1745 *£7,000 — £10,000*

680

681. An extremely functional and tedious example with inkwell, pounce pot and taperstick as in the preceding example, but this time with two pen depressions as well. The only decorative features are the shaped oval base, the armorial and the ball-and-claw feet.
c.1750 *£5,000 — £8,000*

682. A so-called gallery inkstand because of the fret pierced sides and divisions. The base is usually made in one piece and the sides are applied with lap-over joints and there should therefore be a hallmark, not only on the base, but on the sides as well. Although this example measures no more than 5ins. to 6ins. in length, larger examples are found. As with all other pierced work at this date there is always a possibility of damage and repair, and the piercing should be carefully examined.
c.1765 *£2,500 — £3,500*

683. An oblong example with glass bottles having silver tops. Frequently these bottles have been replaced with modern glass. When originally made, the glass would fit neatly into the holders, so if there is any variance from this they are likely to have been replaced. The increased use of machinery in silver production at this date meant that less weight of silver was used. The pierced bottle holders, which will either be bolted or pinned to the base, are removable and therefore should be hallmarked. The corded borders on the stand are stamped on this example and not applied, which is again a saving in materials.
c.1765 *£2,750 — £4,500*

684. There was a vogue for globe inkstands at this period. The example shown here is a particularly elaborate one with Atlas supporting the world on his back, and the globe itself engraved with a map of the world. Occasionally much plainer and simpler examples are found. The owl finial acts as a trigger to release the top two quarter segments, and these fall down to reveal a small inkwell, pounce pot, pen holders, etc. The supports for the globes on these inkstands are often rather weak and are frequently found repaired.
c.1800 *£5,000 — £8,000*

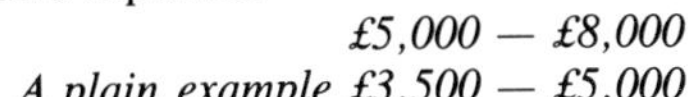
A plain example £3,500 — £5,000

684

683

681

682

685

685. This rather elaborate and heavy design was developed by Smith and Sharp and their successors. They are usually in silver gilt and of extremely heavy quality (60-90oz.). A number of this basic design are known to have been royal christening presents and some are so engraved. Their value is, therefore, out of proportion to other inkstands in this section.
c.1800 *£22,500 — £35,000*

686

686. A shaped oval example, with gadrooned borders and fluted panel feet. Note the bottle holders and tops are all hall-marked as they should be at this date. The bottle holders are not soldered to the stand but held by wire pins on the under-side. In contrast to the preceding example, this is one of the smallest inkstands one is likely to find from this period, and contains probably no more than 15oz. of silver.
c.1800 *£3,000 — £4,000*

687. A shaped oblong example, this time with central taper-stick in the form of a miniature chamber candlestick, quite a common feature from now on. The conical extinguisher is however a replacement. The original would probably have had matching tongue and dart borders. The taperstick will lift off to reveal a container for wafers.
c.1810 *£3,500 — £5,500*

688. A heavy George IV example with bold gadroon and foliate borders, the shape still basically the same but rather more elaborate. The extinguisher on the taperstick is chained to the sconce to prevent it being mislaid.
c.1820 *£4,000 — £6,000*

687

688

689. An amazingly involved and ugly, yet good quality inkstand made by the man who was one of the earliest exponents of 'Victorian' extravaganzas. Edward Farrell produced numerous creations from 1815 onwards which look as though they should have been made in the 1840s. He copied from antique styles, both Dutch and German, and often used well-known Tenier's scenes and figures.
c.1825 *£6,000 — £9,000*

690. From the reign of William IV onwards, inkstands tend to be more delicate and less weighty, and, for a period, normally all have two glass wells flanking the central wafer box and/or taperstick. The inscription on this piece is later and this will detract from the value, but it is otherwise in good condition. Look out however for damage to the feet on this type of inkstand, which are fairly flimsy. The bottle holders will be held on by small nuts and technically should be marked. Note that the extinguisher to the taperstick is missing. It should be attached to the chain dangling beside the handle.
c.1835 *£2,250 — £3,500*

691. With the recently revived interest in collecting items relating to sport, this inkstand would command a competitive price. It was presented in 1842 to a member of Clapham Cricket Club and was made for them by Benjamin Smith. Again the design is delicate with pierced foliate and floral feet. The covers to the inkwells have wickets and cricket bats as finials.
c.1840 *£4,000 — £6,000*

692. A rather plainer example with contemporary inscription, this time with just a taperstick of the early 18th century type, and no wafer box. Bottles on these inkstands are quite often badly chipped as they stand out from the stand itself and are easily knocked.
c.1850 *£1,750 — £3,000*

689

692

691

690

693. An unusual inkwell in the form of a skep with rustic branch feet.
c.1850 £2,000 — £3,000

694. This inkstand was designed by Emile Jeannest (1813-1857) who came to England in about 1845 and was originally employed by Mintons of Stoke-on-Trent as a ceramic modeller. In 1849 or 1850 he transferred to Elkington and Co. as head of their art department. The fact that this piece can be identified from original designs will add to its value. It is quite large, measuring 15ins. across, and weighing 45oz.
c.1855 £3,000 — £5,000

695. This inkwell cum taperstick, modelled as the foot of a Roman centurion, is one of those unusual designs that command high prices. It is parcel gilt which gives much more depth and life to the piece. It is of similar weight to the preceding example and would probably command a similar price.
c.1855 £2,500 — £4,000

696. An inkwell with ribbed circular tray. Quite a number of inkwells are found from this date. This one has a frosted glass bottle.
c.1860 £1,200 — £2,000

693

694

695

696

697. A bird's eye view of a single well inkstand in the form of an apple, 6½ins. in diameter and weighing 10oz.
c.1865 *£1,500 — £2,750*

698. A heavy oblong inkstand with Roman lamp taper stick flanked by two inkwells with Adam revival decoration, on heavy claw feet. A rather cumbersome piece.
c.1875 *£2,000 — £3,500*

699. Replicas of early George III gallery inkstands were very popular at this time. Naturally the piercing on most of these is in better condition than the 18th century originals, and they are nearly always bigger and better than George III examples.
c.1890 *£2,000 — £3,500*

699

697

699

698

Mirrors

700

Silver framed mirrors are comparatively rare and where they do exist were probably made to go with a full dressing table set.

Hallmarks: as they are so rare, there is no hard and fast rule, and in fact many mirrors are completely unmarked.

Condition: obviously the existence of the original glass is an asset, but examine the mirror generally for any later reinforcement, patches or repairs which may have been carried out.

Fakes: I have not come across any, but obviously if a mirror is unmarked one should make sure that it appears to be as old as it is stated to be.

700. This unmarked toilet service with dressing table mirror is not as complete as some examples which have two large caskets or comb boxes, several small bowls and other accessories. The mirror has shaped cresting, which is detachable.
c.1680 *Mirror (double if hallmarked) £12,500 — £17,500*
The set (treble if hallmarked) £90,000+

701

701. Another mirror with a rather plainer border, but similar decorative cresting. The applied leaves at the angles of the frame act as both decoration and shields for the solder joints.
c.1680 *(double if hallmarked) £12,500 — £17,500*

702. A part toilet service with popular chinoiserie decoration. The almost square mirror has detachable shaped cresting. Mirrors like this are usually wooden backed and are not always hallmarked, although with cresting of this type one would hope to find a full set of marks on it. The applied leaf motifs at the angles are typical.
c.1685 *Mirror (double if hallmarked) £25,000 — £35,000*

703. This unusually small example (about 12-15ins. as opposed to 24-30ins. in height) is not typical and was perhaps intended to be hung on the wall, unlike the majority of silver framed mirrors which were intended as easel mirrors for the dressing table.
c.1700 *(double if hallmarked) £6,000 — £9,000*

703

704. A very plain rectangular example with part toilet set in silver gilt. Note the volute feet, a feature used on George I and George II mirrors.
c.1720 *Mirror (double if hallmarked) £8,000 — £12,500*

705. This shaped dressing table mirror has cast and chased armorials applied at the top, and, as with most 18th century and earlier mirrors, was no doubt made especially for a lady of nobility.
c.1750 *(double if hallmarked) £12,000 — £16,000*

706. An unusual mirror made by Frederick Kandler with a quiver and bow at the top.
c.1775 *Mirror (half if unmarked) £20,000 — £30,000*

707. In the early 19th century mirror plateaux for table centre decorations are found. This example (approximately 36ins. long) , in silver gilt, is by Paul Storr and is heavily decorated with vine motifs. There are many more examples in Sheffield and electro plate than there are in silver. A number of centrepieces made by Elkington and Co. later in the century came with their individual plateaux which were irregularly shaped to look like rock pools (see 710). This plateau would perhaps have been used with a centrepiece or epergne flanked by candelabra, but it is doubtful that all the pieces would have been *en suite.*
c.1820 *£35,000 — £45,000+*

707

706

704

705

708

708. Another example (45ins. long) by the same maker, this time in two sections and rather more elaborate. There are examples made in three sections as well, but they are not necessarily more expensive because they are larger.
c.1825 *£40,000 — £50,000+*

709. An attractively shaped and decorated silver gilt dressing table mirror with the maker's mark of Mortimer and Hunt, successors to Storr and Mortimer. The cresting is pierced with a monogram below the ducal coronet, again emphasising that silver of this type was only made for the grandest households.
c.1840 *£10,000 — £15,000*

710. A smaller mirror plateau only 25ins. in diameter, much more suitable for the centre of a dining table in a modest house. It is attractively modelled to simulate a pond with applied cast and chased foliate borders.
c.1845 *£2,500 — £4,000*

711. Silver mounted mirrors were becoming more common by this date, rather than being restricted to stately homes. This example is unusually decorated with oval medallions of charioteers and horsemen.
c 1875 *£2,500 — £5,000*

709

710

711

712. Heart shaped mirrors are particularly popular and appropriately shaped for the dressing table. The pierced and stamped decoration is in this case of high quality compared with some of the later examples.
c.1885 *£2,500 — £3,750*

713. Silver framed mirrors are comparatively scarce at any date, but they seem to be practically non-existent between 1780-1880. Here are two late Victorian examples which are basically wooden framed, covered in velvet. The stamped and pierced silver mount is then pinned to the border.
c.1890 *Right £1,750 — £2,750*
Left £2,000 — £3,000

714. This wooden framed mirror has a minimal amount of applied die stamped silver decoration, which is simply tacked on over the velvet background. More often than not the velvet has become either very worn or badly stained and caked with silver polish. These are practically impossible to clean satisfactorily once they have become very dirty, but one in good condition will command a hefty price for the amount of silver involved.
c.1900 *£1,250 — £2,000*

714

712

713

715

715. Another die stamped mirror in art nouveau taste with butterflies, roses and insects.
c.1915 *£1,250 — £2,000*

716. A more substantial silver mirror made by the firm that seems to have specialised in dressing table sets at this date, namely William Comyns and Sons. 2ft. 6ins. high.
c.1915 *£2,250 — £3,750*

717. A replica of an early 18th century dressing table mirror with plain moulded frame.
c.1915 *£1,200 — £1,800*

717

716

Salvers & Trays
Salvers

Salvers with plain flat surfaces and small feet at the edge are rarely found before the reign of George I. From the seventeenth century until this date salvers on a central foot were the norm, although these are sometimes called tazzas. By the turn of the century a number of these were made with the foot unscrewing. Very occasionally this type will also have three or four small panel feet so that the salver can be used on a lower level. This is the forerunner of the salver we now know. The word 'waiter' is today used only rarely and more commonly relates to small examples of 6 or 7ins. in diameter.

Hallmarks: salvers on a central foot should be marked on the surface of the tazza and have a lion passant on the foot. If this latter mark is missing be very cautious as it is likely that the foot has been replaced at some stage. With salvers on three or four feet there need only be one full set of marks, although occasionally in the early eighteenth century each foot is marked with a lion passant. Trays should again have one full set of marks. Handles are not marked. Some salvers and trays, however, have borders which are applied by a lapover joint and not soldered to the main body. In this case there should at least be a lion passant and preferably a maker's mark on the border. At a later date the monarch's head and date letter should both appear. In nearly all cases the marks will be in a roughly straight line.

Condition: salvers and trays are perhaps the most common candidates for having armorials or crests removed. Always test the centre to see that there is no thinness. A number have been later chased and should you come across an example with chasing it is sensible to compare it with other examples to try and establish whether or not the chasing is contemporary. Look carefully at the area between the centre and the border for any splits or holes. Sometimes when clumsily put down or loaded with items too heavy for the piece, a foot gets bent and distorts the rim, and sometimes the border splits. This area therefore should be examined for any damage or repairs. The soldering at the feet on eighteenth century examples, however, is often left in a rough state and unless there is any obvious sign of damage, clumsy soldering does not necessarily indicate a later repair.

Fakes: the most common fake is where a salver has been refashioned. The most frequently used types are the plain circular salvers of the 1780s and 1790s. These were often chased and given an applied border of scrolls and foliage at a later date and might also have had decorative feet added. These are usually easy to spot, firstly because the date indicated by the hallmark is not the date that the style suggests, and secondly because the hallmark is often distorted or at a peculiar angle. If the border and feet have 'additions marks' they are legally saleable, but not particularly desirable. If they do not have these marks they have to be submitted to an assay office before they can be sold. Some oval salvers have had handles added to convert them to trays.

718. This type of salver on a single foot was made to accompany a porringer and cover. The high relief embossing of fruit, flowers and foliage is typical of the period. It is however apt to have holes because of the depth of the chasing and should be examined carefully by being held up to the light. The engraved armorials are in the correct style for the period. The tied branches, sometimes called plumage, are the main form of cartouche used at this date.
c.1670 *£6,000 — £9,000*

718

719

719. The gadroon border on this example (about 12ins. in diameter) is embossed and not applied and therefore is not very sturdy. There is a similar border to the foot. Repaired splits or damage to the border will halve the price. The foliate mantling is here used as the cartouche.

c.1700 *£4,000 -- £6,000*

6ins. £1,250 — £1,750

9ins. £1,800 — £3,200

720. The quality of many salvers has improved by this date and the gauge is usually fairly heavy. The border has an applied moulded wire. Occasionally on these heavier salvers the foot unscrews and will be cast rather than raised. There may be applied cut card work around the thread (723), which adds weight to the value. The style of cartouches now changes once again, and this is a typical example of the period with scrolling strap-work and foliage around fish scale motifs. The armorials are those of the widow of a baronet. A baronet bears a badge of a hand in a shield which can be seen at the centre of the left hand armorial. A widow bears her armorials in a lozenge.

c.1710 *Per oz. £165 — £265*

720

721. A very simple oblong salver or tray with raised border. Practically no merit in the design, but the quality will usually be very good. A coat of arms would have helped tremendously, but by virtue of its early date, a high price will still be demanded. Sometimes on bracket feet, only occasionally with no feet at all.

c.1710 *Per oz. £225 — £325*

722. A similar salver to 720 with armorials in a less ostentatious cartouche, yet very effective and strictly in the baroque style.

Hallmarked 1717 *Per oz. £150 — £220*

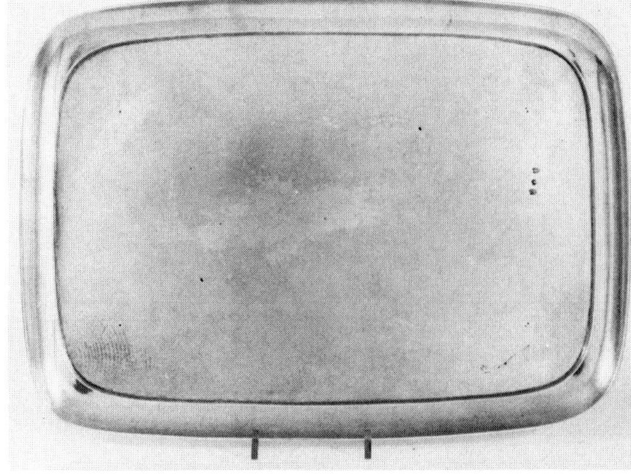

721

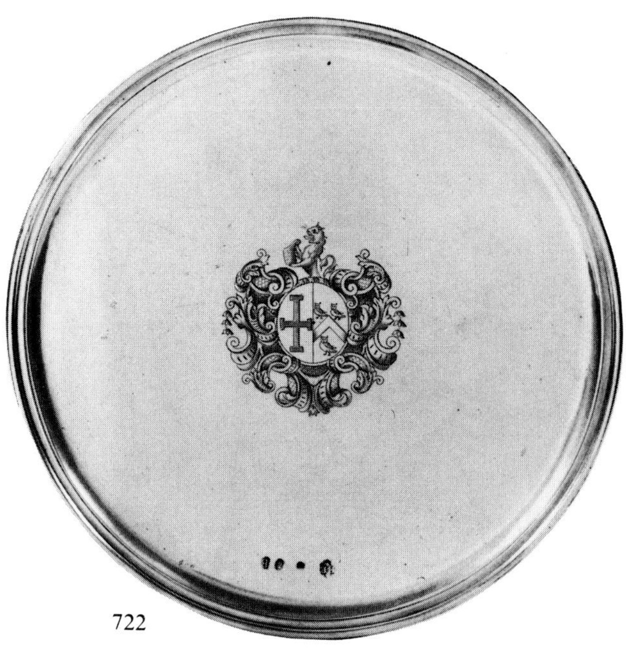

722

723. A pair of small waiters, 6ins. in diameter, made by Pierre Platell, Paul de Lamerie's master. One is illustrated upside down to show the applied cut card work around the foot, which unscrews as discussed in caption 720. The cartouche around the crest has two semi-cherubs incorporated into the design. This more interesting engraving was inspired by Simon Gribelin, the French born engraver and designer, who came to England in the late 17th century. The additional band of engraved scroll work and diaper below the border gives more body to the design and is here used at a much earlier date than one would normally expect.
Hallmarked 1717 *£13,000 — £22,000*

724. Octafoil salvers are found between 1710-1730. They are comparatively rare and command high prices. They usually stand on four panel or bracket feet. It is probable that many have perished and indeed a number of those that have survived are badly damaged and split at the incurved points. Always examine very carefully. The engraving is again typical of the period. The use of a shell at the top of the cartouche and a human mask at the base was popular and common to many examples of this period.
c.1720 *Per oz. £300 — £550*

725. An unusual oblong salver. By this date any four sided salver will normally have incurved angles. The engraving is in the manner of William Hogarth and will form the major part of the value. Hogarth was apprenticed to Ellis Gamble who was also responsible for some fine cartouches. Four simple bracket feet will be the norm.
c.1730 *Per oz. £240 — £375*

726. A small waiter, 5 to 6ins. square, of thin gauge with a very simple widow's coat of arms. All contemporary but not particularly good quality.
c.1730 *Per oz. £190 — £250*

726

725

723

724

727. A salver of similar size but far superior quality from the workshop of Paul de Lamerie and improved by the fine engraved decoration. The use of brickwork and architectural forms in the cartouche makes the piece more important. The engraved decoration below the border is reminiscent of a formal garden. William Hogarth is again likely to have been the inspiration behind the design.
c.1735 *Paul de Lamerie £20,000 — £30,000*

728. A fine salver, 12ins. square, with engraving typical of Paul de Lamerie's workshop. He was a master of the use of asymmetrical design and one of the greatest exponents of the rococo. From this date onwards armorials are no longer always in a formal cartouche. The boldly sweeping scrolls and foliage begin to take over and are supreme by 1745. A rather unusual feature on this piece is the use of a banner for an inscription. The armorials in the top left and bottom right hand corners are probably a later addition.
c.1735 *£45,000 — £70,000*

729. This example is by Robert Abercrombie, one of the most prolific salver makers, and is engraved with contemporary armorials. Still of formal design, but again the use of forward and reversed scrolls gives a more flowing cartouche. The feet can just be seen protruding and are of the shaped hoof type.
c.1740 *Per oz. £100 — £175*

730. This example shows a commonly used type of border which is often termed 'Chippendale'. It consists of a shallow curved semi-oval followed by a short straight section between two concave notches. The engraved armorial is similar to that on 729.
c.1740 *Per oz. £100 — £175*

727

728

729

730

731. The large plain area on a salver gives an opportunity for the engraver to explore his art to the limit. The band of masks, baskets of flowers, diaper and scrolls shown here are of the finest quality. When the engraving is of this calibre the price may easily be double that of a similar but less well executed example. In addition to this decoration, the border has cast and applied work of shells, masks and scrolls, indicating a very heavy quality. The feet are also cast scroll and shell type. The central cartouche is attributable to the engraver, Joseph Sympsone and is again finely executed.
c.1740 *Per oz. £100 — £175*

732. Another common type of border is shown here with scroll motifs interspersed by shells. Also from this date flat chasing was occasionally used. This differs from engraving by being hammered up on the surface rather than being cut into it. The cartouche around the armorial is, however, still engraved and of a more formal baroque design, which does not naturally mix with the rococo scrolls and rocaille decoration of the chasing.
c.1740 *Per oz. £75 — £100*

733. A large salver measuring 18ins. in diameter, the forerunner of the two-handled tea tray. The balance between the border, band of flat chasing and the cartouche is as near perfect as possible.
c.1750 *Per oz. £75 — £100*

734. Yet another large salver, this time with pierced, cast and applied border. This type of border is occasionally attached by a lap joint and not soldered to the main section. If this is the case there should be a lion passant and/or maker's mark on the border as well as the full set of marks on the centre. The quality of the border decoration and the finely engraved cartouche is slightly let down by the less effective band of flat chasing. The panel feet will be pierced and cast, echoing the border design.
c.1750 *Per oz. £70 — £110*
(times six+ if by Paul de Lamerie)

734

733

731

732

735. An even larger salver measuring 22ins. in diameter, with very attractively engraved cartouche showing the revival of the influence of Chinese designs and motifs. The outer border is cast and applied to the rim.
c.1755 *Per oz. £70 — £110*

736. A pair of small salvers with scroll and shell rims which were commonly used. The armorial engraving is insignificant and probably added later. The band of chasing however is contemporary.
c.1755 *Per oz. £70 — £110*

737. An example with cast and applied border. The decoration is now running away from the more involved examples of the high rococo.
c.1760 *Per oz. £70 — £115*

738. The salver itself has now reverted to very simple form with applied gadroon border, which is common to so many articles of domestic silver at this date. The engraving of the cartouche around the armorial is however still showing the influence of rococo design. Usually on shell terminated feet.
c.1765 *Per oz. £70 — £110*

735

736

738

737

739. By now the more simple classical designs brought to the foreground by Adam are apparent. The armorial is in a simple formal shield within a small bright-cut cartouche. The border is less pronounced and is applied with simple bands of beading and the piece is supported on ball-and-claw feet.
c.1775 *Per oz. £70 — £120*

740. Over the next twenty to thirty years a number of very plain circular salvers were again produced without any shaping to the border. The applied border wires are either of beading or reeding. The armorial engraving is still in the same style as 739. The feet from this date are usually plain tapering panels with scrolled toes and the same borders as the salver.
c.1780 *Per oz. £70 — £120*

741. Oval salvers were produced for the first time at this date and today they are much more sought after than their circular counterparts. This example, which is just engraved with a crest below an earl's coronet in the centre, may perhaps have been made as part of a set, including a two-handled tray. The tray would almost certainly have been engraved with the full coat of arms of the earl.
c.1785 *Per oz. £90 — £150*

742. Salvers gave the engraver ample opportunity to explore the full extent of bright-cut work. The mixture of swags and formal bands produces a very impressive effect. The art of armorial engraving was occasionally more detailed and a drapery cartouche intended to imitate a nobleman's ermine cloak was sometimes used.
c.1790 *Per oz. £100 — £175*

742

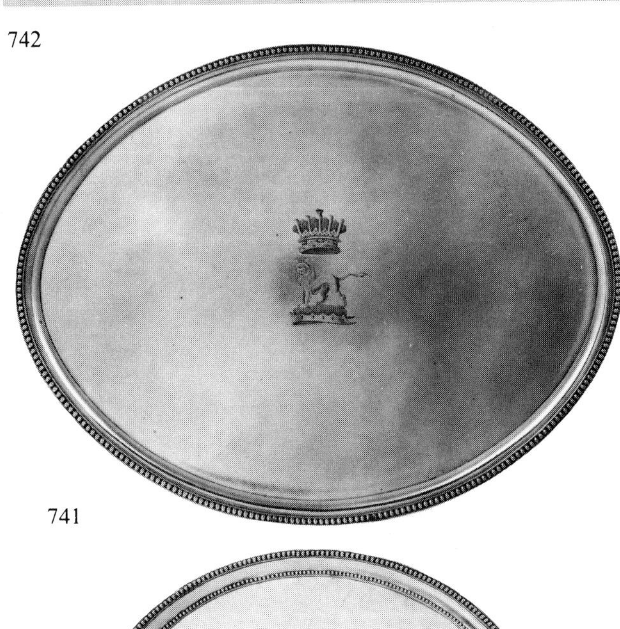

741

739

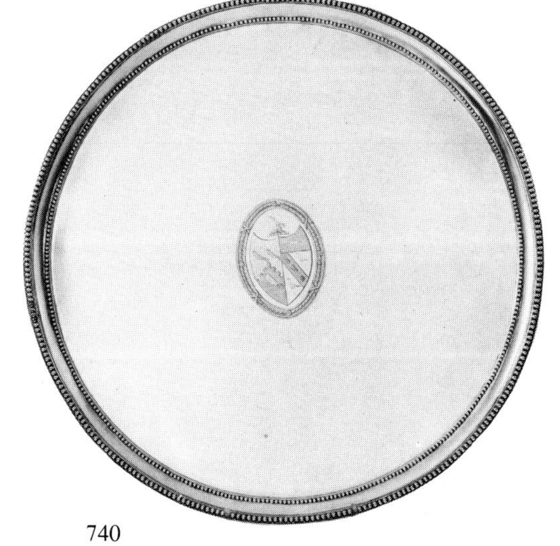

740

743

743. A small 8ins. salver showing the use of reeding to the border, the engraving still in the same style.
c.1795 *Per oz. £70 — £110*

744. A small oval salver which shows the re-introduction of the gadroon border after an absence of about 20 years. The coat of arms is that of a widow engraved within a lozenge. Quite frequently on plain and straightforward pieces of silver no cartouche was used at all at this date.
c.1800 *Per oz. £95 — £150*

745. The oblong shape, which was used for articles like teapots and salt cellars, was also used for salvers. This one is engraved only with a crest and is on four tapered panel feet with scroll toes.
c.1805 *Per oz. £80 — £125*

746. The nobility's patronage of Rundell, Bridge and Rundell encouraged the production of some fine quality pieces including heavy silver gilt salvers on feet. This is the first time since the early 18th century that a salver on foot is found in English silver. The border is cast and applied. The armorial engraving is given a grand appearance by the addition of very fine engraved work. Top quality engraving is comparatively rare on silver of any period, and can increase the price of a standard article many times. This example was made for the Duke of Richmond and Gordon, and reflects the extravagances of the period.
c.1810 *Per oz. £290 — £475*

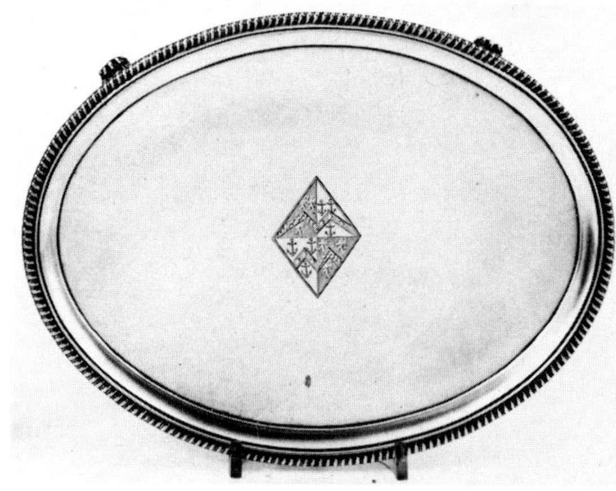

744

745

746

747. The engraved armorial here echoes the style of the late 17th century and early 18th century. The main difference between this and the earlier type is that the armorial is in an irregularly shaped surround. With the gadroon and shell border one will always get heavy panel feet, usually decorated again with a shell of the same type. These heavy designs were produced mainly by silversmiths from the Rundell, Bridge and Rundell stable, such as Paul Storr, Benjamin Smith, Digby Scott and Philip Rundell.
c.1815 *Per oz. £80 — £125*
By Paul Storr, per oz. £150 — £250

748. Pairs of salvers are found in most periods from the early 18th century onwards, but sets of three are not as common. In spite of this a set of three will not fetch a price substantially higher than the total of the individual values. The centre of these are engraved with the simple crest of a marquess enclosed in an engraved representation of the chain of office of the Nova Scotia baronets.
c.1825 *Per oz. £75 — £100*

749. A salver with multiple reeded border unusually decorated with foliage at intervals. The engraved armorial is of a baronet which can be identified by the small engraved hand on the left hand side of the coat of arms. The demi-lion rampant crest above the shield is sitting in a ducal coronet, but this does not mean that it is the crest of a duke. Only when a coronet is engraved above all the heraldry does it signify a particular nobleman.
c.1820 *Per oz. £75 — £100*

750. The combination here of an octafoil salver with a rococo revival cartouche is drawn from two different periods of the 18th century. The addition of combined reeding to the border gives an individual detail which indicates this later date. The feet are decorated with flowers. This was in fact made by Paul Storr in 1834.
1834 *By Paul Storr, per oz. £130 — £200*
By another, per oz. £75 — £100

750

749

747

748

751

751. These salvers also draw on ideas from the 18th century with flat chased decoration below a scroll and shell border. The main differences between these and the original is that they have more involved decoration and are on panel feet in place of the 18th century volute or ball-and-claw.
c.1840 *Per oz. £42 — £70*

752. Naturalistic elements were popular in the mid-19th century and here flowers and entwined leafage form the border in cast and chased work and engraved decoration in the centre. Apart from bright-cut engraving in the late 18th century, this is the first time that engraving is really popular as a form of decoration in salvers; the majority rather than the minority are now decorated with engraving or chasing.
c.1850 *Per oz. £42 — £70*

753. A scroll bordered salver with tightly engraved fruit, flowers and foliage. The detail is immaculate for a piece of silver which is mass-produced. Although by this date machinery was used much more, there is no reduction of the quality which is still of high standard.
c.1860 *Per oz. £42 — £70*

754. This pierced border with medallions and husk swags echoes Adam designs. The engraved work however is more in keeping with contemporary styles.
c.1870 *Per oz. £38 — £65*

752

753

754

755. Another example with pierced border, this time not influenced directly by earlier designs. Much more attractive engraving and a more pleasing result. Unfortunately the crest has been removed from the centre, but this has been cleverly executed and not left the piece thin. The price will however be likely to be near the lower end of the range.
c.1875 *Per oz. £38 — £65*

756. This is in the style of the 1780s with a simple beaded border. Bright-cut engraving was also used at that period, but not in such vigorous tones as are used here. The feet on this example are more decorative than would be found in the 18th century.
c.1875 *Per oz. £38 — £65*

757. Yet another reproduction of an early design. The scroll and shell border is typical of the third quarter of the 18th century.
c.1895 *Per oz. £27 — £42*

758. This example incorporates the gadroon border of the 1770s but has more involved flat chasing than one would expect in the 18th century. The inclusion of birds and animals in the chasing is a feature often more common to Irish silver, but this salver is London made by Charles Stuart Harris.
c.1900 *Per oz. £32 — £48*

758

757

755

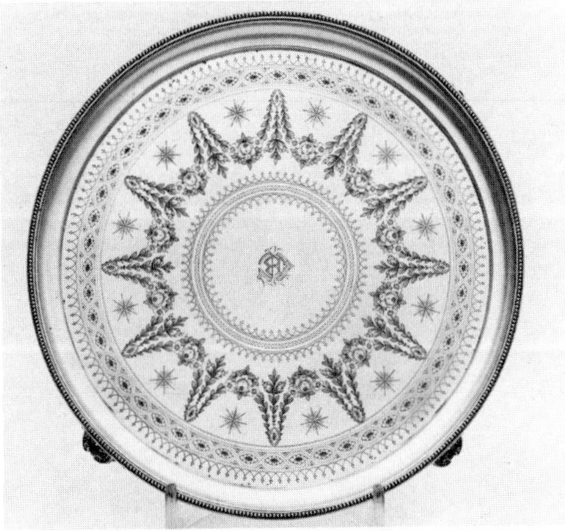

756

Trays

Trays were not to make their appearance until the late eighteenth century and this word is used when there are two handles. In the early part of the century some oblong salvers were made, and these have occasionally been called trays (see 721).

Information on hallmarks, condition and fakes will be found on p. 225, in the introduction to **Salvers.**

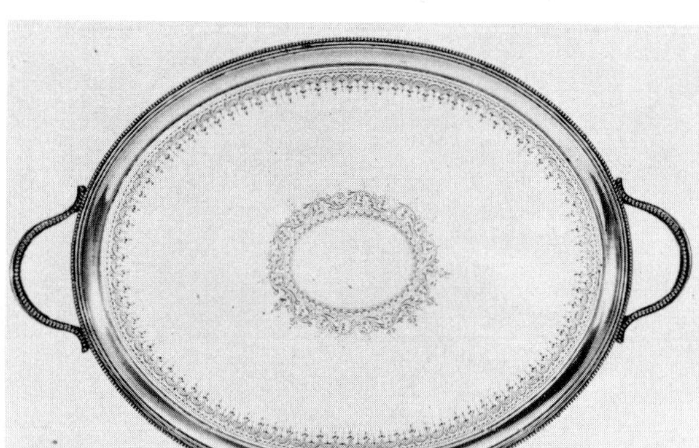

759

759. At about the same time that oval salvers were introduced, the two-handled tea tray made an appearance. Their style mainly followed that of salvers, with much of the decoration and applied work being of similar nature. This one has the beaded border and delicate bright-cut work found at this period.
c.1785 *Per oz. £75 — £120*

760

760. A tray of very similar form, but with bright-cut engraving of much finer detail and greater depth. The armorials are also impressively engraved and surrounded by a handsome drapery cartouche. All these points add up to a more distinctive piece and therefore higher value. The reeded border incidates a slightly later date.
c.1795 *Per oz. £95 — £145*

761. The gadroon border again indicates the date, and in conjunction with the band of bright-cut engraving makes the piece transitional and unlikely to date after about 1805. Handles from now on will usually have extra decorative motifs such as the leaves on this example.
c.1800 *Per oz. £75 — £120*

762. As we have already seen in the development of salvers, the richest patrons of the arts commissioned some extravagant pieces of silver. This silver gilt tray with its cast and applied border is no exception. The centre is engraved with the armorials of the original owner, who was an earl.
c.1810 *Per oz. £275 — £450*

761

762

763. The oblong form was used on trays just in the same way as it is used on salvers. The finely engraved armorials of an earl give this piece a presence which it might otherwise lack.
c.1810 *Per oz. £60 — £90*

764. The gadroon border has here given way to a simple tongue motif interrupted at intervals by shells. The handles however have retained the gadrooning. This type is quite often on heavily cast lion paw feet headed by shell motifs. It is also typical of the work of Paul Storr.
c.1815 *Per oz. £60 — £100*
By Paul Storr, per oz. £150 — £250

765. This has finely engraved armorials echoing the late 17th century style. The interesting shaped border has applied scrolling foliage and flowers pierced out at intervals. This gives a lighter look to the piece which is in fact still of good heavy quality.
c.1855 *Per oz. £60 — £100*

765

764

763

766. A revival of the style of the 1780s and 1790s, the main difference being that the beaded border is much bolder and the bright-cut engraving is more naturalistic.
c.1860 *Per oz. £35 — £50*

767. A large tray given as a presentation piece which is realistically engraved with roses and fruit, enclosed in ovals and roundels. The effect is almost of eight framed still-life pictures, which was a popular expression of design at this period. The shaped border has three or four different bandings, giving a massive look to the piece.
c.1880 *Per oz. £35 — £50*

768. The use of the pierced gallery on tea trays was comparatively common in the late 18th century in conjunction with a mahogany centre. Silver examples at that date however are extremely rare. They are more common at this period with pierced pales and swags below beaded borders. A coat of arms in the centre would give the piece more appeal.
c.1885 *Per oz. £30 — £45*

766

767

768

769. A very heavy tea tray produced by Walker and Hall of Sheffield weighing 175oz. The vine decoration is die stamped and applied, the inscription engraved, and the foliate decoration flat chased.
c.1895 *Per oz. £30 — £45*

770. A more attractive and more desirable tea tray with delicately scrolling border emphasised by the flat chasing. An inscription at this date has to be historically very significant to add to value. This is also lighter than 769, weighing 120oz., which again will make it easier to sell as anything over 140oz. becomes too heavy to use, except to be permanently on a table top.
c.1900 *Per oz. £30 — £45*

771. Another example produced by Walker and Hall. Their distinctive maker's mark struck in a pennant can be seen. The tray is based on late Georgian designs although the flat chased vacant cartouche indicates a much later date. Of lighter weight than 770 but rather more masculine, it is not likely to be as easy to sell.
c.1910 *Per oz. £25 — £40*

771

770

769

Some additional illustrations, showing the changing styles in armorials between 1685-1825, may be seen over the next three pages. A later coat of arms can adversely affect the value of a piece. It is therefore a great asset if the collector is able to determine whether the engraving is 'right' or not. The only way to obtain this knowledge is by experience gathered from endless comparisons. These illustrations, together with the examples shown on the salvers and trays, should provide a good base from which to learn.

c.1685

c.1685

Dublin 1715

c.1717

c.1724

c.1725

c.1735

c.1735

c.1740

c.1755

c.1745

c.1765

c.1745

c.1765

c.1750

c.1770

c.1770

c.1790

c.1795

c.1795

c.1810

c.1810

c.1815

c.1825

Table Silver

Before the eighteenth century the only items of table silver made in any quantity were spoons and therefore they are shown first in this section. This is followed by a variety of table silver arranged alphabetically and the section ends with sets of table silver. Silver forks are rare prior to the eighteenth century, and it is now unusual to find sets of table silver dating earlier than the late eighteenth century. Some silversmiths specialised in making table silver only, and are recorded in the registers at Goldsmith's Hall as 'spoon makers', this being the term used from the sixteenth century onwards.

Hallmarks: London made table silver should bear a full set of marks, except for some teaspoons and smaller items which may omit the town mark. Provincial pieces are also sometimes found without town marks and/or date letters, and occasionally have a maker's mark only.

Condition: always feel the bowls of spoons to see that they have not worn thin with use and examine the tines on forks very carefully. It is obviously not desirable to have forks with worn tines and occasionally you will find tines which have been tidied up by trimming off parts of the ends and then polishing them down into a sharp point. Knives, which rarely survive in good condition, had steel blades which were fixed into a hollow silver handle. Many of these have had the blades replaced by stainless steel which is of course much more practical

Fakes: at the turn of this century collecting old silver first became fashionable and many seal top spoons and other early types were made from 18th century table spoons by hammering the bowl into the old fashioned fig shape and hammering the stem into a thin shaft and then applying a seal or an apostle at the top. These can be spotted by the fact that the hallmarks all appear on the stem. As you will see, all early finial spoons should have the town mark in the bowl with the other three marks on the stem. Rat-tail pattern spoons are always popular and some plain bowled Hanoverian spoons have been later applied with rat-tails. It is usually possible to discern a seam and the rat-tails themselves are often bolder than the original types. Three-prong forks which are the earliest type are occasionally made by cutting and re-hammering the bowl of a spoon or by applying an old shaft to new tines. The tines on these are flimsy, so avoid any that bend fairly easily under the pressure of thumb and forefinger. Sometimes sets of 'early' spoons are cast from one original. A good test is to lay them side by side and see if the marks are all in the same position on each stem. If they are, then carefully test the stems by applying pressure. If they bend, then they are probably cast.

Spoons

772. Apostle spoons were common from the 15th century to the beginning of the 17th century. As their name implies the terminal figure represents one of the twelve apostles and should carry a device or emblem which indicates that particular apostle. These three examples are all London made and one should examine the place where the terminal figure is applied to the top of the shaft carefully. On London spoons this is always done by a 'V' joint as can clearly be seen in the illustration. On provincial made spoons the joint is normally a lap joint, that is to say, one should be able to see a seam across the back of the shaft about ¼in. below the capital, and seams down the sides of the stem which meet this. If one of these types of joints is not visible, it is quite possible that the apostle may have been added at a later date. Also carefully examine the figure and try if possible to compare it with other known examples. The nimbus, or terminal disc, is usually either pierced in a cartwheel fashion or cast with the holy dove and variations are either unusual or wrong on London spoons, though there are variations on provincial spoons. As you can see the town mark appears in the bowl of the spoon, and the other three marks should be on the back of the stem. The earlier the spoon, the more the bowl tapers.

Pre-Elizabethan £4,000 — £6,000+
Elizabethan £3,500 — £5,500+
James I £2,500 — £4,500+
Charles I £2,250 — £4,250+

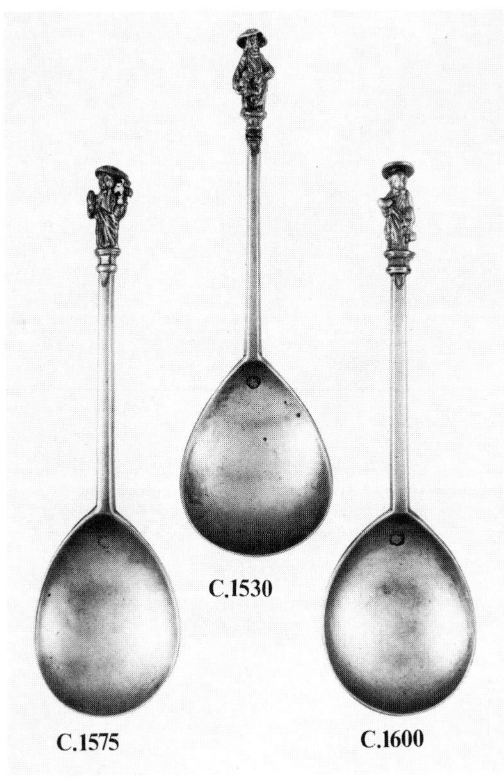

772

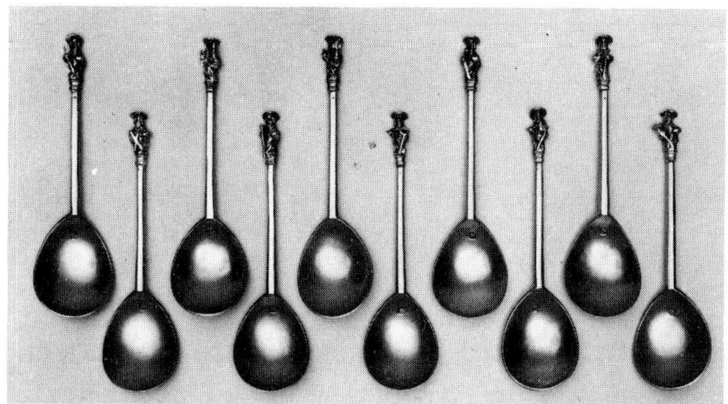

773

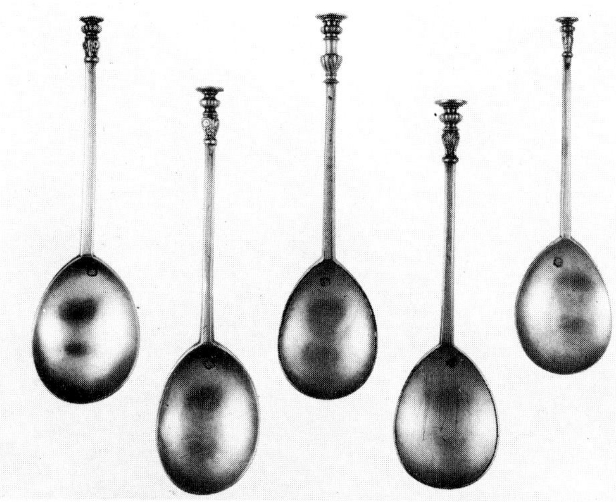

774

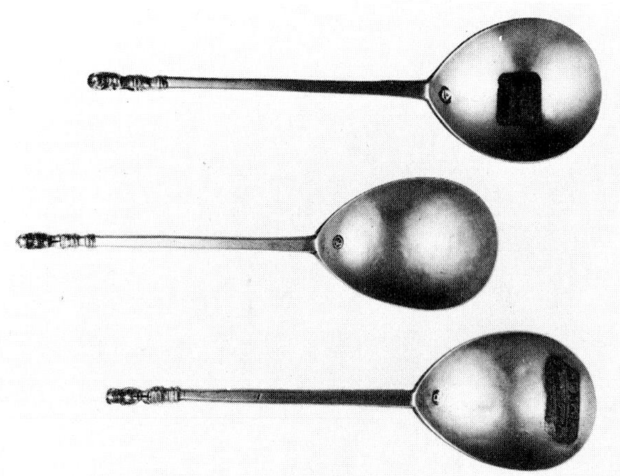

775

773. The likelihood of a full set of twelve apostle spoons and a master spoon being found for sale is extremely remote and therefore anyone who becomes interested in the subject has to collect the different spoons individually. Seven of these are by the same maker, now identified as Daniel Cary (D enclosing C). They were offered in the London salerooms in 1966 and are London marked, seven 1606 and three 1609.
1606/1609 *The set £35,000 — £50,000+*

774. Seal top spoons are found during the same period as apostles and are the most common type of spoon. These seals are applied in the same way as the apostles. Very early examples have seals which are shallow in depth, but by the Elizabethan period the large baluster vase type is used (centre spoon). Late Elizabethan and 17th century examples normally have a scroll decorated vase below lobed knop and plain nimbus. The nimbus is often pricked, engraved or stamped with the owner's initials. The backs of the bowls are also sometimes pricked with contemporary dates and initials. All the decorative terminals on these early spoons are cast, whilst the stem and bowl are hand wrought. Often the bowls are very thin and worn at the edges from use and they should be priced at a much lower level than one in good condition.
Elizabethan £1,500 — £3,000+
James I £1,000 — £2,500+
Charles I £800 — £2,000+

775. Lion sejant spoons are the next most common type after seal tops and apostles and here are three provincial examples. They are common over a shorter period: the majority can be dated between 1570 and 1640. The price for provincial spoons varies tremendously in accordance with their rarity. Note that the right hand example has a more worn down bowl than the others.
1570-1640 *London £2,500 — £5,000+*
Provincial £2,000 — £3,500+

776. Maidenhead spoons are also found during the period that lion sejant spoons are common. Illustrated here are two examples of the usual dessert spoon size, the one on the left being London made and that on the right provincial, and three much smaller examples, presumably made for children. The smaller size is extremely rare and the price is correspondingly high. Poor condition however can reduce the price considerably. The example on the far right has a substantial repair to the bowl and is worth only half the left hand spoon.
Left to right:
c.1630 *£2,500 — £5,000+*
c.1610 *£2,500 — £5,000+*
c.1610 *£2,750 — £5,500+*
c.1600 *£2,000 — £3,500+*
c.1610 *£1,250 — £2,500*

777. From the late 16th century the plainer slip top spoon is commonly found (left hand example) until the mid-17th century when the so called 'puritan' spoon (centre), which has a very plain flattened stem, was introduced. The bowl of the spoon is now developing into the form that we are all used to. The spoon on the right of this photograph has a stump top, c.1600, a feature rarely encountered; the two smaller slip top spoons are probably children's, and are also rarities.

Slip top £2,500 — £4,500+
Puritan £1,500 — £3,000
Stump top £2,500 — £4,500+

778. The trefid spoon is so called because of the triple moulding on the terminal. They are found from the Charles II period until the early 18th century although some smaller examples were made as christening spoons in the Channel Islands up until the mid-18th century. Early examples are fairly plain with perhaps just pricked initials and a date at the terminal and a small 'V' moulding at the junction of the handle and bowl. By 1680 the bowl is applied with a rat-tail, a feature which was used on spoons right into the 18th century. The most desirable trefids are those which have stamped lace decoration on the front of the stem and on the back of the bowl.

Plain trefid £400 — £1,200
Set of six £4,500 — £9,000
Lace decorated trefid £600 — £1,500

779. By the turn of the 17th century the trefid becomes less pronounced and this set of twelve spoons have bowls which are very similar to present day examples. When these were sold through the London salerooms in 1974 they made a price which was indicative of their rarity and superb condition. As you can see the bowls are very thick and the hallmarks clearly struck. The engraving of the crest is naïvely attractive and this is probably the earliest date at which table silver will be crested.

Set of twelve £9,500 — £18,000

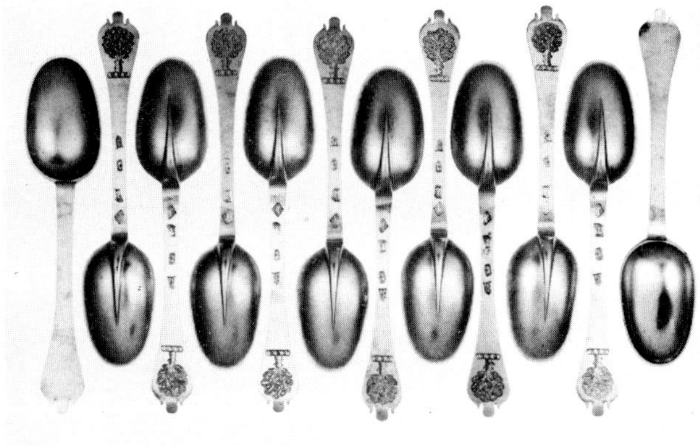

779

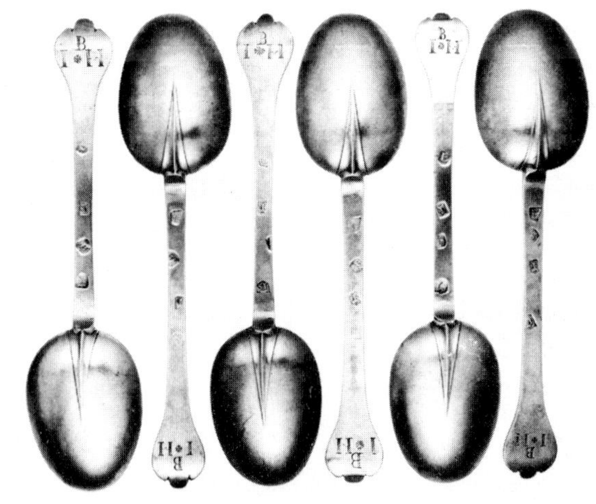

778

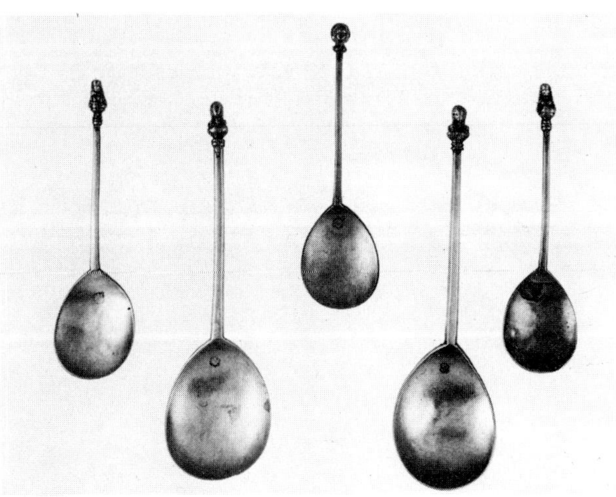

776

777

Caddy Spoons

780. Individual caddy spoons were made from 1780 onwards and come in numerous designs, and some collectors concentrate on caddy spoons alone. Rare examples, such as those in the form of a jockey's cap, can command at least four or five times that of the more ordinary types. Always be careful to see that there is not a seam at the junction of the handle and the bowl, as this could indicate that it has been made from the terminal of a teaspoon, with an added bowl.

£100 — £300

780

Serving Spoons

781. Longer handled serving or hash spoons with tubular handles were first introduced in the late Charles II period and were made up until about 1725. They are usually either marked on the inside of the bowl or on the side of the bowl and should have a lion passant and maker's mark on the handle. They measure 14ins. or so in length.

Hallmarked 1719 *£2,000 — £4,000*

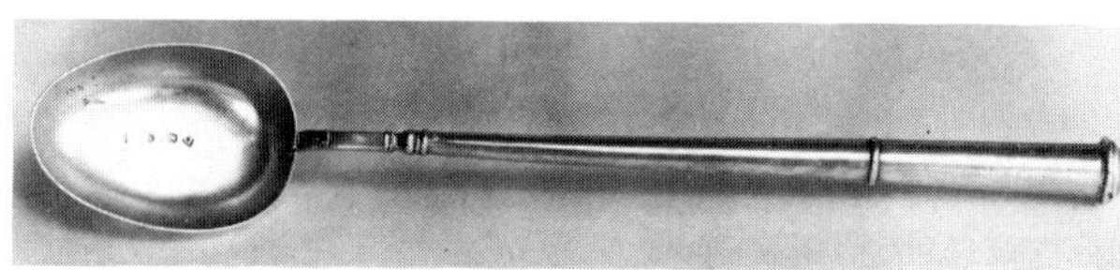

781

782. Early serving spoons, some 13ins. to 15ins. in length, are much sought after and large bottom marked examples appear as late as 1760. However the rat-tail is not normally found after 1730. An attractive crest or coat of arms is a great advantage and can add 20% or 30% to the price.

Queen Anne £1,000 — £2,000
George I £800 — £1,500
George II £600 — £1,200

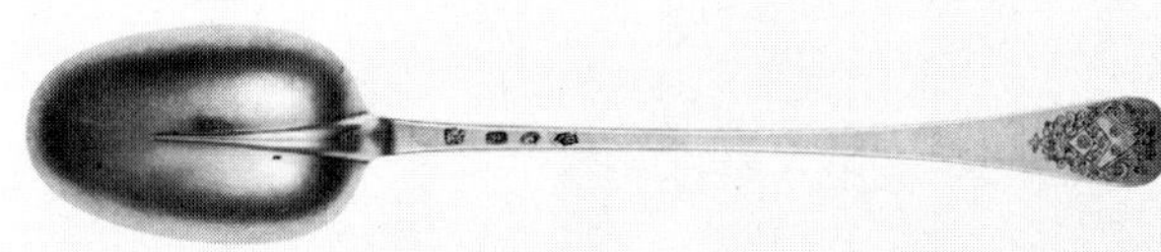

782

783. The Onslow pattern was occasionally used in the early George III period for serving implements such as long handled spoons, soup ladles and sauce ladles, and will usually command twice the price of a comparative Old English pattern piece. Cheese scoops (centre) were made in silver with bone or ivory handles from c.1790 until 1840. Their design varies very little except that on some later examples there is a sliding pusher to remove the cheese from the blade.

Serving spoon £200 — £400
Cheese scoop £175 — £300

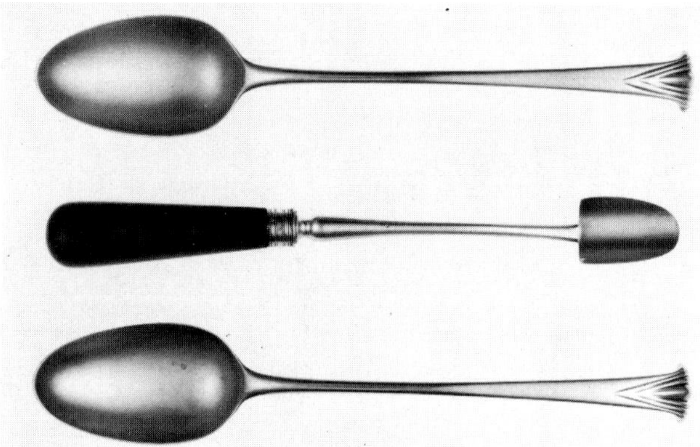

783

784. Table spoons with decorated bowl backs can command high prices because they are unusual. These examples have just a shell motif on the back of the bowl but the price is 50% more than a plain Hanoverian spoon.

c.1740 *Each £100 — £200*

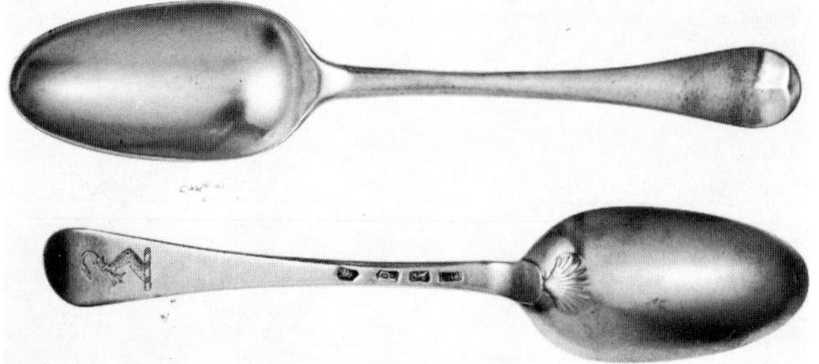

784

Fish Slices

785. The fish slice was first made in silver in the second half of the 18th century, the early examples having triangular blades, usually pierced with scrolling motifs and often engraved as well. Always examine these carefully for any applied reinforcements which are sometimes needed when some of the pierced work becomes damaged or broken.

c.1760 *£750 — £1,500*

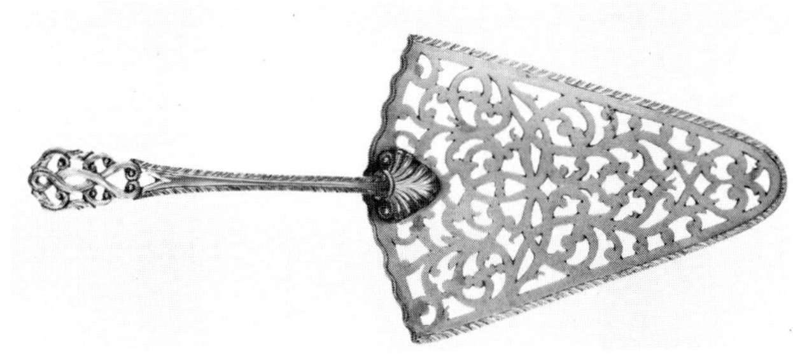

785

786. A group of unusual fish slices which are truly collectors' items. They could command very high prices but I consider the following to be realistic estimates.

Top to bottom
c.1850 *£250 — £425*
c.1805 *£225 — £400*
c.1850 *£425 — £650*
c.1780 *£425 — £650*
Right hand example
c.1775 *£550 — £1,200*

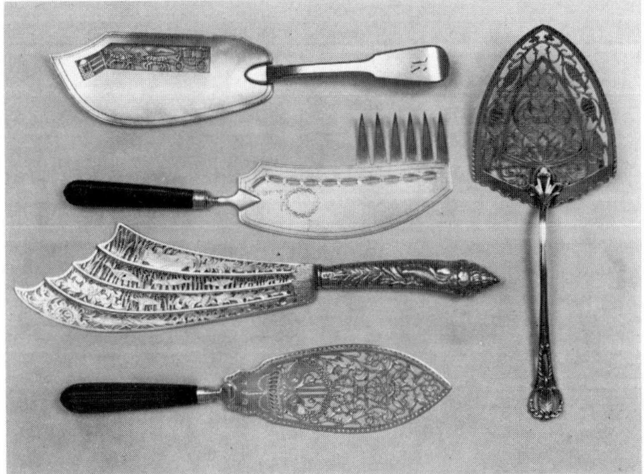

786

787. It became the norm in the 19th century when a foundation stone was officially laid by some dignitary to present him or her with a ceremonial trowel, suitably inscribed. These do not command high prices unless they are of particular artistic merit or of great historical interest. Occasionally an ordinary fish slice, which could be bought from any silver retailer, was used for the presentation, rather than commissionning a specially made trowel.

Left to right:
£275 — £475
£250 — £425
£250 — £425
£350 — £600
£250 — £425

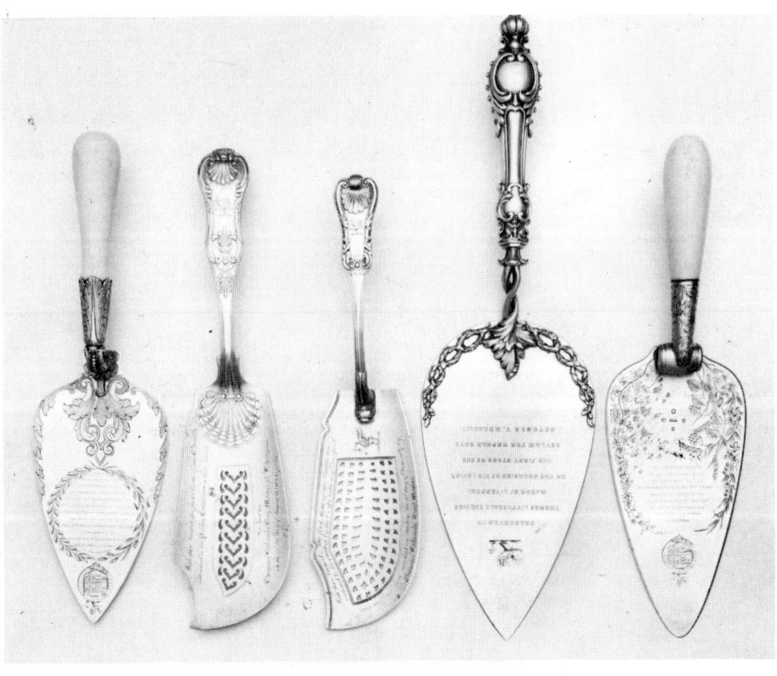

787

Ladles

788

788. The 18th century saw the introduction of punch ladles which are very popular today. They differ from sauce ladles and soup ladles in that they have turned wooden or twisted whalebone handles. The earliest example (a) is shown on the left with circular bowl. These were superseded by those with egg shaped bowls (e) in about 1735. By 1745 double lipped and chased examples are the norm (b). After 1760 is is quite common for punch ladles to be made from silver coins and often the original milled edge of the coin is visible on the bowl of the ladle. Occasionally the bowl will also be inset with another coin. When this is the case the ladle is rarely hall-marked as the appearance of the piece, having been made from coinage, was proof that it was silver. Circular bowled examples, some chased with flowers and/or inset with coins (d) were popular between 1760 and 1780, when oval ones took over.

(a) c.1720 — *£475 — £800*
(b) c.1745 — *£225 — £400*
(c) c.1780 — *£175 — £275*
unmarked £90 — £150
(d) c.1780 — *£175 — £275*
unmarked £90 — £150
(e) c.1735 — *£425 — £750*

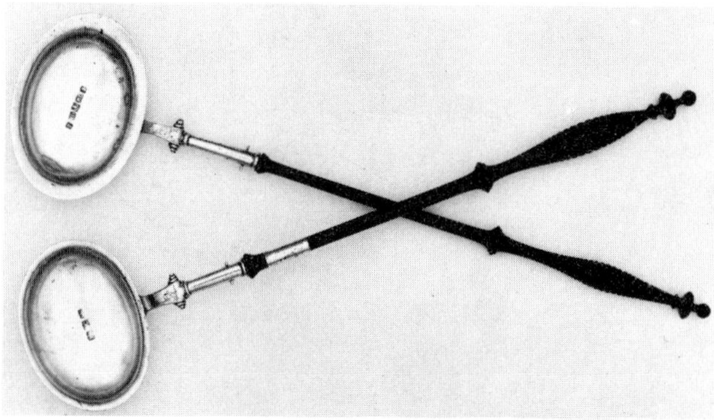

789

789. Scottish provincial punch ladles are very much sought after, mainly because of the rarity of their hallmark, but they are unlikely to date before 1800.

Dundee c.1810 — *Each £550 — £800*

790. Small examples of punch ladles are called toddy ladles. They are nearer in size to a sauce ladle. London examples date between 1795 and 1820. They were particularly popular in Scotland and, like these, are often found in sets of six.

c.1840 — *Scottish £450 — £650*
Unmarked £225 — £350

791. All-silver Scottish toddy ladles are also found and are in fact just like a sauce ladle. Quite often found in sets of six, and sometimes numbered.

c.1800 — *Edinburgh set of six £300 — £500*
Provincial set of six £500 — £1,000

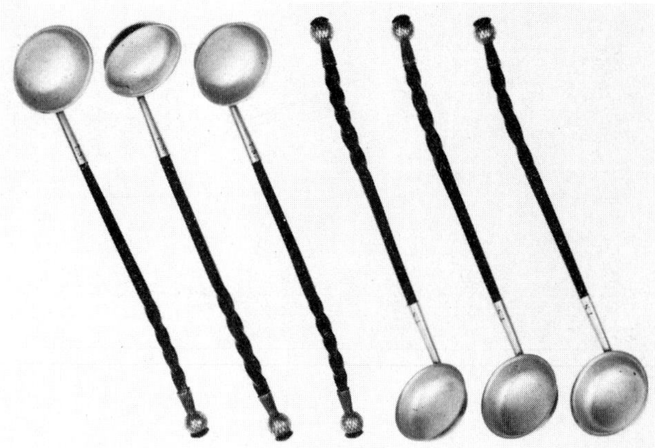

790

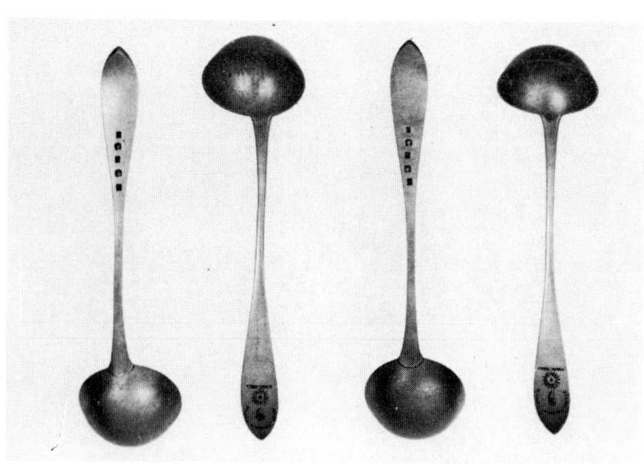

791

792. Soup ladles are so often sold individually that it is worth mentioning them as a separate item here. They are however normally always in the style of the contemporary sets of table silver and individual prices are illustrated on the table of patterns in this section (see No. 805).

Old English George III £250 — £500
Old English Victorian £250 — £500
Fiddle George III £250 — £500
Fiddle Victorian £225 — £400

793. The marrow scoop, used for removing the marrow from the bone, was made in great quantities in the 18th century. It seems likely that only one or two were provided with a service for a dozen people and therefore were used communally. The earlier examples have fatter and shorter bowls.

Queen Anne and George I £200 — £375
George II £180 — £300
George III plain £120 — £200
George III decorated £150 — £300
Early Victorian £120 — £160
Late Victorian £80 — £150

794. Mote skimmers were a necessary part of tea equipage in the 18th century when tea leaves were of irregular size. When a tea leaf got into the cup it would be skimmed from the top. The pointed terminal served to clear the spout of the teapot, should it become blocked. Early examples have a plain needle type handle, but by 1740 the spearhead moulding is typical. The pierced decoration varies very little and is usually as shown in the form of saltires and scrollwork. Often with only maker's mark and/or lion passant.

Clearly marked £100 — £200
Poorly marked or unmarked £60 — £120

792

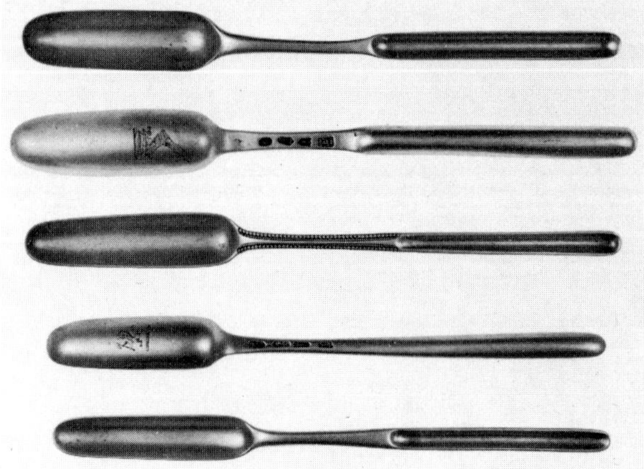

793

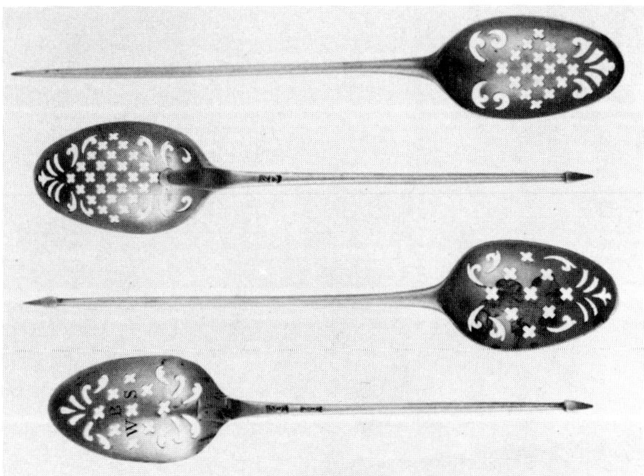

794

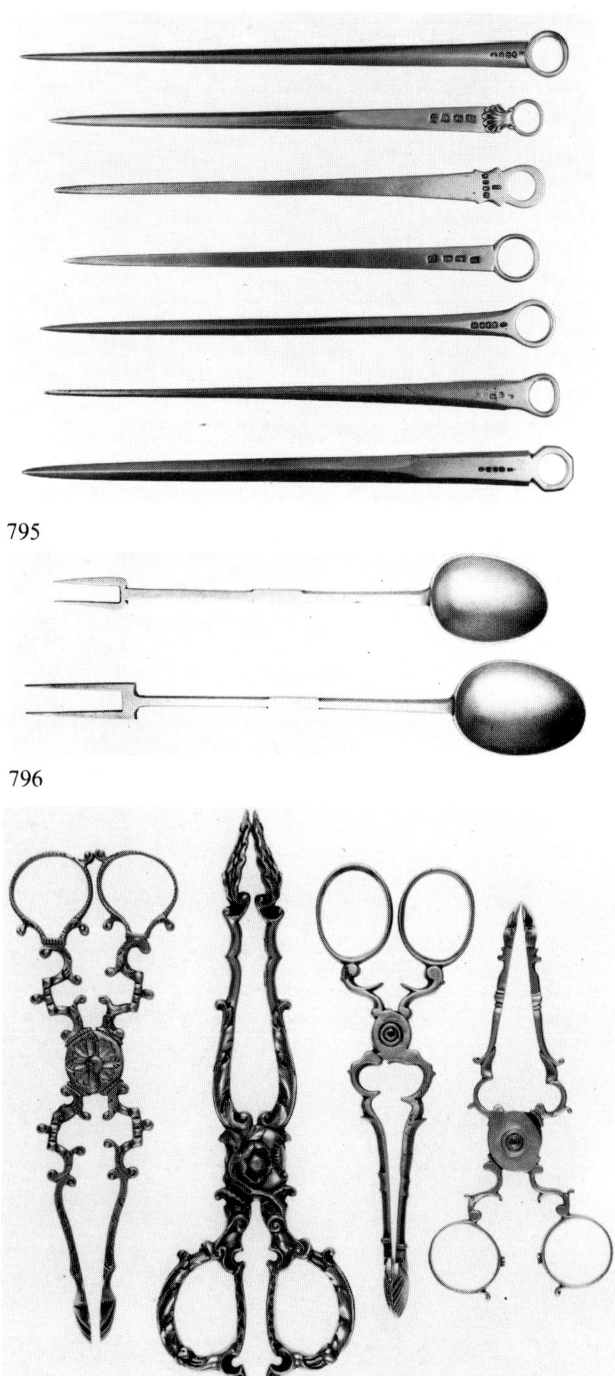

795

796

797

Skewers

795. Meat skewers are found in their greatest quantity between 1780 and 1840 and vary very little in form. They are now often sold and used as paper knives. Some have been later hammered out and flattened to make them more practical, but this detracts from value. Small skewers of 6ins. or less are called poultry skewers and are rarely hallmarked.

£250 — £550
Poultry skewers £60 — £120

Sucket Forks

796. Occasionally sucket forks will be found. This is an implement with a teaspoon bowl at one end and a two-pronged fork at the other. These were only made at the latter part of the 17th and early 18th century and are of great rarity. They are normally only marked with maker's mark. The stem is quite flat, although sturdy, and the gauge of metal is the same throughout.

£600 — £900
c.1690 *Fully marked £900 — £1,800*

Sugar Nips & Sugar Tongs

797. Sugar nips, which made their appearance in the 18th century, are of scissor form, although some early examples are in the form of fire tongs. They are not normally fully hallmarked, usually only having lion passant and maker's mark, either on the finger rings or on the terminal grips. There is a likelihood of repair to the stems and one should look out for any rough soldering. The larger pair illustrated here date from 1830 and these are sometimes called 'grape tongs', although I think they would be impractical if used for that purpose.

George I £150 — £275
George II and III £100 — £200
'Grape' tongs £300 — £600

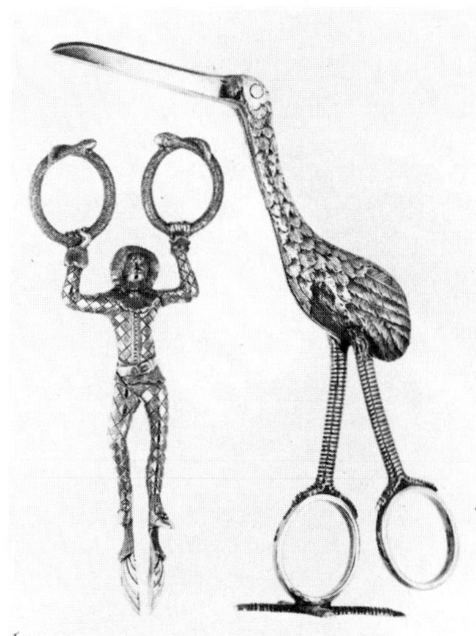

798

798. Novelty sugar nips in the form of a harlequin with entwined serpent finger rings were made both in the mid-18th century and copied in the Victorian period, as were those in the form of a stork.

18th century harlequin £275 — £500
19th century harlequin £125 — £250
18th century stork £275 — £500
19th century stork £125 — £250

799. By 1770 sugar tongs mainly replaced sugar nips, as they were less costly to produce. These do not match sets of table silver until after 1800, the earliest type of tongs being of pierced scrollwork design. By 1780 they are of simple form with bright-cut engraving.

£40 — £120
By Hester Bateman £100 — £200

799

Sets of Table Silver

800. Occasionally small spoons of teaspoon size, forks and knives can be found which were originally made to fit in a shagreen covered wooden case. They are often silver gilt and sometimes referred to as 'sucket' or 'sweetmeat' spoons or forks. The engraving is an extremely attractive additional feature but they usually have either maker's mark only or no mark at all.

c.1690 *Per piece £250 — £400*
Six spoons £1,750 — £3,000
Six knives, spoons and forks £6,000 — £9,000

800

801. After the trefid spoon (No. 778) the dog nose terminal is used. Sets of table silver were now becoming common in grand households. The rat-tail is still used on the bowls whilst the forks have three prongs. The knives illustrated here are called 'cannon handled' and are of the corresponding period.

c.1705 *6 table spoons £1,250 — £2,000*
6 dessert spoons £1,750 — £3,500
6 table forks £1,750 — £3,500
6 dessert forks £2,000 — £4,000
6 table knives £1,750 — £3,000
6 cheese knives £1,750 — £3,000

801

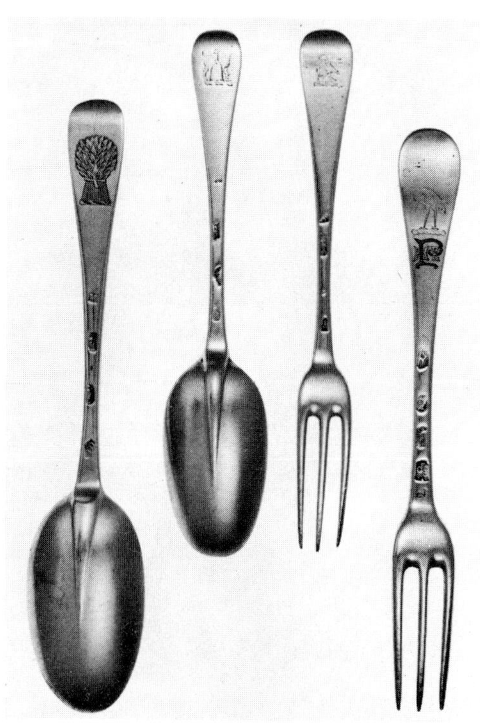

802

802. The next step was the plain rounded terminal, together with the rat-tail bowls, usually called either rat-tail pattern or Hanoverian pattern. As with No. 801 the great majority of these were made during the enforced Britannia period (1697-1720) and more often than not the condition is not good and the hallmarks are often worn. Shown here are four samples from a made-up set; as you can see each piece has a different crest and the table fork in addition has a rather ugly Victorian monogram.

c.1710 *48 pieces £12,500 — £25,000*
6 table spoons £800 — £1,500
6 table forks £1,500 — £2,500
6 dessert spoons £1,250 — £2,250
6 dessert forks £1,750 — £3,000

803

803. By the 1730s the rat-tail is rarely found and shown here is a sample from a matched Hanoverian pattern service. The forks are still three-pronged but the spoons now have a plain drop moulding at the back of the bowl. The corresponding knives have octagonal pistol handles and steel blades. These silver handles, if they have a clear mark, will only bear a maker's mark and lion passant. Very often the handles are split and repaired so that good examples are rare and can command high prices. The scimitar type blade is the original, but these blades are often replaced by stainless steel in the shape of a modern knife because it is more practical.

c.1730 *72 pieces £18,000 — £30,000*
6 table spoons £750 — £1,250
6 table forks £1,500 — £2,500
6 dessert spoons £1,250 — £2,000
6 dessert forks £1,750 — £3,000

804

804. By the 1770s the Old English pattern is introduced. This differs from the set shown in 803 by having the terminal to the spoons turning down instead of up. The gauge of silver is usually less and the spoon bowls become slightly more pointed while the forks become four-pronged. This illustration is of Old English Thread pattern which differs from Old English by having a reeded band around the border.

From c.1780 onwards the Assay Office marked table silver near the top of the stem as opposed to on the stem just below the bowl, and hallmarks are generally much clearer because there is more space on which to strike them. On early examples when the marks were struck on the thin part of the stem they distorted the form of the piece and therefore the silversmith had to hammer this back into shape, hence the hallmarks themselves are often squashed and distorted, and become very much more easily rubbed and worn. It is comparatively rare to get a set which is all the same date and all by the same maker and obviously prices vary tremendously depending upon the exact make-up. There is a premium if it is completely matching, but if not the price should be calculated by adding up the price for individual dozens or half dozens.

Old English

Set by the same maker and same date of 60 pieces comprising 12 tablespoons, 12 table forks, 12 dessert spoons, 12 dessert forks and 12 teaspoons	*£6,000 — £12,000*
6 table spoons	*£350 — £600*
6 table forks	*£350 — £600*
6 dessert spoons	*£450 — £900*
6 dessert forks	*£500 — £1,000*
6 teaspoons	*£120 — £240*
Old English Thread *(as illustrated)*	*plus 35%*

805. These are some of the more common patterns found from the early 19th century. They are all much heavier than Old English and Fiddle patterns and consequently command a higher price. Sometimes completely made-up sets are found with as many as twenty different dates and makers. It is not possible to give prices for sets of this type except to say that they will be considerably less than a completely matching set. If the condition is poor as well, then the price will be closely related to the silver value.

The price range given is for late Victorian or 20th century at the bottom end, up to late Georgian at the top end.

	Fiddle Thread	***Fiddle Thread and Shell***	***Hour Glass***	***King's***	***Queen's***
60 piece set, all same maker and date	*£6,000 — £12,000*	*£6,000 — £12,000*	*£6,000 — £12,000*	*£6,000 — £12,000*	*£6,000 — £12,000*
6 table spoons	*£325 — £550*	*£325 — £550*	*£325 — £550*	*£325 — £550*	*£325 — £550*
6 table forks	*£325 — £550*	*£325 — £550*	*£325 — £550*	*£325 — £550*	*£325 — £550*
6 dessert spoons	*£450 — £800*	*£450 — £800*	*£450 — £800*	*£450 — £800*	*£450 — £800*
6 dessert forks	*£450 — £900*	*£450 — £900*	*£450 — £900*	*£450 — £900*	*£450 — £900*
6 teaspoons	*£120 — £240*	*£120 — £240*	*£120 — £240*	*£120 — £240*	*£120 — £240*
Soup ladle	*£200 — £400*	*£200 — £400*	*£200 — £400*	*£200 — £400*	*£200 — £400*

805

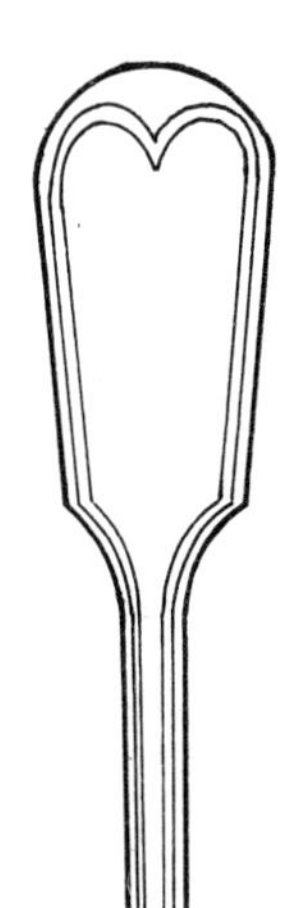
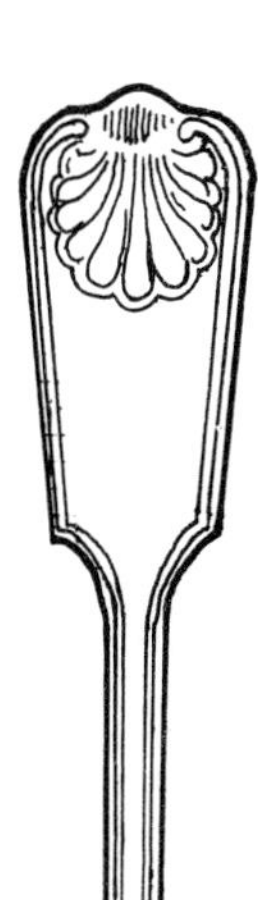
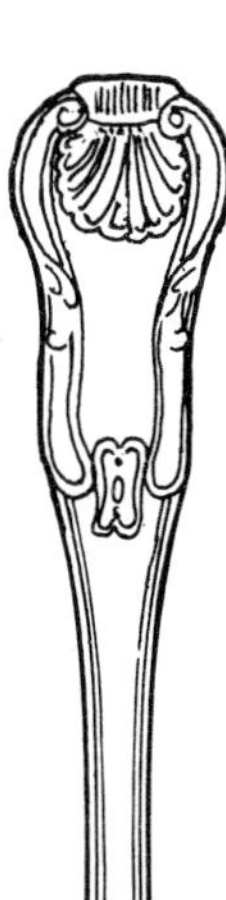

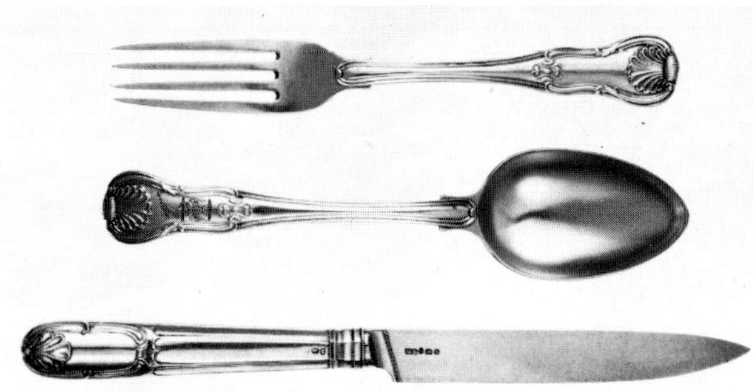

806

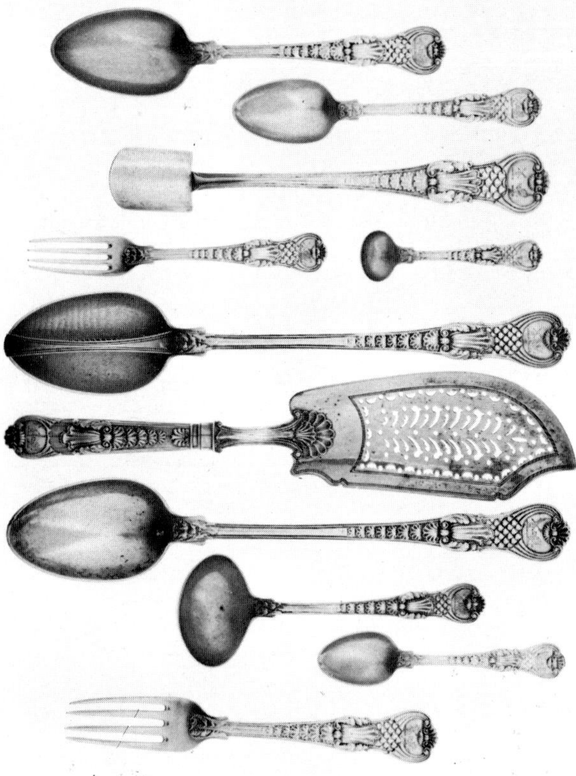

807

806. During the latter part of the 18th century it became fashionable to have silver gilt table silver for dessert. This usually involves having a dessert knife, dessert spoon and fork, although services are often comprehensive with extra items such as serving spoons, ladles and grape scissors.
c.1810 *36 piece hour-glass pattern £3,000 — £6,000*

807. Naturally some sets of table silver come with a variety of serving implements and here is a set in the Coburg pattern which, in addition to the five main items, has a sauce ladle, serving spoon, fish slice, straining or dividing spoon, salt spoon and a cheese scoop. These pieces are often found sold separately and they will add a corresponding amount to the price of a set. This pattern was mainly used during the first thirty years of the 19th century, and is often by Paul Storr.
c.1815 *60 piece set £10,000 — £15,000*
60 piece set by Paul Storr £35,000 — £55,000
Sauce ladle £100 — £180
Sauce ladle by Paul Storr £300 — £550
Serving spoon £225 — £325
Fish slice £250 — £450
Straining spoon £200 — £325
Salt spoon £35 — £50
Cheese scoop £200 — £350

808. Vine pattern dessert services I always think are very uncomfortable to handle, but are usually very finely forged and decorated. The marks on this pattern are often found on the back of the spoon bowl and just above the tines on the back of the fork. This is because of the obvious danger of distorting the decoration when marking, which would then be very difficult for the silversmith to rectify upon return from the Assay Office.
c.1825 *36 piece set £4,000 — £7,000*
Grape scissors £400 — £650
Serving spoon £350 — £600
Ladle £150 — £275

808

809. Many new and varied designs were created during the 19th century. This set of Princes pattern was a popular design used between 1850 and 1870.

60 piece set £6,000 — £12,000
6 table spoons £300 — £500
6 table forks £300 — £500
6 dessert spoons £300 — £500
6 dessert forks £350 — £550
6 teaspoons £120 — £240
Sauce ladle £80 — £140
Salt spoon £30 — £40

810. Table silver, like many other areas of domestic silver manufacture, was copied from earlier styles in the mid-19th century. Georgian beaded pattern is extremely rare and can command astronomical prices if it is 'right'. More often than not, however, it is Old English pattern which has had the beading added. If the beading goes down the splay of the fork to the top of the tines (see illustration) it is definitely Victorian. This set dates from the 1870s and is more clumsy than the 18th century table silver. There is less weight of silver than in 809 and the price should therefore be lower.

c.1870 *60 pieces £5,000 — £10,000*
6 table spoons £275 — £400
6 table forks £275 — £400
6 dessert spoons £275 — £400
6 dessert forks £275 — £400
6 teaspoons £120 — £240

811. An extraordinarily complete set of mid-Victorian, dog nose pattern table silver in the Queen Anne style.

c.1880 *84 piece (including knives) £6,500 — £11,000*
Butter knife £35 — £65
Pair of fish servers £180 — £350
Soup ladle £200 — £350
Serving spoon £150 — £200
Sauce ladle £60 — £100
Sugar sifter £60 — £100
Cream ladle £50 — £90
Salt spoon £25 — £35
Mustard spoon £28 — £38

811

809

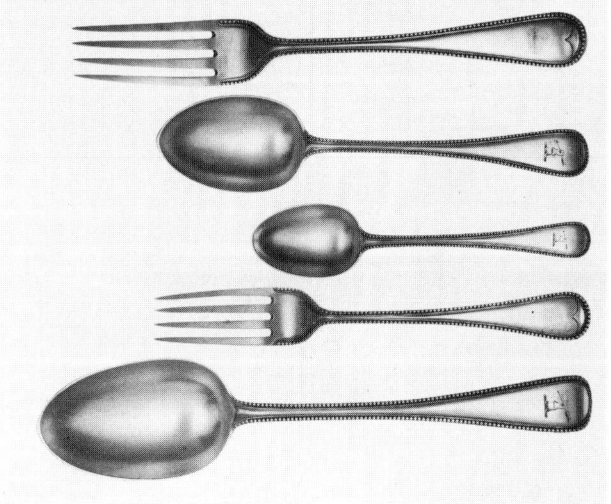

810

Tea & Coffee Wares

Coffee Pots, Chocolate Pots & Hot Water Jugs

A coffee pot, c.1730, with 19th century hit-and-miss trellis decoration.

A coffee pot from c.1735 which has been chased at a later date, creating thin patches which have been badly repaired.

Coffee and chocolate were both introduced into England in the mid-seventeenth century, and were to become, by the end of the century, an important part of social life, with more than four hundred coffee houses in London alone. The earliest known English silver coffee pot is hallmarked 1681 and is in the Victoria and Albert Museum.

It is quite likely that the pots on the following pages were used for both coffee and chocolate, but when found in a catalogue the only pots which will be termed 'chocolate' pots are those which have a removable finial for inserting a swizzle stick. Also included in this section are hot water jugs which again were quite possibly used for coffee or chocolate. In catalogue terminology they are distinguishable by having a defined short spout or lip at the rim, rather than a long spout starting from halfway down the body.

Hallmarks: these pots can be marked either on the base or the side. If on the base they will be scattered around the centre point. If on the side they will be in an almost straight line. If you find a coffee pot with marks in a straight line on the base, or three in a straight line and the maker's mark in a different place, it is likely to be what is known as a 'duty dodger'. The pot will have been made at the period it belongs to stylistically, but the marks may have been taken from another hall-marked piece, usually of a seventeenth century date, and then inserted into the base so as to avoid paying the duty levied per ounce when the piece was hallmarked. This temptation was greatest between 1719 and 1758, when the duty (at 6d. per ounce) payable on a pot of approximately 25 ounces would have been a great deal of money.

Lids should be marked with the maker's mark and lion passant, although it is acceptable to have only one mark. After 1784, however, there should be three marks, maker's mark, lion passant and monarch's head duty mark. The finials on chocolate pots are removable and should ideally be marked with the lion passant, although this is not always the case.

Condition: if there is no armorial engraving or initials, check to make sure that nothing has been erased and that there are no thin spots. Look at the handle sockets for any reinforcements or repairs. Check the hinge to the lid to see that this has not been strained and repaired or reinforced. See if the finial is damaged. If original, this will always be cleanly soldered on to the lid, and there should be no obvious signs of where this has been done from the inside. Look at the spout to see that it is not split at the seam and that there is no later added solder around the junction with the body. Lastly, check the foot to make sure that this is the original and is not repaired. Breathing over the whole surface should reveal all variations in colour and any later solder or patches. If the coffee pot is decorated be certain that this is contemporary, something which you can only discern with practice (see illustrations on p. 256).

Fakes: apart from the work of duty dodgers (see above), the most common fakes are those made from tankards. These can usually be discovered by judging the proportions. Tankards are generally shorter and fatter than coffee pots and if a coffee pot looks particularly dumpy then it may be a converted tankard. Another way of telling a fake is by checking the lid marks. If there are four or more hallmarks on the lid, then it is almost certainly a converted tankard as coffee pots only have three or fewer hallmarks.

The top illustration on the opposite page is a coffee pot, c.1730, with nineteenth century hit-and-miss trellis decoration. Eighteenth century coffee pots are never decorated all over in this way. The bottom illustration opposite is of a later chased coffee pot which dates from c.1735 when it is very unlikely to find any chased decoration in high relief. This chasing is more restrained than the majority of decorated pieces and is perhaps not as unattractive as some. It is undoubtedly later and because the chasing has been added it has created thin patches in the body which have been repaired by the local blacksmith with lead solder! Very unsightly and should be sold at a rock bottom price.

812

812. This coffee pot shows the influence of Dutch design on English silver due to the ties with Holland during the last quarter of the 17th century, with its embossed flutes or lobes, and floral and foliate decoration. The majority of pots dating before 1715 have handles at right angles to the spout and this continued into the George I period, and occasionally even later. The spout on this piece is raised rather than cast, a feature which died out by c.1720, although cast spouts were being used from c.1710. This is an unusual example, although not particularly attractive.
c.1700 *£15,000 — £27,500*

813

813. Queen Anne period silver was in general of plain and sturdy design. This was due to the enforcement of Britannia standard silver which, because of its higher silver content, would not stand up so well to excessive wear. Design was also influenced by the Huguenots who introduced solid French styles which were taken up avidly in reaction against the fussy embossed Stuart silver of the preceding twenty-five years. This chocolate pot has a hinged spout cover which is a feature sometimes found in the first quarter of the century on raised rather than cast spouts.
c.1705 *£12,500 — £17,500*

814

815

814. This type (this example happens to be from Dublin) is the simplest and most common design used during the first quarter of the century. The body is made from sheet silver which is seamed vertically in line with the handle sockets. The applied mouldings around the spout and handle junction are both decorative and functional as strengtheners. These mouldings should be carefully examined because very occasionally they have been added as reinforcements. This type, as with the majority of pots prior to 1715, were hallmarked on the body near to the rim.
c.1708 *£10,000 — £15,000*

815. As with 813, this is a chocolate pot which differs from a coffee pot by having a covered aperture in the centre of the lid. This is because the sediment in chocolate, unlike coffee, was to be savoured, and the opening allows for the insertion of a swizzle stick without heat loss. Lids were occasionally attached by a removable hinge pin chained to the body which facilitated cleaning. The decorative work around the spout and handle is a rare feature in this form and is known as cut card work.
c.1710 *£15,000 — £27,500*

816. Octagonal coffee pots are probably the finest and most sought after examples of this period. The form is indicative of heavy quality because of the need to withstand knocks and wear on the additional stress points. Spouts from this date are usually cast in two halves and this example has the so called 'duck's head' terminal. Coffee pots at this date are hallmarked either on the underside or on the body.
c.1720 *£20,000 — £35,000*

817. This is a plain pot with the handle opposite to the spout which now becomes more commonplace than the spout at right angles to the body which was invariably used until 1715. This is probably as late as one will find a high domed cover. The thumb piece, which is usually only found with side handles, is also no longer used (see 812, 813 and 815).
c.1725 *£8,000 — £12,000*

816

817

818. A slightly shallower domed lid is now more typical, the spouts invariably cast and as with 816 and 817 with a quite pronounced swan's neck curve. Handle sockets begin to be more adventurous with scroll and drop mouldings. The oval plaque at the lower socket could be a later reinforecment, or the silversmith's afterthought. Careful examination for any heat marks or rough soldering should reveal the truth.
c.1728 *£6,000 — £11,000*

819. Lids with an even lower dome, and occasionally bun shaped, are now a prevalent feature. Spouts temporarily straighten up, with handle sockets still occasionally very simple. The design of this pot is simple to the point of being dull. It is a chocolate pot with detachable finial, its only interesting feature. A contemporary coat of arms could add another £1,000 to the price.
c.1730 *£4,500 — £8,000*

820. A coffee pot from the same period incorporating a plainer lid and scroll handle sockets. Armorials would again enhance the value.
c.1730 *£4,500 — £8,000*

821. Lids begin to have more complex mouldings and spouts again become slightly more curved. This example is hallmarked on the body, although it is more common to find marks underneath at this date. As can be seen, armorials make a marked improvement on the overall appeal.
c.1735 *£4,500 — £8,000*

821

820

818

819

822

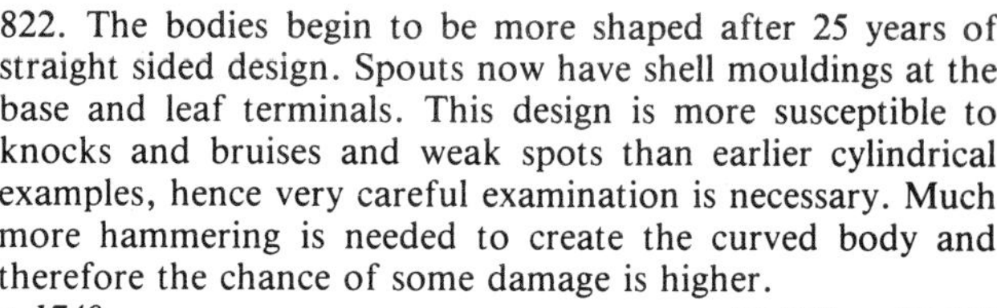

822. The bodies begin to be more shaped after 25 years of straight sided design. Spouts now have shell mouldings at the base and leaf terminals. This design is more susceptible to knocks and bruises and weak spots than earlier cylindrical examples, hence very careful examination is necessary. Much more hammering is needed to create the curved body and therefore the chance of some damage is higher.
c.1740 *£4,000 — £6,000*

823. A ribbed and sturdier example of the same period as 822 with an asymmetrical rococo armorial, although not bold enough to add substantially to the value. This is a period of transition from the more formal baroque engraving seen on the previous example to the flamboyance of the rococo period.
c.1740 *£4,500 — £8,000*

824. Flat chasing was used from the 1740s. This example by Paul de Lamerie incorporates a fine cast upper handle socket and almost equal plain and decorated areas. Later chased pieces tend to be covered with a profusion of flowers, scrolls and matting. The armorial engraving is rather weak in comparison with the fine chasing.
c.1745 *£45,000 — £75,000*

825. Full blown rococo chasing and slightly higher domed lids are found at this period. The lids quite often wrap over to fit the outside of the rim rather than having a sleeve which fits inside it. Occasionally this type of lid is found without a hallmark, although of course the body will be marked. The lack of any armorial engraving in the cartouche detracts from the value and careful examination should be made to see if there has been an erasure.
c.1747 *£3,500 — £5,500*

823

824

825

826. Bodies are now beginning to take on a more baluster shape. This example has three hallmarks on the body and the maker's mark is underneath, a feature occasionally found between 1745 and 1760. At the same time the foot, which is cast and applied, begins to spread more. The soldering around the inside of the foot is often left rough. This is not, therefore, necessarily a sign of restoration.
c.1755 *£3,500 — £5,000*

827. This is another chased rococo example featuring gadrooning on the foot which was introduced at this time. This pot has rather weak armorial engraving which does not compare with the slightly Chinese style of the chasing. Some chasers went even further with chinoiserie designs, incorporating figures, mystical creatures and prunus.
c.1757 *£3,500 — £5,500*

828. This is a more elaborate example showing rococo decoration at its height, with the spout as part of the integral design, unlike the preceding example which had an adapted shell and leaf decorated spout. The foot is also cast in a shaped design to complete the creation! Wood finials were not common at this date.
c.1760 *£3,500 — £5,500*

829. More pear shaped bodies are now common. The example on the left is a much more simple design and tends to be slightly lighter in weight, and for this reason less valuable. The pot on the right has gadrooned mouldings around the lid and foot and is one of the most sought after types of this period.
c.1765 (left) *£3,250 — £4,500*
c.1770 (right) *£3,500 — £5,500*

829

828

826

827

830

830. This is a hot water jug of the same period as the coffee pot on the right in 829, differentiated by the short spout. The simple silver strap handle has lost its original cane or leather covering. These are lighter and less desirable than contemporary coffee pots and therefore less valuable.
c.1770 *£2,250 — £3,250*

831. This is a Dublin example with less refined chasing than one would fine on a London made pot. It has, however, a certain charm which appeals to some people. Dublin continued to produce this type of chasing long after London had ceased to do so. Dublin makers were also fond of using animals in their decoration.
c.1775 *£3,500 — £6,000*

832. This shows the beginning of the influence of Adam on design. The urn shaped, neo-classical design of this example has beaded borders which were introduced at this date and prevalent until 1795. Covers now have a more peaked dome and a raised foot to lift the body higher from the table.
c.1775 *£3,000 — £5,000*

833. A hot water jug, again showing the influence of Adam. This is a good quality piece with alternate plain and matted stripes with a girdle of drapery swags. The entwined serpent handle is unusual and not very happy with its wicker covering. Lids on these jugs tend to have lower domed covers.
c.1775 *£2,750 — £4,500*

831

832

833

834. Another hot water jug with beaded borders, but reverting to the much plainer earlier style, the foot again being lower. The engraved crest under the spout slightly breaks up the very plain line.
c.1780 *£2,000 — £3,250*

835. This is as late as one sees a baluster coffee pot in the 18th century. Beaded borders are still used, but the cover and finial, being similar to 833, are the only influence of Adam in this piece.
c.1785 *£3,250 — £5,000*

836. A hot water jug with ivory handle rather than wicker covered, and a rather more elaborate body with slender pedestal foot. This again shows the slightly lower domed lid found on hot water jugs. This type is also occasionally found with bright-cut decoration.
c.1785 *£2,250 — £3,750*

837. An ovoid coffee pot with crest enclosed in an attractive bright-cut floral cartouche. The fan fluting on the lower body is less obtrusive and more attractive than the lobing introduced within the next ten years. This example is made by John Schofield, a sought after maker.
c.1790 *£2,500 — £4,500*

837

834

835

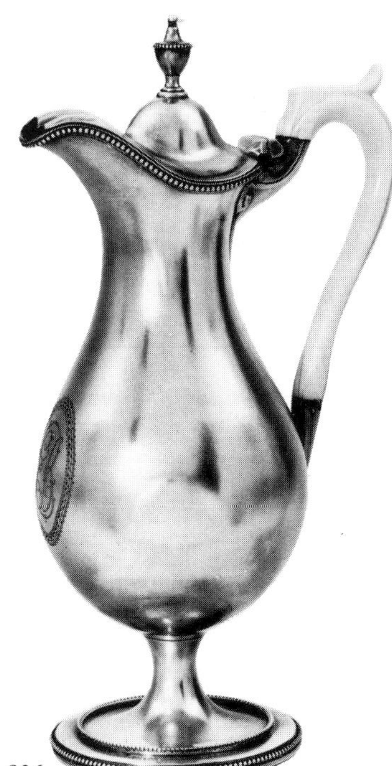

836

838

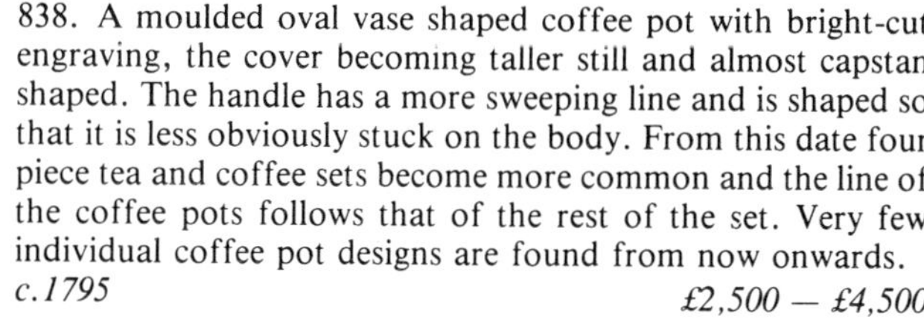

838. A moulded oval vase shaped coffee pot with bright-cut engraving, the cover becoming taller still and almost capstan shaped. The handle has a more sweeping line and is shaped so that it is less obviously stuck on the body. From this date four piece tea and coffee sets become more common and the line of the coffee pots follows that of the rest of the set. Very few individual coffee pot designs are found from now onwards.
c.1795 *£2,500 — £4,500*

839. This is a slightly more refined version of the last example because of the absence of heavy lobing. Note the drapery cartouche which is bright-cut engraved and a very dominant feature.
c.1795 *£2,500 — £4,500*

840. A circular vase shaped coffee pot with the rather ugly lobing which was used extensively in the last 25 years of George III's reign. The thin waisted pedestal foot is still in evidence. Reeded border wires are used during this period.
c.1795 *£2,250 — £3,250*

841. The vase shaped body has now become rather more squat and the bright-cut engraving less intricate. This example has a silver handle, which is by no means usual, with ivory fillets to prevent heat conduction. A silver handle should be examined to see whether it is hallmarked. After about 1805 they should be, and therefore make sure that they are contemporary as later silver handles tend to detract slightly from the price. Wooden and ivory handles are often replaced but they age quite quickly and, assuming they have been well made in the right style, this should not be detrimental.
c.1800 *£1,750 — £3,000*

839

840

841

842. The oval shape now gives way to oblong. The bright-cut engraving is still in evidence, but usually by this date is much more formal, omitting the scrolling floral designs depicted on No. 838. The handle on this piece has obviously been replaced by someone who was unsympathetic to the design as it does not balance with the spout. This would probably reduce the value.
c.1805 *£1,500 — £2,750*

843. The body is now even more squat and more obviously oblong than the previous example. Ball feet are introduced at this period, although more often found on teapots, and are used until c.1820. Coffee pots now follow the shape of teapots, but are rather larger and are raised higher from the table by a pedestal foot.
c.1810 *£1,250 — £2,250*

844. An oblong coffee pot. The pedestal foot has now gone and spouts temporarily become shorter and are no longer of the swan neck type. The lobing is still used and handles for a short period, c.1800-20, are angular, although this is not a definite rule.
c.1815 *£1,250 — £2,000*

845. A coffee jug on a lampstand by Paul Storr, showing the influence of ancient designs discovered by archaeologists in Egypt at this time. Gadrooned borders were reintroduced, usually with the extra embellishment of intermittent shell and leaf mouldings. The stand and the burner, with its separate cover, should all bear hallmarks, although the full set of marks will only be found on the main piece.
c.1815 *£3,500 — £5,750*
By Paul Storr £7,000 — £12,000

845

844

842

843

846

846. The same type of coffee pot but probably not intended to have a lampstand because the foot spreads from the body rather than being the rim foot seen on the previous example.
c.1815 *£2,250 — £3,750*

847. A ribbed baluster example with the silver handle now found on the majority of pots rather than the stained wood or ivory handle. Check to see that they bear the same hallmarks as the main piece. One should find the monarch's head, the lion passant and the maker's mark.
c.1830 *£1,500 — £2,500*

848. A baluster coffee pot almost imitating the early George III style, but rather fatter and with a larger spout. Decorative flower finials now become common.
c.1830 *£1,250 — £2,250*

849. A coffee pot of very similar shape to 848, but with embossed flowers and foliage. There is no engraving in the cartouche so examine carefully for any erasure. The chasing is restrained compared with that found on later chased coffee pots.
c.1835 *£1,250 — £2,000*

847

848

849

850. A compressed vase shaped example. This shape first comes in at about 1825, but becomes rather fatter as the years go by. It is no longer fashionable by 1860. Reeded girdles like this should be looked at carefully for any lead repairs. The hallmarks should appear on the base, lid, finial and handle. Any lack of hallmarks on these will certainly indicate repair or replacement with the exception of some provincial pieces.
c.1840 *£1,000 — £2,000*

851. A coffee pot with flat chasing of rather indifferent design. The feet with scroll and rocaille motifs are quite common at this period and would be cast and applied. Note that the lid does not close properly, showing that the hinge has been strained. There is no engraving in the cartouche and this may have been erased, so check for any thinness. Ocasionally a cartouche which has a chased surround is patched, and the solder-line is hidden so close to the chasing that it is not distinguishable without very careful examination.
c.1850 *£1,000 — £2,000*

852. A tapered cylindrical example with a flat flush hinged lid. which should be examined for any reinforcements or repairs. The engraved decoration is typical for this era. This type of pot can quite often be badly dented around the base and, if it has been restored, there may be solder repairs where the metal has split.
c.1865 *£1,000 — £2,000*

852

850

851

853

853. A sturdier example with vertical ribs. The handle is almost an exact replica of 852 but in this case there is an applied rim foot which will make the piece much more sturdy and should prevent any damage to the base. Again there is a vacant cartouche which should be examined for any erasure. The cover has an applied hinge which is also of sturdier design.
c.1870 *£1,250 — £2,500*

854. A late Victorian replica of a George III coffee biggin (1795-1815), so called because of the use of a burner, biggins originally being camp fire pots. The stand and pot are considered two separate pieces for hallmarking purposes at this date, and therefore all five marks are found on both pieces, whereas on a George III example the lampstand hallmarks would omit the leopard's head townmark.
c.1880 *£800 — £1,600*

855. The decoration on this pot shows the influence of the art nouveau movement but the basic shape has not been adapted to this inspiration. The handle is the only part which shows some natural movement and sympathy with the embossed work.
c.1900 *£1,000 — £1,750*

856. A hot water or coffee jug with neo-Celtic design as made by Omar Ramsden and Alwyn Carr. This is a piece of individual design and will fetch more per ounce than a pot from one of the larger manufacturers. Popularity for Ramsden and Carr waxes and wanes, but there is no doubt that in the long term their pieces will hold and increase in value.
c.1910 *£4,000 — £6,500*

854

855

856

Teapots

Although tea has been drunk in China for perhaps 4,000 years, it was not introduced to Europe until the seventeenth century. Indeed Samuel Pepys records in his diary on 25th September, 1660, that he 'did send for a cupp of tee (a China drink) of which I never drank before'. It is thought to have been first sold in England by Thomas Garroway of Exchange Alley, London, in 1657 and he recommended it then for 'gravel, scurvy, loss of memory, looseness, griping of the guts and colic'.

Although there are a few seventeenth century teapots extant, there is very little likelihood of finding one dating before 1710. The earlier the teapot the smaller they tend to be as tea was a very expensive commodity until the middle of the reign of George III.

Apart from the teapots shown in this section, more examples may be found under **Tea and Coffee Sets** on p. 290.

Hallmarks: teapots are usually hallmarked on the base, only occasionally on the side of the body, and there should be maker's mark and lion passant on the lid, plus monarch's head and date letter after 1784. If the handle is silver, this should also bear these marks. If the finial is silver and detachable, it should bear lion passant and maker's marks.

Condition: a teapot has generally been subjected to a great deal of use and should be examined very carefully. If at all possible it is quite a good idea to fill it with water and see whether it leaks. Failing this, very careful overall examination should be made, especially of the areas around the spout, the handle junctions and the base. Look carefully for any erased engraving and breathe heavily over the whole surface to see if there are any patches. If the interior is covered with a heavy layer of tannin then the examination should be all the more thorough. If the interior on the other hand is clean it should be easier to spot any defects.

Fakes: there are so many English made teapots in existence that it is difficult to believe that there would be a market to encourage anyone to fake a teapot. There are of course early eighteenth century duty dodgers. The bullet teapot is the most likely candidate but, if you take heed of where a piece should be hallmarked, it is unlikely that you will go far wrong. I have however recently seen a small bullet teapot which was made from the base of a George II mug, but the construction was very poor and stylistically the piece was not quite right. In addition the lid only had a maker's mark. Apart from these, there are some teapots which bear hallmarks for c.1800 which are stylistically from the early Victorian period. It appears that it became common to send one's old Georgian teapot to the family silversmith and ask for a more fashionable replacement. Some of the more unscrupulous silversmiths obviously just re-fashioned the piece.

857. Early teapots were of small capacity because of the rarity of tea. This Queen Anne example is the most common type found in the first twenty-five years of the 18th century. Although this one has an octagonal curved spout, they do occasionally come with plain spouts. The spout is cast in two halves, soldered together and applied. The stand-away hinge is often repaired where it meets the upper handle socket and this area should be carefully examined. There are some octagonal teapots of the same proportions as this example.
c.1715 *£9,000 — £18,000*

857

858

859

858. As with coffee pots, the octagonal shape is usually very sturdy and this example has a double moulding at the waist which gives it a more distinctive air compared with the plainer pear shape of the preceding type. Occasionally the lids are cast but the majority are hand raised. The spout and finial, however, are cast and applied.
c.1720 *£17,500 — £35,000*

859. The pear shaped body was superseded by this squatter version with the lid now set into an almost spherical body. The finials are now often detachable with a wooden knop. Sometimes the lids are completely detachable but more often have an applied hinge.
c.1725 *£13,500 — £27,500*

860. A typical Scottish teapot of the period, the body being formed as an almost perfect sphere. The foot is higher than contemporary English examples and the silver handle is also a common Scottish feature. The straight spout is indicative of the early date. The crests are probably later although they are typically Scottish with motto banners above.
c.1725 *£2,750 — £4,500*

861. The bullet shaped teapot is probably one of the best known types of the George II period. The best examples usually have a finely engraved band around the shoulder and this one in addition has an attractive contemporary coat of arms. The cast and applied foot is now slightly larger. The lid has a cleverly concealed or flush hinge which is difficult to distinguish as the engraver has continued the decoration over this area.
c.1730 *£5,000 — £9,500*

860

861

862. A much plainer bullet teapot still with a concealed hinge. The area around the hinge should always be carefully examined as they are often strained, reinforced or patched. Although the coat of arms is stylistically correct, it has been added later. This is apparent by the sharpness and stiffness of the engraving.
c.1735 *£2,750 — £5,000*

863. Bullet teapots are not found much after this date. The spout and handle mouldings are more decorative and the engraving is in typical rococo style. A more honest piece than 862 and should therefore command a higher price in spite of the later date.
c.1745 *£3,250 — £5,500*

864. Two teapots with very similar petal moulding to the spouts. This is a feature used by Exeter silversmiths. The lids on these provincial pots are quite often detachable rather than hinged and, although the engraving on the right hand example is quite fine, it is more usual to find the rather sketchy engraving apparent on the left hand example.
c.1730 *Left £3,250 — £5,000*
Right £3,750 — £5,500

865. Another Scottish example. The same body shape was used in Scotland over twenty years but examples from this date have shell moulded curved spouts. Note that there is a repair to the handle and that the hinge has been re-soldered. Small repairs can take 10% off the price if they are clumsily executed.
c.1735 *As shown £2,250 — £3,500*

865

864

863

862

866. Again Scottish but rather more squat than 865, indicating the later date. It is also flat chased with fruit and flowers which is typical of the rococo decoration used between 1740 and 1760. Again a silver handle is used unlike London made examples where wood or ivory is the more common material.
c.1740 *£2,250 — £3,500*

867. The inverted pear shape body was used in Scotland and England. This pot could have been made by a silversmith from either country, apart from the fact that the silver handle will indicate that it is Scottish and the extraordinary bird finial is an unusual feature normally only found on Scottish examples. The flat chased decoration is again typical of the period. One would expect to see some engraving in the cartouche and there is a likelihood that this has been removed.
c.1750 *£2,250 — £3,500*

868. The drum shaped teapot is the next type found. These can date from 1760 to 1780. They occasionally have detachable lids and some prettily bright-cut examples can be found. It is the most expensive of George III teapots. The spout and handle sockets are now no longer cast but hammered up from sheet and seamed. Always examine the seams for any splits or repairs. The flat base is liable to be worn.
c.1770 *£2,250 — £3,500*
A good bright-cut example £2,750 — £5,000

869. From now on the oval form is popular for about twenty-five years. This very simply made pot has beaded borders which are only found over a fifteen year period. The flush hinge should be examined to see whether it has been strained or reinforced.
c.1780 *£1,350 — £2,250*

866

867

868

869

870. Although the shape is very similar the overall effect is dramatically different. The bright-cut engraving brings the whole piece alive. This has the maker's mark of Hester Bateman whose mark will always command a very competitive price.
c.1785 *Hester Bateman £2,250 — £3,750*
By another £1,750 — £2,750

871. The flattening machinery in use from the latter quarter of the 18th century enabled silversmiths to use a minimum amount of metal. Although the capacity is on a par with a modern teapot, the weight of silver used is perhaps only two-thirds that of some of the smaller teapots made earlier in the century. The bright-cut engraving is used as a decorative feature which enables the silversmith to get away without using any cast or applied work except for the reeded border wire.
c.1795 *£1,000 — £2,000*

872. This illustration shows three examples. The one on the left is an unusual teapot decorated with vertical 'staves' and horizontal reeded 'hoops' simulating a barrel. The centre example shows the re-introduction of the circular shaped pot. Vertical lobes are used as a form of decoration. The coat of arms is very simple without any cartouche, typical of this period. The slightly earlier pot on the right combines both lobing and a band of bright-cut engraving and the form is octagonal with a higher domed lid than was found over the previous fifteen years. Many flat based teapots were found to scorch the tea table and therefore independent teapot stands were made so that this could be avoided. These are collected in their own right today and can be priced very close to an inferior teapot.
Left: c.1790 *£1,400 — £2,750*
Centre: c.1805 *£1,200 — £1,800*
Right: c.1795 *Teapot and Stand £1,750 — £3,000*
Teapot only £1,250 — £2,250
Stand only £400 — £600

870

871

872

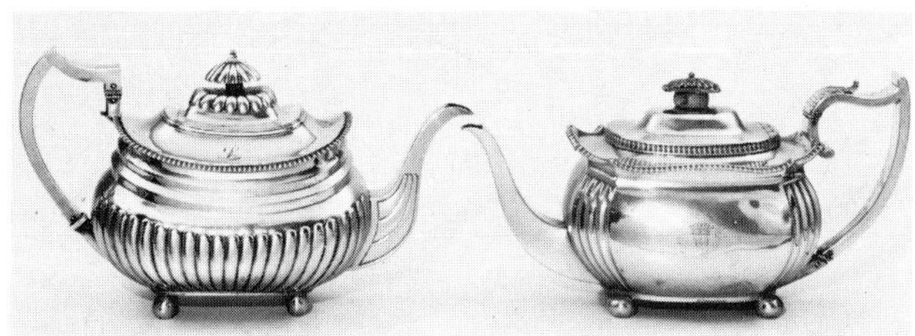
873

873. Rather cumbersome oblong bodies were used between 1800 and 1820 and bun feet were applied rather than using teapot stands. This type is perhaps one of the least popular of all Georgian teapots. For the first time it becomes common for London made examples to have silver handles. Gadroon borders and lobing or fluting are common features on this style, two examples of which are illustrated.
c.1810 *Each £700 — £1,150*

874

874. A heavier quality now returns with cast spout and foot, cast finials and applied mouldings. Teapots of this design weigh almost twice as much as the type shown as 873 and are usually found to be in much better condition because of this extra quality. The temptation is to think that these are Victorian because of their fussy decoration and it is often not admitted that these designs were used as early as 1815. The naturalistic feature of flowers and buds as finials now becomes commonplace.
c.1820 *Each £900 — £1,750*

875

875. The decoration is more realistic than ever and looks almost as though the flowers and leaves are growing out of the teapot rather than just applied and embossed on to the surface. More restrained in surface decoration than those shown as 874, but more movement and crispness result from the use of bolder leafage.
c.1835 *£800 — £1,600*

876. By this date the majority of teapots were made as part of a set or, if they were individually made, the design followed those of tea sets. This is an attractively engraved example with applied moulding at the rim. The silver handle should of course be hallmarked.
c.1850 *£750 — £1,250*

877. This is rather an unusual design and individual pieces like this from the 19th century can command prices in excess of the more straightforward teapots of 60 or 70 years earlier. The hexagonal body is die stamped with insects and a variety of plants. The spout and handle have realistic bark decoration.
c.1875 *£1,250 — £2,250*

876

877

Milk & Cream Jugs

Milk and cream were not commonly taken in tea and coffee until the early eighteenth century. There are no extant small jugs dating before the Queen Anne period which could have been used for this purpose. Indeed, small jugs are extremely rare even at this early date and usually follow the design and shape of coffee pots. By the 1720s there were cream jugs without lids, the earliest being of pitcher form, either with a simple baluster body or, occasionally, an octagonal body. By the 1740s it was the norm for them to have three legs and this format lasted until the 1760s when the spreading foot was again used. By 1800 the design of cream and milk jugs was influenced by the overall design of tea sets, and individual prices and shapes can be studied in the section on **Tea and Coffee Sets** (p. 290).

Hallmarks: cream and milk jugs are hallmarked on the base, or on the body either under the spout or near the handle. They should always bear a full complement of marks if they are London made.

Condition: such small items are often of fairly thin gauge and therefore very susceptible to damage. Always examine for any splits or repairs at the rim and torn out or patched handles. If the body is decorated with chasing, examine for any solder repairs. The foot or feet should be carefully studied to see that they have not been repaired or bashed up into the body.

Fakes: one of the most common fakes is made by adding a spout to a small christening mug. Although the piece may be 95% original, the addition of a spout will quarter the value of the mug. In the early eighteenth century small pitcher cream jugs have occasionally been made from the body of a caster by the addition of a spout and handle and any clumsy soldering or workmanship on a jug of this type should make one extremely cautious. There are duty dodgers and other examples of milk jugs with let-in marks, and all the normal procedures of examination should be followed.

878

879

878. As already stated in the introduction, this is one of the earliest forms of English milk jug and the style is very much like that of contemporary coffee pots. The foot and spout are usually cast and applied, and covers are hinged. They are extremely rare and may command very high prices.
c.1710 *£6,000 — £10,000*

879. An octagonal jug which by virtue of its construction is heavier than the type shown in 878. Be careful to examine the hinge junctions as they bear a lot of strain and have occasionally come adrift and been resoldered.
c.1720 *£10,000 — £17,500*

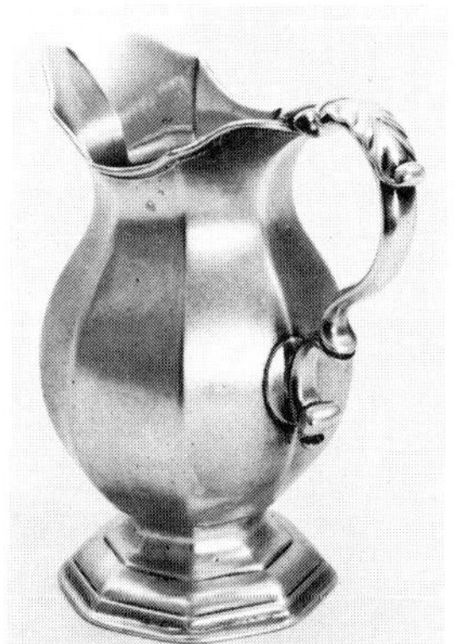
880

880. Smaller cream jugs were introduced in the 1720s with octagonal examples being the rarest. Silver scroll and double scroll handles are the norm, very often with a leaf moulding at the top, a feature which was used extensively over the following 50 years. This type will always be marked underneath the base and it is desirable to see the impression of the marks on the inside of the jug. The applied disc under the lower handle terminal in this case is probably contemporary, but look carefully to see that this is not a later reinforcement or repair.
c.1720 *£4,000 — £8,000*

881. The pitcher shaped jug now becomes common, but again octagonal ones are much rarer than plain ones and can command four times the price, or even more.
c.1725 *Octagonal £3,500 — £6,000*
Plain £750 — £1,500

881

882. A pitcher jug with simple scroll handle, not flattened like those on the preceding examples, but of circular section. The foot is a simple applied ring.
c.1725 *£750 — £1,500*

883. The body now becomes taller and narrower and usually of thinner gauge. Always examine carefully for any weak spots.
c.1730 *£600 — £1,200*

884. Hot milk jugs were occasionally produced as late as this, but are usually on three hoof feet. They are again extremely rare and can have either hinged or detachable lids. Scottish examples also exist but tend to be of plainer design. The quality of this piece is worthy of Paul de Lamerie's work, and his mark could increase the price by five times.
c.1735 *£6,000 — £10,000*
By Paul de Lamerie £32,500 — £50,000

882

883

884

885. The ovoid body with a narrow neck is usually indicative of reasonably heavy quality. The feet and handle are usually cast and applied.
c.1735 *£1,250 — £3,000*

886. A small jug in the form of contemporary brandy saucepans, a design peculiar to Exeter. Examine carefully to see that it has not been converted from a brandy saucepan. There should be no signs of discoloration where the handle socket has been removed. London hallmarked examples are considered to be conversions.
Exeter c.1735 *£600 — £1,000*

887. The rims of jugs are now nearly always waved or of curved shape. Three hoof feet and trefoil headings are common.
c.1745 *£500 — £800*

888. Amongst the more straightforward type of jug shown as 887, others of more distinction were produced. This one has an entwined and chased serpent handle and this one unusual feature has a dramatic effect on the value.
c.1745 *£750 — £1,500*

888

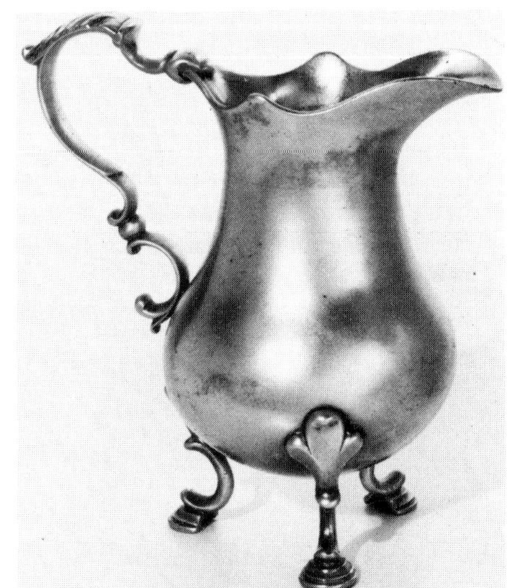

887

885

886

889

890

889. This is a typical example of an Irish made jug. The milk jugs have paw feet headed by masks and this feature is also found on Irish sugar basins. The quality is usually good, although look out for repairs at the rim. The lack of reinforcing wire at the rim on a piece with a wide mouth puts a lot of stress on the metal if it is not of very thick gauge.
c.1745 *£750 — £1,500*

890. Small oval cream boats were only occasionally produced and the majority were of plain design in imitation of the larger sauce boats. This one however is attractively chased with a goat, trees and other motifs which sets it apart from the majority. The clarity and quality of the chasing is a sure sign of contemporary decoration.
c.1750 *£1,000 — £2,250*

891. By this date the majority of milk and cream jugs will have a pedestal or spreading foot. The borders to the rim and the foot usually match (as here) with an applied gadroon wire or sometimes with a simply punched bead edge. The chasing is contemporary. It is not tight and involved like the majority of later chasing.
c.1765 *£500 — £1,000*

892. One maker, John Schuppe, produced cow creamers between 1755 and 1775. It was undoubtedly his specialist trade as little other silver bearing his mark exists. They are comparatively rare and command very high prices. These are not to be confused with late 19th century Dutch cow creamers which are only a tenth of the value. They are always hallmarked on the belly; the lid is usually unmarked.
c.1765 *£9,000 — £16,500*

891

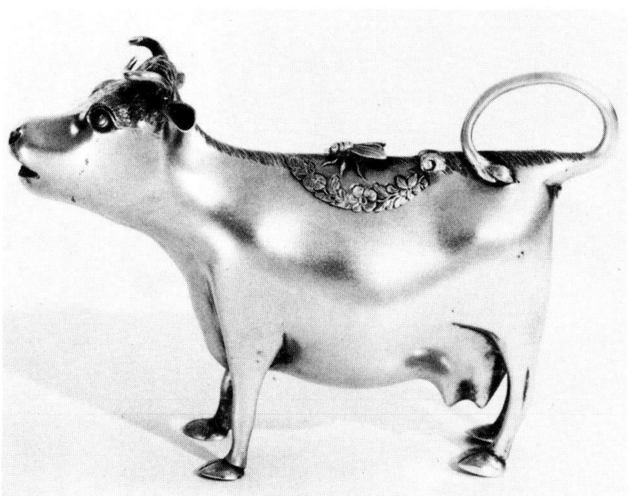

892

893. The form of cow creamers varies very little, but sometimes the decoration is more detailed. This one has textured 'hair'. It seems strange that no other silversmiths took up the design, but pottery cow creamers are, of course, well known.
c.1765 *£9,000 — £16,500*

894. Small cream jugs with floral embossing or decorated with rural scenes were common between 1760 and 1780. A minimal amount of silver was used and no border wires were added. Instead the borders were punch beaded. The scroll or double scroll handles either have leaf capped upper scrolls or applied beaded rat-tails. The examples on the left and right of the photograph date from c.1770, whilst the jug in the centre is between 1775 and 1780. The later date is distinguishable by the higher foot and more curved rim. Although very similar to 895, it is not of such heavy quality.
1760-1780 *Left £400 — £700*
Right £400 — £700
Centre £400 — £700

895. A plain baluster, almost pear-shaped jug, with applied beaded borders. Taller and more elegant than those made in the previous thirty years. A very straightforward design, but this example bears the mark of Hester Bateman.
c.1780 *Hester Bateman £500 — £975*
By another £400 — £700

895

894

893

896

896. The helmet shaped jug was very popular over a period of fifteen or so years. The best ones are decorated with crisp bright-cut engraving. The foot will nearly always be of square pedestal form and the handle a plain reeded loop. Usually hall-marked under the foot in the four corners, otherwise under the lip, or very occasionally on the foot rim. If one is marked in the latter way, look carefully to make sure the mark has not been let in.
c.1790 *£350 — £700*

897. This jug has additional bright-cut floral swags which, as long as the engraving is still crisp, will make it a slightly more popular buy. Features otherwise are practically the same as 896.
c.1790 *£350 — £700*

898. A somewhat plainer example of the same type with its companion sugar basket. These both bear Edinburgh marks. Their value however is comparable with London examples. Note that the cream jug has a dented and twisted foot which must be set against the value.
c.1795 *Jug and basket £1,250 — £2,500*
Jug £350 — £700
Basket £850 — £1,600

897

898

899. Another Edinburgh made piece with a large shaped oval foot, somewhat out of proportion with the overall size. This type of foot was also used by Dublin makers. There is a nasty repair at the junction of the handle and the rim which is a common place for damage. The crest and initials are later. These deficiencies will reduce the value, perhaps by as much as 20 or 30%.
c.1795 *In good condition £350 — £700*

900. This jug shows the next development after the pedestal foot. Jugs are usually flat based until the introduction of the ball feet after 1805. Other examples can be seen under **Tea and Coffee Sets**, p. 190.
c.1800 *£350 — £700*

901. An unusually involved milk jug, cast and chased with game birds. The foliate spout rim and scroll handle are not of sympathetic design and look rather clumsy. The quality, however, is very good and because of the unusual design features, a high price will be demanded.
c.1820 *£650 — £1,100*

901

900

899

Sugar & Other Bowls

This section includes bowls which were obviously used for sugar, sugar boxes, swing-handled sweetmeat baskets, cream pails and some other small bowls.

In the early eighteenth century sugar bowls or sugar boxes nearly always had covers. By the 1730s small bowls which are too large to be called sugar bowls, but too small for use as a punch bowl, made their appearance and were perhaps used for slops. By the 1760s there are swing-handled sugar or sweetmeat baskets, as well as the smaller cream pails. There are many other examples of sugar bowls illustrated under **Tea and Coffee Sets** and you will find individual prices for them there.

Hallmarks: any boxes or bowls with covers should be fully marked on both pieces, usually on the underside and inside the lid. Examples from the George II period with saucer shaped covers are occasionally marked on top, in the centre of the lid. Swing-handled baskets after 1784 should have the lion passant mark on the handle and are most usually marked with the full set of marks on the foot.

Condition: always look at the sides for any erasures and at the feet for any damage where they are soldered to the body of the piece. Make an examination of the rims in case there are any splits. On swing-handled baskets look for repairs at the pivots.

Fakes: on early eighteenth century examples look out for duty dodgers (see introduction to **Coffee Pots,** p. 256). Some late eighteenth century baskets are occasionally chased or pierced later. See also under **Epergnes** (p. 207) where the small detachable baskets are sometimes sold as sweetmeat baskets, but these rarely have any more than maker's mark and lion passant.

902

903

904

902. This small bowl on a rim foot was probably intended for use as a tea or herb cup. It has the popular chinoiserie decoration.
c.1685 *£1,500 — £2,500*

903. Octagonal sugar bowls are very rare and extremely desirable. This example has a nice contemporary coat of arms. They are usually of fairly thick gauge.
c.1710 *£5,000 — £8,000*

904. A pair of two handled bowls with covers, probably from a toilet service, although extremely desirable as separate items. These are silver gilt and again have contemporary armorials and are of heavy gauge. They should be fully marked on bases and covers in the same way as a cup and cover.
c.1710 *Pair £20,000 — £30,000*

905. A so-called sugar box because the form is oblong rather than bowl shaped. Again rare and very desirable. Of heavy quality and partly cast.
c.1715 *£20,000 — £35,000*

906. Another example similar to 905. This one was made in Dublin and, assuming the quality is the same, would fetch rather more than a London example purely because of the rarity of the hallmark.
c.1715 *£20,000 — £35,000*

907. Although the most usual type of early 18th century sugar bowl with detachable lid which, when reversed, can double as a saucer or spoon tray, they are nevertheless fairly scarce. The engraved armorial, although apparently contemporary, is probably engraved later. There is a certain lack of detail and depth to the engraving. This will prevent the piece from making a really top price as the most discerning collectors and dealers will shy away.
c.1725 *£3,500 — £5,500*

908. This slightly later example has a higher dome to the cover which is a normal development, and it is also likely to be slightly lighter in weight. The finely engraved contemporary armorials are an added bonus to this example.
c.1730 *£3,500 — £5,500*

909. A third example of this type, the knop to the domed cover very similar in form to the foot on the bowl. The lack of any engraving makes this piece rather dull.
c.1735 *£3,000 — £4,500*

909

908

907

905

906

910

911

912

910. A ribbed circular example. This is a popular form and usually of quite heavy quality. The two crests are Scottish although the bowl is London made, and these may have been added later.
c.1735 *£1,750 — £3,250*

911. A slightly larger bowl approximately 6½ins. in diameter with flat chased decoration at the rim. This embellishment turns a comparatively plain bowl into an interesting example. The use of bowls which are larger than sugar bowls and too small to be punch bowls has never definitely been pinpointed: it is probable that they were slop bowls. This description will rarely be used by the retailer as it conjures up an unattractive picture! Another name which will *not* be used is 'spitting bowl' which was also a possible usage.
c.1735 *£4,000 — £6,000*

912. This sugar bowl without cover is again Scottish and the scroll border is a distinguishing feature not found on English bowls.
c.1735 *£1,750 — £3,000*

913. A Scottish example of skittle ball shape which is not found in England. The two engraved crests have motto banners above, which is also a typically Scottish feature.
c.1735 *£1,500 — £2,750*

913

914. Yet another ribbed circular bowl, this time of larger size, being approximately 7½ins. in diameter and with contemporary coat of arms.
c.1735 *£4,000 — £6,000*

915. An Irish bowl of typical form. These come in varying sizes from as small as 4½ins. up to about 8ins. in diameter and vary only slightly in shape. The early examples tend to be deeper and less flared. The engraved crest is enclosed within a garter with motto. The garter around the crest is a 19th century feature and therefore this crest is later and will detract from value.
c.1735 *Depending on size £2,500 — £6,500*

916. An Irish three legged bowl, the basic shape of which was used from 1735 right into the 1780s. The later they are the thinner and more flimsy they become. This example is of reasonably good gauge and will be hallmarked on the base. The later ones often have punched bead decoration, which can wear very thin and therefore holes appear.
c.1750 *£750 — £1,500*
A later and thinner example £500 — £800

917. Another Irish example, this time on three legs headed by lion masks. It would be unusual to find an 18th century English example on legs, so if it is not Irish it will either be a rarity or an out-and-out fake.
c.1750 *£700 — £1,300*

917

916

914

915

918

918. This oval sweetmeat basket is a miniature of a cake basket of the same period. The stamped floral decoration is applied to the wirework sides and is vulnerable to damage.
c.1765 *£600 — £900*

919. A largish bowl with stand, approximately 9ins. in diameter, decorated with bands of Vitruvian scrolls, a popular Adam feature. This example is made by Andrew Fogelberg, whose mark is nearly always indicative of good quality, and therefore is much collected.
c.1780 *£4,250 — £6,750*

920. Here are four cream pails, which are quite small and perhaps not as useful as the larger sweetmeat or sugar baskets. They are however quite rare and command good prices.
Left to right:
c.1760 *£650 — £950*
c.1815 *£450 — £650*
c.1760 *£650 — £900*
c.1775 *£650 — £900*

919

920

921. A boat shaped sugar basket by Hester Bateman with attractive piercing and bright-cut decoration. Much sought after nowadays, and popular for use as a sweet basket.
c.1780 *By Hester Bateman £1,250 — £1,900*
By another maker £1,000 — £1,500

922. Another example by Hester Bateman displaying slightly different piercing, and this time with its original blue glass liner, which is missing from 921. This does not seem to add tremendously to the value as they are equally useful as sweet baskets with or without liners.
c.1780 *By Hester Bateman £1,250 — £1,900*
By another £1,000 — £1,500

923. This small basket is made from a cowrie shell. It is too small to be for sugar and may have been intended for salt. It is by Hester Bateman and a collector's piece. The silver mounts are attached by tiny rivets at the base and held by the hinge pins at the rim.
c.1780 *£400 — £700*

924. A miniature cake basket type, pierced and engraved below the reeded rim. These do not hold a great deal and therefore are not as highly priced as other examples of this period.
c.1780 *£600 — £900*

924

923

921

922

925

925. A swing-handled example of an octagonal pedestal sugar bowl with bright-cut engraving.
c.1790 *£1,000 — £1,500*

926. This is slightly later than the similar sugar baskets shown in 921 and 922. Although it still retains a band of bright-cut engraving, it is not pierced. The beaded borders have been superseded by reeding which is again an indication of later date.
c.1790 *£1,000 — £1,500*

927. Another octagonal pedestal sugar bowl with bright-cut engraved decoration.
c.1795 *£900 — £1,250*

928. A very plain and comparatively unattractive example which is later still, but functional.
c.1800 *£700 — £1,000*

926

927

928

929. A heavy circular sugar bowl, perhaps originally part of a tea service, by Paul Storr with lion mask handles.
c.1810 *£1,250 — £2,500*

930. A wirework sugar basket with applied stamped decoration of oak leaves and acorns. Not a very practical shape and usually fairly light, and therefore would not command a very high price. Less florid examples, but of the same basic shape, are found c.1770.
c.1840 *£750 — £1,250*

931. An unusual small sugar bowl of lily design, the foot formed from the stems of the flower and two leaves. It also has a sugar sifter with branch handle.
c.1895 *Bowl and sifter £800 — £1,500*

932. An unusual preserve jar in the form of an apple, the lid hinged from a branch of the bifurcated handle.
c.1895 *£600 — £900*

932

931

929

930

Tea & Coffee Sets

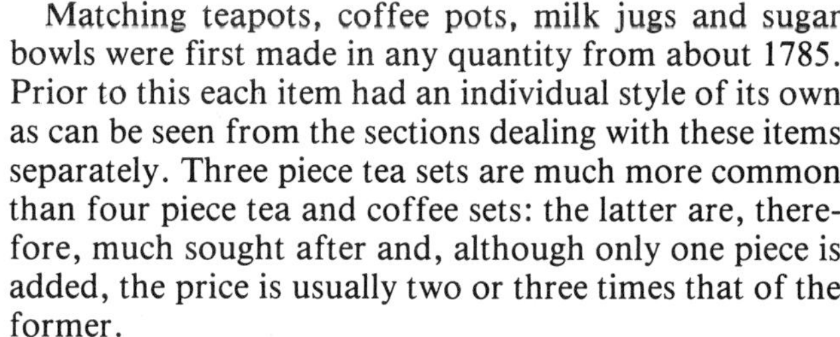

Matching teapots, coffee pots, milk jugs and sugar bowls were first made in any quantity from about 1785. Prior to this each item had an individual style of its own as can be seen from the sections dealing with these items separately. Three piece tea sets are much more common than four piece tea and coffee sets: the latter are, therefore, much sought after and, although only one piece is added, the price is usually two or three times that of the former.

Hallmarks: a set is only a set if all the marks on each piece are the same. Milk jugs and sugar basins should bear one full set of marks. Teapots and coffee pots should bear the full marks on the body with maker's mark, lion passant, date letter and monarch's head duty mark on the lid. Where there is a silver handle or detachable silver finial these should also be marked. Each piece is usually either marked on the base or on the side near the handle.

Condition and Fakes: see remarks under separate sections. If one piece of the set is by a different maker or more than two years different in date, the price should be arrived at by a summation of the individual valuations of each piece.

933

933. The likelihood of one coming across a tea or coffee set in the early 18th century is remote. This heavy octagonal set is extremely fine, although the foliate initials have been added at a later date. The value of something like this is in an entirely different league compared with the later sets which are described in this section.

c.1720 — *£60,000+*

934

934. Even at this date it is unusual to find sets and this one with typical Adam features of rams' masks and husk swags is uncommon. Although coffee pots normally have long curved spouts, it seems probable that the pot here was used for coffee as it came originally from a family collection where it had remained since its date of manufacture. The only other alternative is that it might have been used for chocolate, but there was no teapot or other piece which might have been a coffee pot in the collection.

c.1775

The set £7,500 — £10,000
Coffee jug £3,250 — £5,000
Sugar basket £1,000 — £1,500
Milk jug £650 — £950

935. The moulded wavy sides with bright-cut engraving are an unusual design, although teapots like this are not as uncommon as the other two pieces. The sugar bowl is a transitional type. Under the section for tea caddies you will find sets of two caddies and a sugar bowl with cover which are echoed by this example. There is a teapot stand on four ball-and-claw feet which adds 20% or so to the price of a set.
c.1780 *The set £4,500 — £7,000*
Teapot £1,500 — £2,750
Stand £450 — £700
Sugar vase £1,200 — £1,500
Milk jug £600 — £900

935

936. From 1785 onwards the manufacture of tea and coffee sets becomes more prolific. The new methods of production introduced at this time also meant that the pieces were made with less weight of silver. This set is unusual in that it has two sugar baskets which now take over from the covered sugar vases. It is possible however that one was used as a slop basin. Although the pedestal foot is used on the baskets and the milk jug, the teapot still has a flat base. The teapot stand, which is shaped to the form of the pot, is needed to keep it from scorching the table.
c.1785 *The set £4,500 — £6,500*
Teapot £1,500 — £2,500
Stand £400 — £600
Milk jug £400 — £700
Large sugar basket £1,000 — £1,400
Small sugar basket £800 — £1,200

936

937. The shaped oval body was used extensively over the next fifteen years and bright-cut engraving at the rim and the base of a piece breaks up the rather harsh line. This set has a contemporary coat of arms which probably has been executed by a different hand as it is rather unhappily placed in a shaped octagonal cartouche which may have been intended for initials rather than armorials. From now on the teapot lid is nearly always domed and they get slightly higher as time goes on.
c.1790 *The set £4,250 — £6,500*
Teapot £1,500 — £2,500
Stand £400 — £600
Sugar basket £1,000 — £1,300
Milk jug £400 — £700

937

938. A similar set but slightly later in date. This may be discerned by the more flowing bright-cut engraving and the use of a silver handle on the teapot. The teapot has a straight tapering spout which was superseded by the swan's neck spout over the next five years or so, although this type also continued to be used up to 1805.
c.1795 *The set £4,000 — £6,000*
Teapot £1,500 — £2,500
Stand £400 — £600
Sugar basket £1,000 — £1,500
Milk jug £400 — £700

938

939

939. This plain oval shape with reeded borders lacks character without the bright-cut engraving on the preceding example. The likelihood of a coffee pot being part of a set now becomes greater and it is normally modelled following the same style as a milk jug. The pedestal foot is an area which can be badly damaged over the years and should be examined carefully for any repairs.
c.1800

The set £6,500 — £11,000
Coffee pot £2,250 — £4,000
Teapot £1,250 — £2,250
Stand £350 — £550
Sugar basket £1,000 — £1,300
Milk jug £400 — £700

940

940. Curved spouts are now the norm. Sugar basins still have a swing handle. When sold separately, these are often called sweetmeat baskets although the likelihood is that they were all used for sugar.
c.1800

The set £6,500 — £11,000
Coffee pot £2,250 — £4,000
Teapot £1,250 — £2,250
Stand £350 — £550
Sugar basin £1,000 — £1,300
Milk jug £400 — £700

941

941. Milk jugs by this date begin to have flat bases although coffee pots continued for a year or two on pedestal bases. Sugar tongs were used with sugar baskets, not for the manufactured sugar lumps of today, but for the coarsely cut, unrefined sugar of the 18th century. Silver handles on the teapot and coffee pot are found occasionally, with bone fillets between the handle and the body of the pot to prevent the heat being conducted.
c.1800

The set £6,500 — £11,000
Coffee pot £2,250 — £4,000
Teapot £1,250 — £2,250
Stand £350 — £550
Sugar bowl £1,000 — £1,300
Milk jug £400 — £700

942

942. A more complete set with a small 'bachelor's' teapot. Angular handles were sometimes used and these do not enhance the elegance of the set. However, cone finials give it an added dignity. Sugar basins now usually have a flat base and two handles. The swing-handled basket is not found much later than 1805. The six teaspoons illustrated, which are of the same period, are not by the same maker but have similar bright-cut engraving. Very occasionally sets of bright-cut table silver can be found which included teaspoons but usually sets of teaspoons were made to be sold separately. They were no doubt given as gifts in the same way that six coffee or teaspoons in a case have been given as wedding presents in this century. The larger teapot still has a teapot stand whilst the small one has bun feet and this became more common over the next few years.

c.1800

The set £7,500 — £12,000
Coffee pot £2,250 — £4,000
Teapot £1,250 — £2,250
Small teapot £1,000 — £1,750
Stand £350 — £550
Sugar basin £500 — £800
Milk jug £400 — £700
Teaspoons £200 — £300

943. By 1805 bright-cut engraving was on the wane and chased lobing was introduced. This is a late example of the straight tapering spout. The milk jug and sugar basin are of larger capacity but not yet as big as some mid-Victorian examples.

c.1805

The set £2,500 — £4,000
Teapot £1,000 — £1,750
Sugar basin £400 — £600
Milk jug £300 — £500

944. This oblong shape became popular between 1805 and 1815 and teapots are usually now raised up on feet. This meant the demise of the teapot stand and you are unlikely to find one hallmarked later than 1805. This design of set, incorporating oblong bodies and 'bun' feet, is one of the least popular Georgian types. The condition is often poor and the squared spout in particular may be split or repaired.

c.1805

The set £2,250 — £3,250
Teapot £800 — £1,200
Sugar basin £325 — £450
Milk jug £325 — £450

945. This set is functional but not of great artistic merit. Occasionally from this date lampstands with burners are incorporated. These are normally detachable and should be marked on both the burner bowl and cover. Tea kettles are not often found with a set; usually they were of individual design and performed a similar function to the tea urn.

c.1810

The set £7,500 — £13,000
Coffee pot £2,500 — £4,000
Kettle £3,000 — £5,000
Teapot £800 — £1,500
Sugar basin £400 — £600
Milk jug £400 — £600

943

944

945

946

947

948

946. At this time the use of lobed decoration below gadroon and foliate rims was often used in conjunction with leaf capped angular handles. There is now a uniformity in the type of foot used on each piece.

c.1810

The set £3,750 — £5,500
Coffee pot £1,250 — £2,250
Teapot £750 — £1,250
Sugar basin £350 — £550
Milk jug £350 — £550

947. Curved lobing was also used and an additional feature was the reeded or moulded girdle. The cast border mouldings are now more decorative with flowers or foliage. The feet are also more fussy with leaf flanked shells and anthemions being the most popular design. The panel feet remain common right through to the Victorian era.

c.1815

The set £3,250 — £5,000
Coffee pot £1,000 — £2,000
Teapot £700 — £1,150
Sugar basin £350 — £550
Milk jug £350 — £550

948. Circular services take over from oblong ones at about this time. This example was made in Dublin but incorporates features common to London made sets. Although there are two sugar bowls, one perhaps being a slop basin, this does not add 25% to the price, as the extra bowl is superfluous for modern day use. Handles now tend to be more elegant and this one takes a nice scrolling form.

c.1815

The set £2,250 — £3,500
Teapot £700 — £1,150
Sugar bowls, each £350 — £550
Milk jug £350 — £550

949. Another Irish set in the circular form. Although basically of the same shape as 948, it is plainer. It has good quality cast borders and interesting mask terminated handles on the milk jug and sugar basin.

c.1815

The set £2,000 — £3,000
Teapot £700 — £1,150
Sugar basin £350 — £550
Milk jug £350 — £550

949

950. Paul Storr, under the auspices of Rundell, Bridge and Rundell, produced some fine pieces in designs based on Roman antiquity. The teapot in this set is adapted from the shape of an oil lamp. The quality is very heavy and the majority of the decoration is cast and applied. The handles are formed as curved twisted serpents which on the teapot and coffee jug are cleverly fashioned in both silver and ivory. Sometimes found in silver gilt, which would increase the prices given below by 30%.

c.1815 *The set £30,000 — £40,000*
Coffee pot £8,000 — £15,000
Teapot £4,500 — £7,500
Sugar basin £1,500 — £2,750
Milk jug £1,500 — £2,750

951. Another Paul Storr three-piece set based on the same designs, but much simpler. The teapot handle has probably been replaced (see the handles on the preceding set) as the original would have been more likely to have followed the form of those on the milk jug and sugar basin.

c.1815 *The set £7,500 — £12,500*
Teapot £3,000 — £5,000
Sugar basin £1,500 — £2,250
Milk jug £1,500 — £2,250

952. The classical compressed vase shape is used again with girdles and florets. The hot water jug on lampstand took over from the larger tea kettles on lampstand for a period, although some sets are known with both. Tea kettles were to re-appear in the 1830s. It is unusual to have a covered sugar basin, but in this case it is indicative of the fine quality of the set.

c.1825 *The set £7,000 — £10,000*
Jug £3,000 — £5,000
Teapot £1,200 — £2,000
Milk jug £400 — £800
Sugar basin £600 — £1,000

950

951

952

953

954

955

953. Still of the same proportions, but now more elaborately embossed with flowers and foliage. The hot water jug could obviously have had a dual purpose and may have been used for coffee, hence these are sometimes sold separately as coffee jugs. The feature which differentiates between a pot and a jug is that the coffee pot has a long curved or straight spout emanating from the belly of the body, whilst a jug has a shorter spout on the same lines as a milk jug.
c.1825

The set £6,000 — £8,500
Coffee jug £2,000 — £3,500
Teapot £800 — £1,600
Milk jug £400 — £750
Sugar basin £400 — £750

954. The floral decorated border on this set is stamped and applied. Because of the method of manufacture, the gauge of silver at the borders was not particularly thick and you will often find that this type is repaired or full of holes if it has had a substantial amount of use. This type of applied decoration was the innovation of Sheffield manufacturers, and they also stamped out the feet in two halves and soldered them together before applying them to the body.
c.1825

The set £2,000 — £3,500
Teapot £650 — £1,100
Sugar basin £350 — £500
Milk jug £350 — £500

955. At various periods Chinoiserie decoration was revived and here is an example chased with scenes amongst floral motifs. The chinaman's head thumbpieces reinforce the design, but the overall effect is not very imposing. Usually of heavy quality in spite of this lack of good design.
c.1825

The set £2,250 — £3,750
Teapot £800 — £1,600
Sugar basin £400 — £700
Milk jug £400 — £700

956. The decoration on this set is more involved and has even less of a clear theme, with Rubenesque cherubs flanking the cartouches, as well as a chinaman finial on the teapot. It is noticeable that the sugar basin has quite a bad dent and repair at the cartouche. Always examine this area carefully on this type of set as it is comparatively easy to patch the area if it becomes worn or damaged and disguise the seam in the chased decoration.
c.1830

The set £4,750 — £7,500
Coffee pot £2,250 — £3,500
Teapot £800 — £1,600
Sugar basin £400 — £700
Milk jug £400 — £700

957. A more restrained design with arches and bouquets of flowers. Although there is a period from 1815 to 1825 where teapots and coffee pots often have wooden or ivory handles, by 1830 they are again normally always made of silver.

c.1830

The set £2,250 — £3,500
Teapot £750 — £1,500
Sugar basin £350 — £650
Milk jug £350 — £650

958. The decoration is now less intense and the use of larger foliate motifs gives a clearer design. Finials on the other hand become more decorative in the form of sprays of flowers and leaves. It is more usual now for each piece to be raised on four individually cast feet rather than the spreading feet seen in 957.

c.1835

The set £4,250 — £6,750
Coffee pot £1,750 — £2,500
Teapot £750 — £1,500
Milk jug £350 — £650
Sugar basin £350 — £650

959. The use of decoration is very similar but the waved borders indicate a slightly later date. The milk jug is now often taller and proportionately similar to the coffee pot rather than the sugar basin.

c.1840

The set £4,250 — £6,750
Coffee pot £1,750 — £2,500
Teapot £750 — £1,500
Sugar basin £350 — £650
Milk jug £350 — £650

960. A pleasing and fairly plain design which is not compatible with the popular belief that all Victorian silver is highly ornate. The feet, handles and rims however are a giveaway of the period.

c.1845

The set £2,250 — £3,500
Teapot £750 — £1,500
Sugar basin £350 — £650
Milk jug £350 — £650

956

960

959

958

957

961

962

963

964

961. Very occasionally extremely plain designs were used and presumably followed the purchasers' instructions. This set was made for a Continental family and bears their coat of arms, which has been stamped and applied rather than engraved. This is an unusual feature which will not necessarily add to the value unless the original owner was someone of particular note.
c.1845
The set £1,750 — £2,750
Teapot £600 — £1,150
Sugar basin £300 — £550
Milk jug £300 — £550

962. Another plain design but again with typical scrolling handles and decorative feet indicative of the early or mid-Victorian period, and further embellished with scroll and diaper panels. The teapot and coffee pot have rather ugly melon finials which are in fact contemporary and intended as part of the design.
c.1845
The set £4,250 — £6,500
Coffee pot £1,250 — £2,000
Teapot £750 — £1,250
Sugar basin £350 — £550
Milk jug £350 — £550

963. Fussy floral and scroll decoration was often used on sets of the period.
c.1850
The set £1,500 — £2,750
Teapot £600 — £1,200
Sugar basin £300 — £500
Milk jug £300 — £500

964. Occasionally an adapted melon form is used in the design of individual pieces. The engraving at this date is quite detailed but does not have a lot of depth and is liable to wear down comparatively quickly with use. Anything with worn decoration should be avoided.
c.1855
The set £1,650 — £2,750
Teapot £600 — £1,200
Sugar basin £300 — £500
Milk jug £300 — £500

965. A five piece set with the same sort of engraving, but with elaborate Gothic mouldings at the borders. It is unusual to have an extra teapot, which probably adds 25-30% to the value.
c.1860
The set £4,750 — £7,500
Coffee pot £1,250 — £2,250
Teapot £750 — £1,250
Small teapot £600 — £1,000
Sugar basin £300 — £500
Milk jug £300 — £500

966. One of the most elaborate Victorian designs, sometimes called 'Louis quatorze'. Occasionally at this date very large services would be made by one firm and might include muffin dishes and toast racks and other items. A tea kettle on lamp-stand was a more usual additional piece. More often than not they have swing handles but this example is fixed and therefore has ivory fillets in the arch to stop heat conducting.

c.1865

The set £6,500 — £9,000
Tea kettle £2,750 — £4,000
Coffee pot £1,250 — £2,250
Teapot £600 — £1,200
Sugar basin £300 — £500
Milk jug £300 — £500

967. A five piece Scottish set based on the design of the bullet teapots made in Scotland in the mid-18th century, but more elaborately chased than those examples. The spreading foot is again used on tea and coffee sets and the use of individual feet does not recur for another twenty years or so.

c.1865

The set £4,000 — £6,000
Coffee pot £1,200 — £2,000
Hot water jug £1,200 — £2,000
Teapot £600 — £1,100
Sugar basin £300 — £450
Milk jug £300 — £450

968. This small set, perhaps intended for use as an early morning tea or coffee set, is typical of the lengths silversmiths went to to please their clients. It is engraved with a monogram below a royal coronet and was probably made to order for one of the European royal houses. Having created a design for an individual client, the maker often repeated it to sell in retail outlets. Although of good quality the effective engraving lacks detail and is in the main mechanically executed by engraving concentric lines to give the outline of flowers and foliage. Some detail is then hand engraved to give a little depth.

c.1870

The set £4,000 — £6,000
Salver £1,750 — £3,000
Coffee pot £750 — £1,500
Teapot £550 — £1,000
Sugar basin £250 — £450
Milk jug £250 — £450

968

967

965

966

969

970

971

969. A very plain set with simple loop handles, with nothing really to recommend it. Purely a functional example.
c.1870
The set £900 — £1,500
Teapot £400 — £750
Sugar basin £200 — £350
Milk jug £200 — £350

970. In contrast a prettily engraved octagonal set. Each piece is still flat based. Engraving by this date is definitely the most dominant form of decoration.
c.1870
The set £4,000 — £6,000
Coffee pot £1,250 — £2,000
Teapot £750 — £1,250
Sugar basin £325 — £475
Milk jug £325 — £475

971. The basic form of this set echoes some of the late 18th century styles but the engraved decoration and scrolling handles are unmistakably Victorian.
c.1870
The set £2,250 — £3,500
Coffee pot £750 — £1,500
Teapot £500 — £800
Sugar basin £225 — £375
Milk jug £225 — £375

972. Again it can be seen from the teapot that this is based on a George III style, and the bright-cut engraving is also very reminiscent of that period, but the monogram of Gothic letters and the angular handle are not.
c.1870
The set £2,750 — £3,750
Coffee pot £800 — £1,600
Teapot £550 — £850
Sugar basin £225 — £375
Milk jug £225 — £375

973. The engravers of this period were particularly fond of using motifs such as fronds of fern and in this case have incorporated them with the floral swags used in the 1780s and 1790s by the Bateman workshop and others. A wooden handle is sometimes used on the teapot at this period.
c.1875
The set £1,000 — £1,800
Teapot £450 — £750
Sugar basin £200 — £325
Milk jug £200 — £325

972

974. Designers had drawn on all resources to create new designs for the Great Exhibition of 1851. This initiated the revival of antique forms and the decoration on this set is in the form of friezes of Roman warriors and chariots.

c.1880

The set £3,000 — £4,500
Coffee pot £1,200 — £1,800
Teapot £600 — £1,200
Sugar basin £275 — £400
Milk jug £275 — £400

975. The influence of Japanese designs in all areas of the arts was strong at this period and some very fine engraving was produced. Occasionally this is incorporated with parcel gilding (partly gilt) giving greater depth and variety. On some smaller pieces the imitation went further by copying the use of applied leaves, butterflies and insects in different colour golds.

c.1880

The set £1,200 — £2,000
Teapot £500 — £800
Sugar basin £200 — £350
Milk jug £200 — £350

976. This set shows the influence of Indian culture, the circular bodies being chased with bands depicting the signs of the zodiac. The exchange of business generated by the presence of the British in India encouraged these designs, which no doubt produced a topic of conversation at the tea table. These sets are not very popular today as they are compared with Indian made examples which are considered to be of poorer quality, but in fact are often well made.

c.1890

The set £1,500 — £2,250
Coffee pot £600 — £900
Teapot £350 — £550
Sugar basin £175 — £300
Milk jug £175 — £300

976

975

974

973

977

977. Irish silversmiths also revived earlier styles. The cream jug and sugar basin are in George II style but although the teapot and tea kettle obviously match these, no comparable examples were made in the 18th century.

c.1900

The set £2,250 — £3,500
Tea kettle £1,200 — £1,800
Teapot £500 — £800
Sugar basin £200 — £300
Milk jug £200 — £300

978

978. Many sets were made in this style, which is often called 'Queen Anne'. This term derives from the use of the curved lobing, which in fact was first used in the late 17th century on porringers. The shape, however, is nearer to some late George III designs.

c.1905

The set £1,250 — £2,000
Coffee pot £500 — £800
Teapot £250 — £500
Sugar basin £125 — £250
Milk jug £125 — £250

979

979. A Glasgow made set with finely chased scrolling foliage and flowers on a matted ground.

c.1910

The set £1,250 — £2,250
Coffee pot £650 — £1,100
Teapot £275 — £550
Sugar basin £125 — £275
Milk jug £125 — £275

980. This set bears the distinctive mark of Omar Ramsden made in partnership with Alwyn Carr in 1913, with the usual hammer finish and Celtic type ornamentation inset with semi-precious gems. The tray has a wooden base and silver border and handles.

1913

The set £12,000 — £20,000
Tray £4,000 — £6,500
Coffee pot £4,000 — £6,500
Teapot £2,250 — £3,500
Sugar basin £750 — £1,500
Milk jug £750 — £1,500

980

981. A Georgian style four piece set manufactured by William Hutton and Sons Limited. Very simple and not of particularly heavy quality.
c.1915
The set £1,250 — £2,000
Hot water jug £500 — £850
Teapot £225 — £500
Sugar bowl £125 — £250
Milk jug £125 — £250

982. Some very good quality sets were made between the wars. This one is based on a George II design, the teapot and milk jugs being true replicas, whilst the coffee jug and sugar bowl are adaptations of the same theme.
c.1925
The set £2,000 — £3,500
Coffee jug £600 — £900
Teapot £300 — £600
Large milk jug £150 — £275
Small milk jug £125 — £200
Sugar basin £150 — £275

983. This five piece set again echoes an 18th century design of c.1800. The original however would have been unlikely to have had gadroon borders, the coffee pot and hot water jug would not have been in this form, but more probably of vase shape on a pedestal foot.
c.1930
The set £1,750 — £3,000
Coffee pot £600 — £850
Hot water jug £400 — £700
Teapot £225 — £500
Sugar basin £125 — £250
Milk jug £125 — £250

984. An extraordinary design, typical of some of those produced by the Arts and Crafts Movement, and one which could really have only come from this period.
c.1940
The set £5,000 — £8,500
Tray £1,500 — £3,000
Coffee pot £750 — £1,250
Teapot £600 — £1,000
Sugar basin £350 — £650
Milk jug £350 — £650
Caddy £750 — £1,250

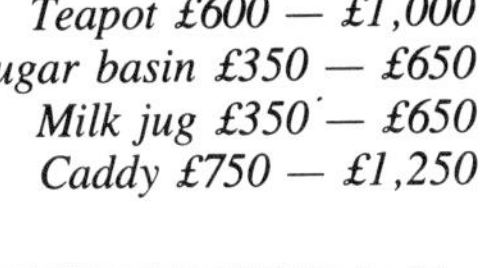

981

983

982

Tea Caddies, Sugar Vases & Biscuit Boxes

Tea was an expensive commodity in the eighteenth century and, apart from thc cost of the raw material, there was a tax on tea. This produced a need to be very sparing and make sure that no tea was wasted, and therefore the tea caddy was adopted. The earliest examples have sliding bases to facilitate easy filling, and sometimes have a lead liner. The detachable lid or cap was used for measuring the tea. By the mid-eighteenth century sets of two caddies and a sugar bowl, all in the same design, were fitted into a case, either made of wood or covered in shagreen and usually with silver mounts. Some of the more decorative examples are shown on the following pages. The late eighteenth century saw the introduction of the single tea caddy with its own lock and key, whilst by the nineteenth century the relative cost of tea had come down and there was no longer need to lock it away.

This section also includes some biscuit boxes and sugar vases. Biscuit boxes are found from the late nineteenth century and vary in size and design. There is no stylistic development and each example must be valued according to individuality and merit.

Hallmarks: there should be one main set of hallmarks on the body and a lion passant and maker's mark on the lid. Early eighteenth century examples with sliding bases and detachable caps rarely have a mark on the cap.

Condition: all the usual examination of the surfaces should be made. Hinges in particular should be looked at carefully. Occasionally those which had integral locks have had them removed. Look carefully at this area. Finials are often replaced with examples which are not in keeping with the style.

Fakes: in the early eighteenth century one particular maker, John Newton, who was a specialist caddy maker, dodged paying duty (see introduction to **Coffee Pots,** p. 256) by either stamping his maker's mark four times, or by using his maker's mark and a small lion passant only. Any incompletely marked caddy should be avoided when there is uncertainty about its authenticity.

985. An octagonal tea caddy with a removable domed cap and a sliding section at the shoulder for filling the caddy. These will usually be marked on the base and on the sliding shoulder, but are very rarely marked on the removable caps.
c.1715 *£2,000 — £3,250*

986. A pair of larger caddies similar to 985 with detachable caps, but with a sliding base. The section where the moulded foot slides away can be seen in the illustration. This type should be marked fully on the side of the caddy and with maker's mark and lion passant on the sliding base. The extremely bold armorials are a little out of period as the helm and foliate mantling was not really seen in heraldic engraving after about 1705.
c.1720 *Pair £5,000 — £8,000*

985

986

987. An oval variation of the first example with sliding shoulder and detachable cap. Not as popular as the octagonal form.
c.1725 *£1,500 — £2,750*

988. An oval variation of the second example with sliding base.
c.1730 *Pair £4,000 — £7,000*

989. A rectangular caddy with hinged lid. The hinge is usually concealed in the moulding around the edge of the lid. This type is often of very heavy quality and therefore more desirable. Again with nice contemporary armorials.
c.1730 *£3,500 — £6,000*

990. From this date onwards it becomes comparatively common to find caddies in sets, usually two caddies and a larger box used for sugar. These examples are very finely engraved, not only with contemporary armorials, but with border decoration of scrolls and simulated waterfalls. The lids are of the sliding variety and have hinged shell finials. These would certainly have originally been in an oblong mahogany or shagreen covered case, the finials being hinged so that the depth of the case could be reduced. They should be hallmarked on both bases and lids.
c.1740 *Set of three £15,000 — £20,000*

990

989

987

988

991

992

993

991. Another set of three of unusual bombé form, this time with flat chased floral and scroll decoration which is not as popular as the engraved decoration on the preceding set. The lids are hinged and have fixed shell finials.
c.1740 *Set of three £12,000 — £18,000*

992. A magnificent set of three caddies by Paul de Lamerie, of very heavy quality with cast and chased decoration. The engraving is also very fine and co-ordinates well with the overall design. The shagreen covered case has a lock which is not visible in the photograph and is applied with cast and pierced panels. The applied silverwork on a case of this type is not always found hallmarked, but usually a comparison of workmanship will make it apparent whether or not it is contemporary.
c.1745 *Set with case £140,000+*

993. A pair of oval caddies, very much in the same vein as examples of fifteen to twenty years earlier, but with floral chasing which, although contemporary, is rather ill at ease in this design. The circular sugar bowl and cover however adapt to the decoration more easily. The shagreen covered case is mainly functional; the silver mounts are not at all elaborate but in this instance one can see the lion passant and maker's mark on the lock plate. The shagreen is coming away from the upper lid, which will obviously detract from value.
c.1745 *Set with case £6,000 — £9,000*

994. Another pair of caddies with a circular sugar bowl. This type was almost entirely produced by Samuel Taylor, who was a specialist caddy maker and his maker's mark is almost as fussy as some of his designs with very scrolling and intricate initials 'ST'. Note that the chased decoration provides a cartouche for the engraving. On the caddies there is a full coat of arms and on the sugar bowl a crest. The spreading feet are cast and will have a roughened look on the underside. Frequently the solder will have been left in blobs where the foot has been joined to the body, rather than turned into a tidy border.
c.1750 *Set of three £6,000 — £9,000*

994

995. Another set by Samuel Taylor, very similar to 994, but this time with pierced spreading feet, again cast, and with rather weak flat flower finials. The decoration if anything is even more fussy, but contemporary.
c.1750 *Set of three £6,000 — £9,000*

996. Another set which is rather taller and more slender. The mahogany case with silver mounts is unusual. One would expect a shagreen example at this date.
c.1755 *Set with case £6,000 — £9,000*

997. A set of three 'sugar vases', so called because there are sets of this type known with companion sugar sifters (which look like a pierced sauce ladle) which hook over the scroll handles. The right hand example has had the cover later pierced to form a caster. An unhappy design which looks like a cross between a goblet and a caster. Not very popular, hence the comparatively low price.
c.1755 *£4,000 — £7,000*

998. A set of three rather eccentrically moulded caddies with chinoiserie decoration and hinged lids. The sides are stamped (and therefore rather thin) and chased in separate parts and then soldered together. They are quite likely to have worn through on the raised points. The shagreen covered case has later brass bindings at the corners.
c.1755 *Set with case £8,000 — £12,500*

998

997

995

996

999

999. A set of three, again with chinoiserie decoration which was popular at this time and presumably stemmed from the interest in Chinese art imported by the tea merchants. This caddy design was first used by Paul de Lamerie in about 1745. These are later copies by a different maker, but will still command a good price because of the design.
c.1760 *Set with case £10,000 — £16,000*

1,000. A single tea caddy with pierced oval sugar basket, teaspoons (there are four more in the case), sugar nips and mote skimmer with a fitted shagreen covered case. It is unusual to find a combination like this and the value is likely to be more than if one bought the pieces individually. All the pieces will not necessarily be by the same maker as there were specialist makers for tea caddies, teaspoons, etc.
c.1760 *Set with case £4,500 — £7,000*

1,001. A pair of caddies with chased foliate decoration and detachable lids. This type is usually made from fairly thin gauge metal and one should be careful to examine for any holes through the bodies. The unusual contemporary marquetry case has the owner's initials 'EW' set in below the lock.
c.1765 *Set with case £4,500 — £7,000*

1,002. A set of three, similar in outline to 1,001 but slightly heavier, with engraved cartouche unhappily squeezed in between the chasing. It is more than likely that a coat of arms has been removed and this will detract from value. Be sure that the feet are all intact; these are usually fairly small castings and the odd corner may have broken away. The bud finials are sometimes fitted with a thread and nut, or sometimes soldered direct to the lid.
c.1770 *Set of three £5,500 — £8,000*

1000

1,001

1,002

1,003. A pair of caddies of similar basic outline, but with a much simplified decoration of plain curved flutes.
c.1770 *Set with case £4,500 — £7,000*

1,004. A pair of tea caddies displaying those well known Adam motifs of rams' masks and swags. These are of fairly heavy quality, necessitated by the depth of decoration and applied castings. The female masks and drapery swags between the hoof feet are to my mind an extra embellishment which they could have done without. They are, nevertheless, fine caddies.
c.1775 *Set with case £7,500 — £11,000*

1,005. A set of three vase shaped tea caddies, sometimes called sugar vases, with similar decoration to 1,004. It is likely however that two of the vases would have been used as tea caddies, and perhaps the larger one for sugar.
c.1775 *Set of three £7,000 — £10,000*

1,006. An unusual oval caddy with lock by Andrew Fogelberg. From the 1760s onwards single caddies as well as sets of caddies are found. The single caddies will have incorporated locks, whereas the sets will be in a case which locks. This unusual and rather impractical design has a removable stand or frame with ram's mask terminals to the fluted pillar supports. The hinged lid has a hinged ring finial.
c.1780 *£4,000 — £6,500*

1,006

1,005

1,003

1,004

1,007

1,007. A circular drum tea caddy simulating the design of a tea chest. These are also found of plain cube shape. The four panels are nearly always engraved with pseudo Chinese characters and the borders engraved with scrolling foliage. The finials are formed by a sprig of the tea plant.
c.1770 *£4,500 — £7,000*

1,008. A rectangular example almost in the style of a Chinese pagoda but the sides are chased with English rural scenes. The cast feet and apron should of course be examined carefully for any breaks or damage.
c.1770 *£3,000 — £4,500*

1,009. An oval example of rather dull form with beaded borders, the engraved armorial being the only relief from a very simple design. Always examine the hinge on this type of caddy as it is liable to strain and will quite often have been repaired.
c.1780 *£2,000 — £3,500*

1,010. Another oval example with flush hinged lid, and bright-cut engraved with floral swags and formal borders.
c.1780 *£3,000 — £5,000*

1,008

1,009

1,010

1,011. A more attractive caddy with simple bands of bright-cut engraving between the beaded borders. The fine contemporary coat of arms is a great boon and gives a much more pleasing ovall effect compared with 1,010. This one in fact is by Hester Bateman, whose mark will always add substantially to value.
c.1785 *By Hester Bateman £4,000 — £5,500*
By another £2,500 — £4,250

1,012. A shaped oval example with bright-cut engraving, again by Hester Bateman.
c.1785 *By Hester Bateman £3,500 — £5,000*
By another £2,500 — £4,250

1,013. An octagonal example with extremely good bright-cut engraving almost giving the feeling of the use of different materials, similar to the effect of marquetry in furniture. This decoration trebles the value compared with a plain example. Stained ivory pineapple finial.
c.1790 *£3,500 — £5,500*
If plain £2,000 — £3,250

1,014. A pair of oblong caddies and a pierced sugar basket with blue glass liner, and a fitted case with pierced and engraved mother of pearl veneer. Although the caddies are very simple, this is made up for by the sugar basket and the case.
c.1770 *Set with case £6,000 — £9,000*

1,014

1,013

1,011

1,012

1,015

1,015. A set of three (one is in the case) rectangular caddies with flush hinged lids and bright-cut foliate borders, with an ivory veneered case.
c.1790 *Set with case £6,500 — £9,500*

1,016. A pair of oval examples, again very plain, but compensated for by the decorative veneered ivory case.
c.1790 *Set with case £5,000 — £7,500*

1,017. A pair of silver gilt sugar vases based on Roman designs and made for Rundell, Bridge and Rundell, the Royal silversmiths. These will have the maker's mark of Paul Storr, Scott and Smith or Benjamin and James Smith, and each vase weighs 30oz. and is 8ins. high. This top quality Regency silver can fetch very high prices.
c.1805 *Pair £22,500 — £30,000*
If by Paul Storr £25,000 — £37,500

1,018. A set of three caddies based on an original Lamerie design (compare 999), usually of extremely heavy quality. They are occasionally made by Dublin silversmiths.
c.1815 *Set of three £8,000 — £12,500*

1,019. A rectangular caddy chased with Oriental scenes.
c.1840 *£2,500 — £4,250*

1,016

1,017

1,018

1,019

1,020. A very simple oval caddy with button catch hinged lid.
c.1860 *£800 — £1,500*

1,021. This is a shaped oblong biscuit box which is larger than a tea caddy, being about 7ins. high, and weighing about 32oz. It is manufactured in the Aesthetic Movement style, showing a distinctive Japanese influence.
c.1880 *£2,000 — £3,250*

1,022. Another biscuit box, this time an oval example of similar capacity. The decoration, a combination of contemporary engraving of sheaves of corn around the inscription and a heavier gadroon base on claw feet copied from designs of c.1810, is less impressive.
c.1880 *£1,250 — £2,000*

1,023. This biscuit box displays the classical decoration which was used on many pieces of this period. The stand is fixed and the lid hinged. About 6½ins. high and weighing 25oz.
c.1885 *£1,250 — £2,000*

1,024. A somewhat eccentrically shaped oval tea caddy with scroll borders and scroll chasing. The design is reminiscent of some of the mid-18th century French rococo designs.
c.1895 *£800 — £1,600*

1,020

1,021

1,024

1,023

1,022

1,025

1,025. This unusual biscuit box, almost 8ins. high, was produced by Edwards and Sons of Glasgow and is modelled on a sedan chair. The die stamped rococo decoration is perhaps too fussy for the form of the piece, but because of its unusual nature, it is the type of box which will command a high price.

c.1900 *£1,250 — £2,000*

1,026. A biscuit box made from an ivory tusk with silver mounts and suitably designed handles and finial. Yet another unusual item which will command an individual price. 9¼ins. high.

c.1905 *£800 — £1,600*

1,027. A simply made biscuit box with pierced scroll design and fixed stand on ball-and-claw feet manufactured in Sheffield by Atkin Brothers. The blue glass liner allows less silver to be used, in this case only 14oz.

c.1910 *£600 — £900*

1,028. A double compartment octagonal tea caddy with detachable twin lids. It was manufactured by Nathan and Hayes of Chester, the partners being George 'Teasets' Nathan and Ridley Hayes. As you would expect, many teasets were made by the firm, thus the nickname of the senior partner. The very simple form engraved with a Gothic initial indicates a late 19th or 20th century date. The finials are made of wood and the all-in weight is just under 11oz.

c.1910 *£550 — £1,000*

1,026

1,027

1,028

Tea Kettles

Tea kettles were used for keeping hot water to replenish the teapot. Although there is a record of late seventeenth century examples, the earliest extant date from the Queen Anne period. There are numerous examples made up until the 1770s when the tea urn took over the job of providing hot water. Tea kettles were still made between 1770 and 1840 but they are not as common. The reason for the re-introduction of kettles in the Victorian period is probably because of the discovery of odourless spirit for the burners rather than the use of spirits of wine necessary in the eighteenth century. At first the tea urn was normally heated with an iron core; later on they were heated by burners which also used the new spirit.

Hallmarks: the kettle and stand should both be marked with a full set of marks. The lid and cover of the burners should be marked with lion passant and maker's mark. If the body of the burner is also detachable, this should have a full set of marks. After 1784 the monarch's head duty mark and date letter should also be found on the detachable parts. The swing handles rarely have a visible hallmark, but if there is a mark this is an added bonus.

Condition: the body should always be examined for any erased armorials or initials. Spouts and handle junctions should be examined for repairs. Occasionally the marks on the base of the kettle can be badly rubbed because of repeated cleaning off of the sooty deposits made by the burner. Look carefully at the stand for any repairs to the legs and damage to the aprons. I illustrate here a tea kettle, c.1730, which has been chased later. This is obviously not desirable and detracts substantially from the value. Tea kettles, however, are not as often later chased as other items such as coffee pots and mugs. This example is so obviously of plain outline that the chased scrolls and fruit look completely out of place.

Fakes: there are no common fakes and as long as one is confident that the piece is marked correctly, duty dodgers can be avoided. During the nineteenth century, or even later, some kettles were made up from teapots, but again incomplete hallmarks will normally give the game away.

A tea kettle, c.1730, which has been chased at a later date.

1,029

1,029. The earliest type of kettle normally has a stand which has two hinged carrying handles. This one is unusual because the burner is of brazier form and has three hinged tongues to support the kettle. It will be noticed that the hemispherical feet have ivory pads to stop the heat being conducted to the table. At this date the lids are usually detachable and the handle hinged. The spout is cast in two halves and, rather unusually, has a hinged cover in this example, similar to that on some earlier coffee pots.
c.1705 *£17,500 — £27,500*

1,030. The kettle is still of similar shape, but the stand is more conventional on three scrolling bracket supports. The hemispherical feet have unfortunately lost their insulating buttons. This example has a circular tray stand which is an unusual find. There are early examples in the Victoria and Albert Museum and the Untermeyer collection in New York which have a silver tripod stand the size of a wine table.
c.1715 *£20,000 — £30,000*

1,031. The octagonal shape was used on tea kettles as well as other items of the tea service. The stand is still separate with two carrying handles. The cast octagonal spout was already used on the preceding example, but is more relevant to the design of this piece.
c.1720 *£22,500 — £35,000*

1,032. The almost spherical body superseded the earlier pear shaped bodies at about this date. Very occasionally cut card work is used as a form of decoration. There are no longer any handles on the stands. The handle is now normally completely made of silver and covered with either wicker or leather.
c.1725 *£8,000 — £14,000*

1,030

1,031

1,032

1,033. The influence of rococo design encouraged the use of scrolls and rocaille decoration around the shoulders of tea kettles, and the form of the body is very similar to that of contemporary bullet teapots. The stand is now also more decorative, at the same time being slightly taller and less massive. The apron between the legs is cast, pierced and chased with ribbon work and shell motifs.
c.1735 *£6,000 — £9,000*

1,034. The ribbed bullet shape body is a variation sometimes found and from now on, for a period of twenty years or so, silver finials on the lids are more common. Occasionally triangular kettle salvers are still found with their original kettles. It is likely that many of these have been lost or melted down because of the ignorance of their use. When the kettle salver was introduced the feet no longer needed insulating buttons and, although kettle salvers are only found between c.1720 and c.1750, these insulators were not reintroduced. It is likely that a salver was used which was not originally intended for use with the kettle.
c.1735 *£7,000 — £12,000*
Kettle £6,000 — £8,500
Stand £2,000 — £3,000

1,035. Just as with teapots, the inverted pear shape was used on tea kettles from about this date. The more raised rococo decoration is also typical of the period. It is now common for the stand to be fixed to the kettle with a pin attached to a chain inserted into a hinge on the foot below the spout and an aperture on the opposite side of the foot. Here is another example of kettle salver but few are found after 1755.
c.1745 *£5,000 — £8,000*
Kettle £3,500 — £5,000
Stand £2,000 — £3,000

1,036. A similar example but with more flat chased decoration, including a cartouche for the armorials. The chained securing pins can be seen more clearly on this illustration.
c.1755 *£3,500 — £5,000*

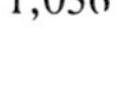
1,036

1,035

1,033

1,034

1,037

1,037. Few kettles were produced between 1760-1795 and those that were are of such individual design that they do not come within the scope of this book. The so called 'hob' shaped kettle was extensively made and like other silver of the period, is not the heavy gauge of earlier examples. The handles are usually fixed, the lids detachable, and the spouts normally hammered up and seamed rather than cast. The stands are either triangular or rectangular and usually have detachable cylindrical burners.
c.1795 *£3,000 — £4,500*

1,038. A small compressed circular kettle with little more capacity than a contemporary teapot. The handle here has a wooden centre.
c.1820 *£1,800 — £3,000*

1,039. A pear shaped example, although similar in shape to George II examples, is of much larger capacity. The stand is on four legs and with four 'U' shaped supports into which pins applied on either side of the kettle slot.
c.1835 *£3,000 — £5,000*

1,038

1,039

1,040. A compressed spherical kettle with light foliate engraving as the main form of decoration. The stand is again attached with chains and pins to the kettle and the handle is fixed rather than being hinged.
c.1845 *£2,000 — £3,500*

1,041. A mid-Victorian example displaying typical floral and foliate chasing on a matted ground, and with the same type of cast flower finial to the lid as is found on tea and coffee pots of the period. A similar example can be seen in No. 966.
c.1865 *£2,000 — £3,500*

1,042. The demand in the latter part of the 19th century was for slightly smaller tea kettles of not much bigger capacity than contemporary teapots. This example is modelled on a late 18th century design of teapot, but has a fixed handle over the lid. It weighs only 27oz. in total.
c.1885 *£1,250 — £1,750*

1,042

1,040

1,041

1,043

1,043. An almost spherical example modelled on the George II bullet teapot with swing handle. Again much lighter than some of the mid-Victorian examples at 32oz. and about $^3/_5$ of the weight of a George II example.
c.1890 *£1,000 — £1,500*

1,044. A heavier design with vertical lobes and gadroon border echoing the late Regency period. 36oz. and made by James Dixon and Sons of Sheffield.
c.1910 *£1,100 — £1,650*

1,045. A somewhat ugly octagonal kettle with fixed handle. This is much heavier and a return to the larger capacity. It weighs 60oz. and measures 15ins. from the foot to the top of the handle.
c.1925 *£1,250 — £2,250*

1,044

1,045

Tea Urns

Tea urns were not commonly made until about 1765. The earliest ones were heated with charcoal. Within the next twenty years the introduction of a central tube into which a pre-heated iron core was placed, allowed more sophisticated designs, and by the turn of the eighteenth century spirit lamps underneath the urn were found to be more efficient, although the iron core method remained popular. There are many more variations of the tea urn in Sheffield plate extant than there are in silver. This is partly due to the fact that an urn made of silver would have been very much more expensive than a plated one, and also that there is a likelihood that obsolete silver urns may have been melted down during the last 150 years.

Hallmarks: a variety of types are all marked in their individual ways, but broadly speaking the main body should bear a full set of marks; the lid of the urn and the heater tubes or lamp covers should be marked with maker's mark, lion passant and, after 1784, monarch head duty mark and date letter. The bases are often also independently marked.

Condition: general overall examination for erased engraving, patches, damage and wear should be made.

Fakes: look out for cups and covers which have had a spigot added.

1,046

1,046. This is the earliest recognised style for a tea urn, the pedestal base being detachable from the ovoid body. The top of the base has a container for burning charcoal and the body has a let-in domed tube which protrudes into the centre to diffuse the heat. This necessitated an awkward construction and a full set of hallmarks was put on the base as well as the body. The marks on the body are often inside the domed tube and can be difficult to read if sooty deposits from use have not been cleaned away. The spigot has a wooden tap which is essential because of the heat.
c.1765 *£4,000 — £6,000*

1,047. A plain version of the same type of urn with very simple beaded and foliate side handles. The spool shaped lid and pedestal base are detachable. The tap on the spigot is wooden and half of it is broken; this is not too serious as it can be replaced without detracting from the value as long as it is done sympathetically.
c.1765 *£3,500 — £5,000*

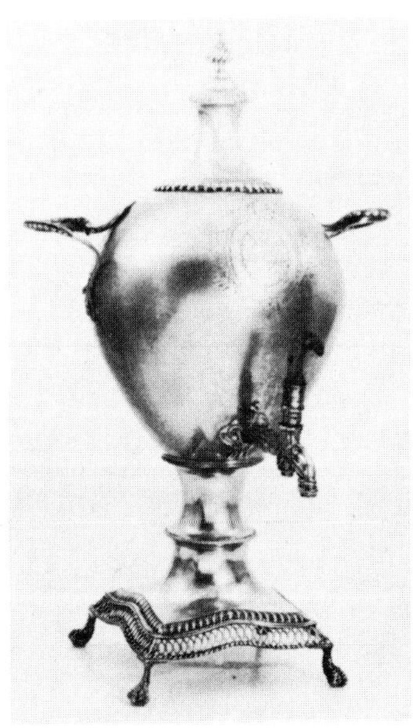

1,047

1,048

1,049

1,048. A fine 'chinoiserie' tea urn with cast and chased decoration. The shape and the gadroon borders are the main indication of the period. It is often difficult for the novice to differentiate between contemporary and later decoration. One of the best indications is the cast and applied work. Although the gadroon borders would be common on a plain example, such decorative handles, spigot, and cast and pierced apron would not. Because these features tie in with the chasing the decoration is likely to be contemporary.

c.1770 *£5,000 — £7,500*

1,049. Even tea urns do not escape the influence of Adam's designs. These two examples are of differing quality. The left hand one has chased husk swags and applied lion mask and drop ring handles, whilst the right hand one has much finer decoration. The goats' masks, swags, anthemion and leaf friezes are all cast and chased. The spigot is ingeniously entwined with a serpent which runs around the whole waist of the urn.

c.1775 *Left £4,000 — £6,500*
Right £5,000 — £8,000

1,050. The vase shaped urn with bright-cut engraving now becomes the norm and high angular or loop handles are used. It can be seen that the proportions are very similar to that of cups and covers of the period. It is therefore necessary to examine an urn like this example carefully to see that you are not buying a converted cup and cover. Check the interior, which on this type of urn has a heater tube with detachable cover which should be hallmarked. Urns of this type nearly always have ball or panel feet unlike cups and covers of the period, which would just sit on the square base.

c.1780 *£3,500 — £5,500*

1,050

1,051. The majority of urns are some 20ins. high. There are however some smaller urns made which are often called 'coffee' urns. Here are a pair in sizes which give a good indication of the relative difference. The flat and concave alternate panels are unusual on a piece of this size and the bright-cut decoration is particularly fine. One of the taps has been replaced which is detrimental to value as it has not been made to match the other. This can be put right however and therefore the value is not likely to be affected by more than 10%.
c.1785 *Pair £7,500 — £11,000*
Larger £4,000 — £5,500
Smaller £3,000 — £4,000

1,051

1,052. A presentation tea urn with full inscription, together with a cup and cover made by the same makers for a similar presentation. Compare this cup with the preceding urns to see the difference. Apart from the fact that there are no feet on this cup, the lid extends right to the rim of the cup, whereas on a tea urn there is a slight collar above the rim into which the lid fits. This urn has a spirit lamp and this now became the more usual way of heating.
c.1795 *Urn £3,500 — £5,000*
Cup £3,500 — £5,000

1,052

1,053. A number of tea kettles were made which have a spigot similar to that on an urn. These are not as popular as the kettles with ordinary spouts but, apart from this feature, the design is very similar.
c.1795 *£2,750 — £4,250*

1,054. Another kettle with spigot which is not quite as unattractive as 1,053. The gadroon borders and contemporary armorials add interest to the plain lines.
c.1805 *£3,000 — £4,500*

1,054

1,053

1,055

1,055. A kettle with a lampstand in early 18th century style. This lampstand however is fixed and not on a separate tray. The crest finial gives the piece a more distinctive air.
c.1805 *£3,000 — £5,000*

1,056. A Dublin made urn with campana shaped body and two side handles. The design is copied from that of a number of contemporary wine coolers. The addition of a square pedestal foot on bun feet and a cover disguise the original form.
c.1805 *£5,000 — £7,500*

1,057. A magnificent silver gilt urn decorated in Egyptian taste and made by Digby Scott and Benjamin Smith for Rundell, Bridge and Rundell, and weighing nearly 200oz.
c.1805 *£60,000+*

1,056

1,057

1,058. Another fine example, this time by Paul Storr and again retailed by Rundell, Bridge and Rundell and bearing their Latin signature. The vertical lobes and gadroon borders indicate the date but the piece does not have the individual design qualities of 1,057.
c.1810 £20,000+

1,059. An uninspired design with an almost spherical body, heavy gadroon borders and unusual claw feet. The armorials are on an applied shield.
c.1815 £3,000 — £5,000

1,060. Another revival of chinoiserie design which was popular at three different periods: 1680-90, 1750-70 and 1820-40. This one was made by James McKay in Edinburgh and is not only of very heavy quality but of extremely fine execution. Again heated by an iron core inside the body.
c.1825 £5,000 — £7,500

1,060

1,058

1,059

Wine

Wine Coasters

Wine coasters are not found until the 1760s when they were made in pierced sheet similar to the work found on cake and sugar baskets of that date. They were normally always made in multiples of two, although it is rare to find sets larger than four. A single coaster will command only 15% to 25% of the price of a pair. The majority have turned wooden bases which occasionally have applied central bosses for the owner's initials, crest or armorials, but examples with silver covered bases do occur, and these are generally more valuable.

Hallmarks: they are nearly always hallmarked around the plain rim of the base, although some of the early pierced examples have the marks scattered around the side on the piercing.

Condition: with the early pierced examples careful examination for any damage to the piercing is necessary. Occasionally the wooden bases will have been replaced. This does not necessarily detract from value, as long as the restoration has been done sympathetically. If however the central bosses on the wooden bases are replaced, the likelihood is that they will have no hallmark, and a later crest or engraving, which is not desirable. There is however no rule of thumb about bosses being hallmarked, and therefore it very much depends on whether the base looks original or not.

Fakes: I do not know of many fake coasters, although cruet frame bases in the 1760s were very similar to pierced wine coasters. They would however nearly always have had screwed on ball-and-claw feet and a central handle, so if the base bears any signs of these having been removed, one should be wary. Cruet frames however were rarely made in pairs and therefore this caution is only given with regard to wine coasters found singly.

1,061

1,062

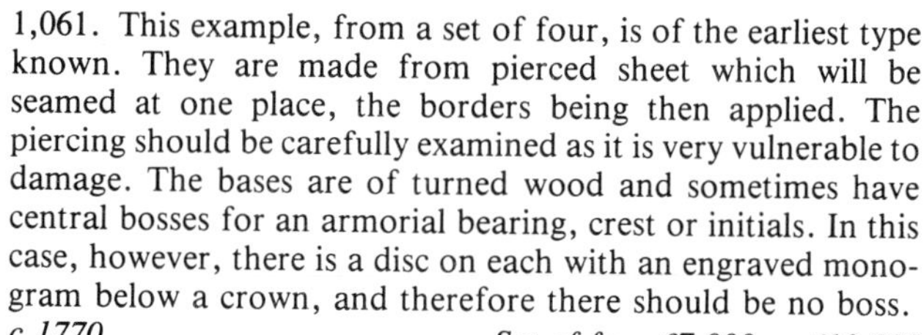

1,061. This example, from a set of four, is of the earliest type known. They are made from pierced sheet which will be seamed at one place, the borders being then applied. The piercing should be carefully examined as it is very vulnerable to damage. The bases are of turned wood and sometimes have central bosses for an armorial bearing, crest or initials. In this case, however, there is a disc on each with an engraved monogram below a crown, and therefore there should be no boss.

c.1770 — *Set of four £7,000 — £10,000*
Pair £3,000 — £5,000
(If silver gilt + 20%)

1,062. The most typical coaster found at this date with simple pierced pales and a small amount of bright-cut engraving. The oval cartouche is not engraved and therefore should be examined for any erasure. The beaded borders are typical for the period. This is one of a Dublin made pair.

c.1780 — *Pair £2,750 — £4,500*

1,063. Another example with pierced pales, but cleverly leaving swags which have been engraved to simulate leafage. This is all done in the piercing and not applied on top of the pales.
c.1780 *Pair £2,750 — £4,500*

1,064. From now onwards the sides are solid for a period. These coasters display the Adam motifs of rams' masks, husk swags and paterae while still having beaded rims. Still no central boss; just an oval with a crest on the side.
c.1785 *Pair £3,500 — £5,000*

1,065. Another example, this time displaying applied work in conjunction with bright-cut engraving. Not as fine as the preceding pair.
c.1790 *Pair £3,250 — £4,750*

1,066. One of a very simple pair of plain coasters with reeded rims.
c.1800 *Pair £2,250 — £4,000*

1,067. A pair of 'jolly boat' double coasters. These are comparatively rare and are mounted on four small castors. They also have a place for the decanter stoppers. This pair is particularly fine and has an anchor at the stern and a coiled rope ring at the bow.
c.1800 *Pair £20,000 — £30,000*
Single £7,000 — £10,000

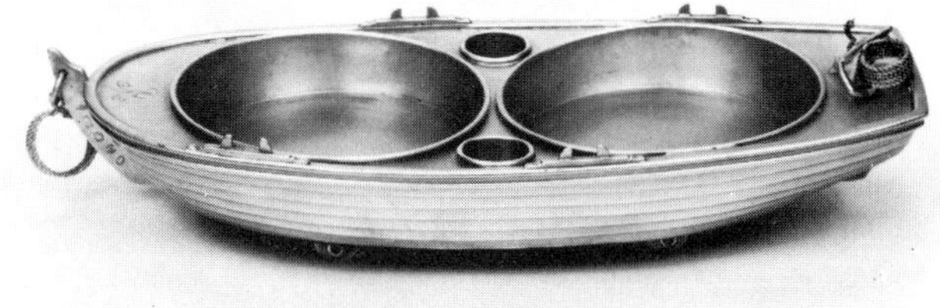

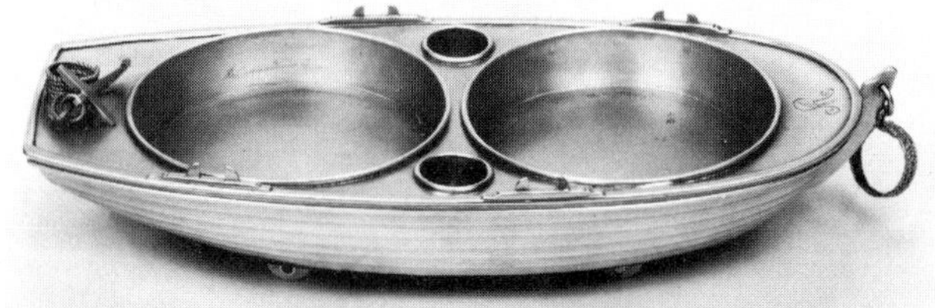

1,067

1,066

1,063

1,065

1,064

1,068

1,068. One of the most expensive type of wine coasters. The sides are cast in sections with grapes and vine leaves below tongue and dart rims. The wooden bases are covered in silver, an additional value point. They also have a fine ducal armorial. They are nearly always silver gilt. All of this type were made for Rundell, Bridge and Rundell, and could be either Paul Storr, or Digby Scott and Benjamin Smith.
c.1805 *Pair by Paul Storr £27,500 — £40,000*
Pair £25,000 — £35,000

1,069

1,069. Three from a set of six of the same quality as 1,068, but of slightly more elaborate design. These are also silver gilt, and instead of having ducal armorials have royal armorials, finely engraved. Stamped with the Latin signature of Rundell, Bridgc and Rundell.
c.1810 *Pair £30,000 — £45,000*
Six £100,000 — £150,000

1,070

1,070. A further example of the heavy elaborate design found at this date, although the quality is not as good as 1,068 and 1,069 because the vine work is lighter and rather fussy. They have reeded wirework sides with applied cast vine motifs. An unusual feature is the small castors. Again these have silver base plates engraved with armorials.
c.1810 *Four £25,000 — £35,000*
Pair £12,000 — £16,000

1,071. This pair is one of the most common types of wine coaster in existence, although these are particularly good examples. Lobed sides and gadrooned rims are typical features. This pair is further embellished with shell and foliate motifs. They will very often have central bosses for crests or armorials, and these are sometimes, although not invariably, hallmarked with the lion passant and perhaps the maker's mark.
c.1815 *Pair £3,000 — £5,000*

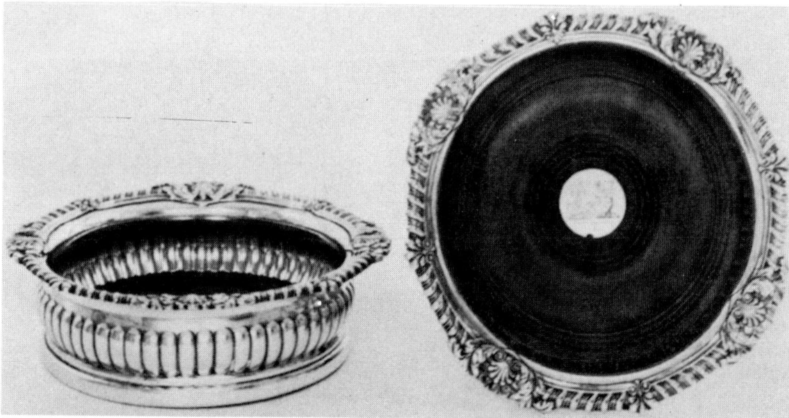

1,071

1,072. A decanter wagon with coasters similar to the preceding example, although a little more ornate. The coasters will usually unscrew from the wagon for use independently. All separate components should be hallmarked.
c.1815 *Single £5,000 — £8,000*
Pair £12,000 — £18,000

1,073. A pair of coasters with pierced vine sides. The decoration at this date would probably be stamped rather than cast and therefore they are not as heavy, or as valuable. Again with silver base plates over the wooden bases.
c.1820 *Pair £3,500 — £5,500*

1,074. A very similar set with turned wooden bases and central silver bosses which are not generally thought as desirable.
c.1825 *Four £10,000 — £14,000*
Pair £4,000 — £6,000

1,075. Two of a set of four plainer examples, but still with vine motifs at the rims. The crested central bosses have a small lion passant mark.
c.1830 *Pair £4,000 — £6,000*
Four £10,000 — £14,000

1,075

1,073

1,074

1,072

1,076

1,076. A rather more fussy Victorian design, still incorporating grape vines. There is however so much detail that the overall effect is rather unimpressive and blurred.
c.1840 *Pair £2,500 — £3,750*

1,077. Unlike 1,076 this example has cast and pierced sides of heavier quality. They are silver gilt and the wooden base is covered and engraved with fruit and foliage. Gilding is always a popular feature on wine coasters and is likely to increase the price by about 25%.
c.1845 *Pair £7,000 — £9,000*

1,078. A pierced pair echoing the earliest examples, but rather more flamboyant, and with the silver base plates decorated with bands of scrolling foliage so popular at this period.
c.1850 *£3,000 — £5,000*

1,079. Very few silver wine coasters were produced in the second half of the 19th century: for some reason the examples that do exist are either Sheffield or electro-plated. This pair of bottle coasters is unusual for the period. The decoration is very simple and all die stamped. They are of smaller diameter than wine coasters, but measure 5½ins., which is between two and three times the height.
c.1885 *£1,800 — £3,000*

1,077

1,078

1,079

Wine Coolers

The earliest surviving hallmarked wine coolers are dated 1698, but they do not become common until the late eighteenth century. Earlier examples are so rare that they can command almost any price. Most wine coolers have a detachable liner and rim. They normally have handles because condensation makes the outside very slippery. The wine cistern of which a number of seventeenth century and later examples survive, is a larger wine cooler for many bottles. The total number still in existence is extremely small; they are as big as a baby's bath and some weigh 2,000oz. or more. The likelihood of one coming on to the market is very remote and the price would be likely to exceed the cost of an average four-bedroomed house. Prices quoted are usually for pairs. A single cooler would fetch approximately 30% of the price of a pair.

Hallmarks: the main body should be fully marked, usually on the base, but occasionally on the side. The detachable liners and rims will normally be marked with everything except the town mark.

Condition: usually the quality is very heavy and condition should be good unless they have been subjected to substantial wear. Sometimes armorials may have been removed which will, of course create thin patches, and so the body should always be examined for any thinness or let-in patches or reinforcements.

Fakes: occasionally a plain liner has had handles and decoration added to convert it to a cooler, but the lack of any liner and rim should point to this. It will also be incompletely marked. I have recently seen the liner from a wine cooler converted to a biscuit barrel by the addition of a hinged lid, but again the lack of any town mark always points to a piece being part of a larger article.

1,080

1,080. Plain pail shaped coolers are one of the earliest designs that one comes across. The simple loop handles which are comparatively flimsy and may have been damaged, should be carefully examined. The chased and applied coat of arms is an unusual feature, but adds some substance to the design. This example is from a pair made by John Schofield whose fine quality pieces are much sought after.
c.1790 *£17,500 — £27,500*

1,081

1,082

1,081. A less impressive type of wine cooler which is lacking its liner and rim. The only thing which is likely to push up the price on this particular piece is the fact that it comes from the workshop of Paul Storr. Like much of his early silver it is fairly simple in design. He had not yet received the encouragement and income from the orders he was to get through Rundell, Bridge and Rundell. The crest is engraved on a later applied foliate cartouche which is out of keeping with the design. This will certainly detract from the value.

c.1800 *Pair £17,500 — £27,500*
Single £5,500 — £9,000

1,082. The Bateman workshop have for once produced an unattractive design. The vertical lobes are extremely harsh and there is not the usual delicacy of line one expects from this source.

c.1800 *Pair £17,500 — £25,000*
Single £4,500 — £8,000

1,083. One of the most obvious forms of decoration for wine coolers is, of course, vine motifs. This example from a fine and heavy pair of coolers has decorative applied work below a laurel wreath enclosing the armorials. The goats' masks, which act as handles, are very impressive and give distinction to an otherwise straightforward design. The hallmarks can clearly be seen on the foot of the cooler and, as with other items marked in this fashion, be certain that the marks are not let in from a piece of table silver. Look carefully for any seams.

c.1800 *Pair £45,000 — £65,000*

1,084. One of a pair of silver gilt wine coolers made under the auspices of Rundell, Bridge and Rundell, and incorporating some of the fine decoration for which they are well known. The unusual entwined serpent handles look rather ungainly but this is certainly one of the most popular periods of English silver at the present time and as long as the item is in good condition, the price will be commensurately high.

c.1805 *Pair £55,000 — £75,000*

1,083

1,084

1,085. A slightly later version of 1,080, using the same basic outline but with lion mask and drop ring handles. The handles and multiple reeding lend a more distinguished look to the design.
c.1810 *Pair £17,500 — £27,500*
Single £4,500 — £8,000

1,086. A simple style which is enhanced by an attractive coat of arms with warrior supporters. The quality of wine coolers is rarely poor, mainly because they would only be ordered by the most élite members of the society of the time.
c.1810 *Pair £20,000 — £30,000*

1,087. A superlative piece of silversmithing from the workshop of Paul Storr with beautifully modelled figures and chariots. In silver gilt, which certainly suits the extravagant design, this cooler illustrates the popularity of classical designs at this period. Coolers like this were almost completely cast in various sections which were then chased to give the finer detail, assembled, and finally gilded. Some fine classical designs by John Flaxman, William Theed and others were commissioned by Rundell, Bridge and Rundell and executed by Paul Storr and others for the same firm.
c.1810 *Pair £100,000+*

1,088. The combination of lobes, lion masks and borders, incorporating gadrooning, shells and foliage was very popular at this period. Paul Storr was perhaps the greatest exponent of this type of design although this example bears the mark of Samuel Hennell. However, the quality is as good as any piece made by the former maker.
Hallmarked 1812 *Pair £22,500 — £35,000*
By Paul Storr £60,000 — £80,000

1,088

1,087

1,085

1,086

1,089

1,089. The campana shaped vase formed the design basis of many objccts and wine coolers are no exception. Again a straightforward design is given more presence by the bacchanalian mask terminals to the handles. A repair is visible inside the rim. Detachable liners and rims are usually of much thinner gauge than the cooler itself and they are sometimes bent or damaged. The damage would have to be substantial for the value to be radically altered.
Hallmarked 1814 — *Pair £22,500 — £32,500*

1,090. Although this piece was made as a presentation cup, its form, without the detachable stand, is very similar to that of contempotary wine coolers. Again silver gilt, and of the finest quality. It is after a design by John Flaxman, R.A., based on the first idyll of Theocritus and is therefore called The Theocritus cup.
c.1815 — *Single, by Paul Storr £70,000+*

1,091. Designs from antiquity were particularly popular during the Regency period. This is a copy of the Warwick Vase; the ancient Greek original was discovered in the late 18th century in pieces and then repaired and eventually sold to the Earl of Warwick. It was frequently copied. The lions' pelts and bearded masks are usually very well modelled and the entwined vine branch handles emphasise the massive form and weight. The depth of the piece however is not as practical as most wine coolers, but the likelihood is that pieces like this would have been for show, rather than for constant use.
c.1815
Pair £22,500 — £32,500
Paul Storr £50,000 — £70,000
Silver gilt plus 25%
Modern copies, per oz. £40 — £60

1,092. Again a fairly squat example with all the type of decoration appropriate for a wine cooler. The mask terminals to the handles are rather unhappily turned on their sides.
c.1820 — *£22,500 — £35,000*

1,090

1,091

1,092

1,093. A pair of wine coolers by Matthew Boulton with contemporary presentation inscriptions on one side and armorials on the other. The manufacturers of Birmingham and Sheffield were extremely cost conscious in an effort to capture the lucrative market on which the silversmiths of London had thrived and had a monopoly for generations. This means that although the overall appearance may be good, the quality is not always up to London standards. These certainly do not have the fine quality of decoration seen on some of the preceding examples. By this date Matthew Boulton, who established a factory in Birmingham employing many hundred craftsmen and artists, had been dead for fifteen years. His name is respected among collectors although many late pieces are only of average quality. In the latter half of the 18th ccentury the factory produced better quality items based on some fine designs.
c.1825 *£20,000 — £27,500*

1,094. An altogether more pleasing design with some good quality decoration and entwined branch handles that encourage a second look. My only criticism of this piece is that the plain foot and knop are out of keeping with the rest of the design.
c.1825 *Pair £22,500 — £30,000*

1,095. An immense amount of work has gone into the casting and chasing of this ribbed baluster cooler, unusually confined to flowers, diaper and spume with no sign of the grape vine.
c.1830 *Pair £50,000 — £70,000*

1,095

1,093

1,094

Wine Funnels

The wine funnel became common in the last quarter of the eighteenth century, although one or two earlier examples do exist. They were used for decanting wines and normally have a pierced platform which in itself is not sufficient to strain the wine properly, and needs a piece of muslin fitted between the pierced section and the spout. There are two main varieties: in one the spout detaches just below the bowl of the funnel, and in the other the main bowl has a detachable inner bowl with a pierced centre. Occasionally there is a further detachable ring which was used for holding the muslin securely.

Hallmarks: a full sct of hallmarks should be found on the bowl, and the detachable spout or inner bowl should have maker's mark and lion passant, and, at a later date, monarch's head and date letter as well.

Condition: the tips of wine funnels are often split, dented or damaged in some way. Sometimes these have been trimmed at a later date because they have become so badly damaged. Apart from this area in particular, general examination should be made for splits, dents or patches.

Fakes: there is no commonly faked wine funnel, but I have seen an example made from the bowl of a wine cup. The construction was so strange that it would have been unlikely even to fool a novice.

1,096

1,096. This is one of the earliest types of funnel with plain conical bowl and no pierced strainer inside. Wine was not decanted as a matter of course at this date. It is therefore possible that this may have been a general purpose funnel, perhaps used for decanting toilet water.
c.1710 *£750 — £1,250*

1,097. Here are two examples with the bowl detaching from the funnel. These are occasionally found with a further small detachable ring inside the rim or bezel, which was used for holding a piece of muslin. The tips of the funnels on both these examples have been trimmed down. The example on the right, with beaded borders, dates from about 1785. This type is often marked on the bulge of the bowl where the marks can become very worn. They are occasionally marked on the underside of the piercing and in the past I have come across them sold as 'unmarked'. The left hand example is about ten or fifteen years later in date with a reeded border, and the maker's mark and lion passant can be seen on the funnel. The full set of marks will be revealed when this is removed from the bezel on the base of the bowl.
Right, c.1785 *£600 — £900*
Left, c.1800 *£600 — £900*

1,097

1,098. Another of the most common types of wine funnel, with detachable inner bowl shown on the right. You can also see that there is an inner ring to hold the muslin, the ring being detachable. As mentioned in the introduction, spouts are very often trimmed. This example has had the upper part of the beak trimmed away. The tip of the spout is bent to prevent aeration of the wine whilst it is being decanted. The applied ribs are purely structural. Curiously, reeded and gadroon borders are often mixed on these small pieces. This is an Exeter marked piece and that is why there is a discrepancy in the number of marks. On a London piece the full marks would be on the outer bowl. Here the maker's mark is on both pieces, but the other marks have been shared out.
c.1790 *£600 — £900*

1,099. Another plain funnel without pierced strainer and perhaps, this was used for decanting perfumes and toilet water.
c.1795 *£400 — £600*

1,100. An unusually large funnel (12ins. high) which must have been specially ordered for decanting into an extremely large decanter. It is made by Paul Storr, who has again outclassed all his contemporaries by making this extraordinary piece.
c.1815 *£7,500 — £10,000*

1,101. It is very unusual for wine funnels to be decorated at all, as they were purely functional pieces. This example was made in Edinburgh and has a companion wine funnel stand. It is rare for a funnel stand to be found still with its original funnel and this may add substantially to the price.
c.1830 *Funnel and stand £1,250 — £2,000*

1,101

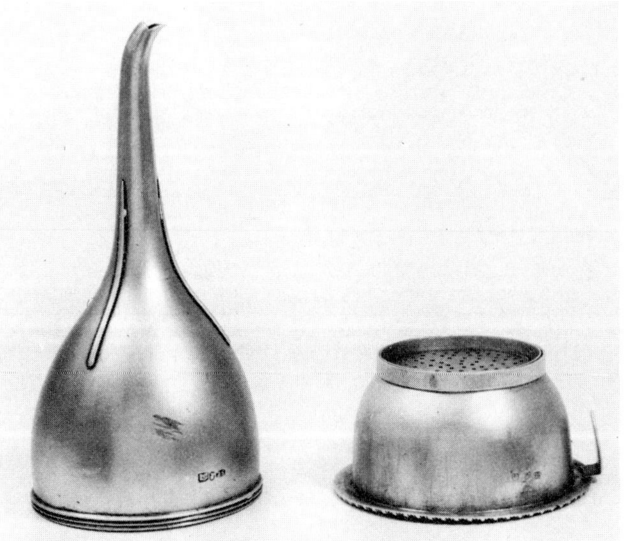

1,098

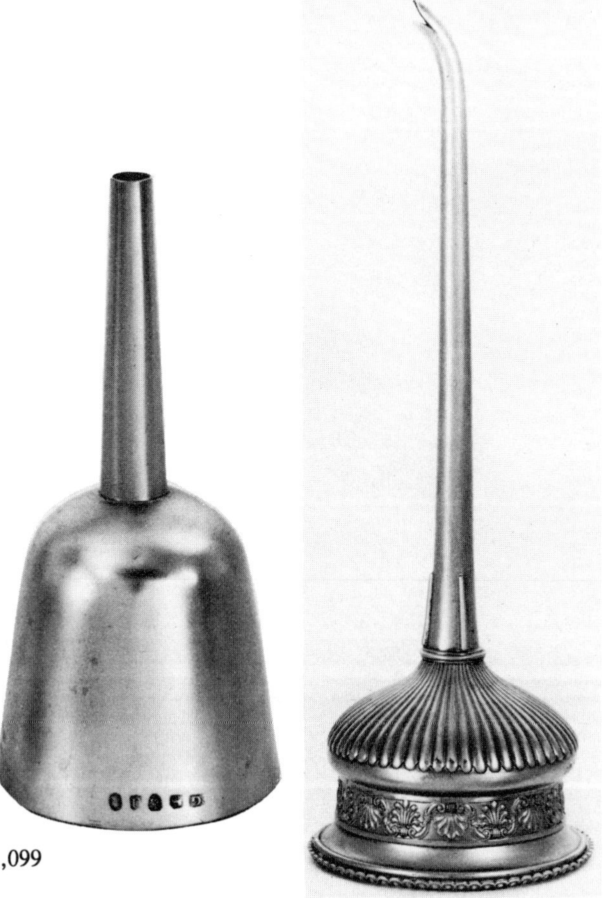

1,099

1,100

Wine Jugs & Flagons

A wine jug made from a mid-18th century tankard.

A wine jug made from a goblet by adding a lid, neck and handle.

This section covers the majority of jugs or flagons used for serving wine, beer or other cold liquids. Perhaps the earliest surviving hallmarked jugs are those which had a companion basin, and date from the late sixteenth and early seventeenth centuries. They rarely come on to the market and, if and when they do, command prices beyond the reach of most pockets. In the mid-seventeenth century cylindrical flagons were produced in fairly large numbers, mainly for use in churches. A number of these have filtered on to the market at different times, but are not usually very popular. The eighteenth century saw a demand for silver jugs which lead to the development of various styles. In the middle of the nineteenth century glass claret jugs with silver mounts were an additional line to the all-silver examples.

Hallmarks: the seventeenth century flagons, which are the first items with which we are concerned, will either be hallmarked on the base or the side, and on the lid with a full set of marks. The handle should have a maker's mark only. Covered jugs from the eighteenth century onwards should have a full set of marks either on the base or the body and a lion passant and maker's mark on the lid. Jugs without covers will of course have only one set of marks.

Condition: careful overall examination is necessary especially for any erased engraving, torn or damaged handle sockets, and repairs to the spouts or feet. Also look carefully for any additions or alterations.

Fakes: one of the most common conversions is from a tankard to a jug. The baluster example shown with lobed and fluted body and flat lid is converted from a mid-eighteenth century tankard. The form has been most cleverly disguised and there is very little to give away the fact that it is altered. Quite often there are obvious hammer marks which is not a good sign, and will indicate that the piece has had later work. The style and decoration is in no way similar to any authentic eighteenth century design. More often than not the hallmarks will be distorted, which is of course a give away.

Another conversion occasionally found is the addition of a lid, neck and handle to a goblet. The size will of course be small compared with other jugs and the likelihood is that there will be no mark on the lid. Goblets are quite often marked near the lip and therefore if hallmarks appear on the body of the piece, a careful diagnosis of the design and construction may reveal this later alteration.

1,102. A pair of cylindrical flagons which were undoubtedly used in a church. Flagons of this type rarely have a spout and should there be one, examine it very carefully as it may be an addition. Some of these have obviously be subjected to a great deal of use over the years and may have been extensively restored. Look out for patches where bad damage has been repaired.
c.1685 *Each £18,000 — £30,000*

1,103. Cylindrical flagons were also made for church use throughout the 18th and 19th centuries. The later in date they are, the less collectable. This example has a thumb piece and handle very similar to contemporary tankards.
c.1720 *Each £12,000 — £18,000*

1,104. Covered jugs of this design are normally of very heavy quality. The attractive coat of arms makes a great deal of difference to the overall appearance and will certainly enhance the price. The foot and handle are both cast and applied, and the spout has a hinged cover.
c.1715 *£27,500 — £45,000*

1,105. It would be unlikely for a fine piece like this to come on to the market more than once in a decade. It is a silver gilt ewer by John Hugh le Sage, which would have had a companion dish. The piece is almost entirely cast and is of very heavy quality, weighing 155oz. It is in Louis XIV style and adapted from designs by Jean Marot. A few other pieces exist in this manner by Huguenot silversmiths associated with the Court of Versailles.
c.1725 *70,000 — £100,000+*

1,105

1,104

1,102

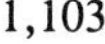

1,103

1,106

1,106. The plain baluster beer jug was introduced at about this time and remained popular in a variety of styles over the next 50 or 60 years. The handle and feet are again both cast and applied. It is extremely likely that all plain jugs of this type would have had a coat of arms and, indeed, the lack of them would make the jugs uninteresting.
c.1725 *£12,000 — £18,000*

1,107. This pair is in the same vein as 1,104. The almost cylindrical neck with a girdle above the belly of the body is peculiar to this period. Note that there are heart shaped and oval reinforced plaques on the handle junctions, which in this case are certainly contemporary, but always look carefully at this type of moulding in case it is a later patch.
c.1725 *Pair £35,000 — £50,000*

1,108. An Irish example of the baluster beer jug of the most simple design. This jug is again of very heavy quality, weighing 40oz. and has a much smaller rim foot. Early Irish pieces of top quality are rare and prices will be high.
c.1735 *£25,000 — £35,000*

1,109. The engraved arms which are contemporary add an interesting feature to the design. The engraver has not only used an asymmetrical cartouche in the typical rococo style, but has also engraved them at an angle. A pair of jugs, because of rarity value, commands a price nearly three times that of a single one.
c.1745 *Pair £40,000 — £55,000*

1,107

1,108

1,109

1,110. The baluster body is not quite so pronounced by this date and the foot has a much narrower collar. The handle is now decorated with a leaf capping.
c.1750 *£7,000 — £11,500*

1,111. Robert Calderwood was one of the master craftsmen of Irish silver and this piece probably ranks amongst his best. The cast and chased caryatid handle displays the sort of movement that one expects of rococo silver. The applied leafy scrolls to the body are perhaps not quite so adventurous.
c.1760 *£15,000 — £22,500*

1,112. Again the shape is the same, but the addition of shell moulding at the upper handle terminal and the engraved floral cartouche indicate this slightly later date. Always examine the moulding below the spout carefully as occasionally this becomes worn and a hole may appear.
c.1765 *Single £7,000 — £11,500*
Pair £25,000 — £37,500

1,113. An almost pear shaped beer jug which is not very attractive. The gadroon bordered foot is sometimes used over the next ten or fifteen years and the handle will occasionally have a second reverse scroll at the heel.
c.1765 *£6,000 — £9,500*

1,113

1,112

1,110

1,111

1,114

1,114. The armorials on this jug are typical of the period with a ribbon tied shield surrounded by floral sprays. The foot is similar to the preceding example but the curved lobes are a feature which is comparatively unusual and not particularly popular.
c.1775 *£6,000 — £9,500*

1,115. A much more elegant design of jug, typical of the Adam period. The delicate bright-cut engraving makes the piece extremely attractive. The goblets which are not by the same maker, are from the same period and no doubt would have been used with a jug of this type.
c.1785 *Jug £3,000 — £4,500*
Goblets £2,000 — £3,000

1,116. The caryatid handle is again used on this example as it has been at various periods throuout the 18th century. The mask below the spout is 'Lameriesque', but the winged demi-figures holding lyres are more in the style of the classical revival of this period.
c.1800 *Pair £25,000 — £40,000*

1,117. An extraordinary pair of ewers made by Edward Farrell who drew on many 17th century designs and pieces for inspiration. The bodies are cast and chased with sea gods. These are in the manner of Dutch work of the early 17th century.
c.1820 *Pair £45,000 — £70,000*

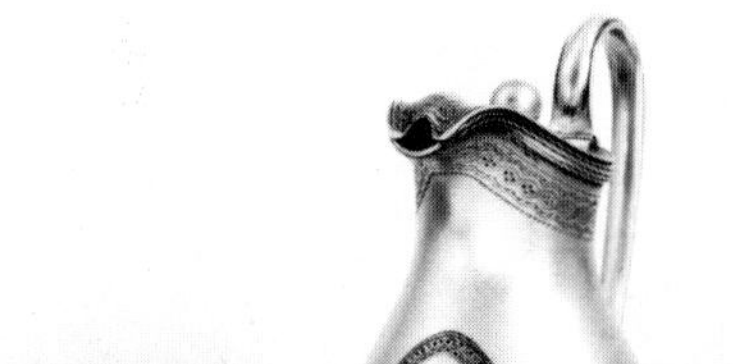

1,115

1,116

1,117

1,118. This jug is appropriately cast and chased with the infant Bacchus astride a donkey, with grapevine motifs cleverly incorporated into the design. It is very heavy, due to the fact that the body is cast, and is by Paul Storr, whose work is practically always of fine quality.
c.1830 *£25,000 — £35,000*

1,119. This wine ewer by Joseph Angell was designed for the Great Exhibition of 1851. The vine motifs, and cherubs climbing ladders and standing on barrels, are all applied to the plain hexagonal shape. Weighing nearly 50oz., it is the sort of piece which will command a price commensurate with its individuality.
c.1850 *£5,000 — £8,000*

1,120. A beautifully balanced ewer displaying inspired use of the scroll. The decoration is mainly chased but with applied cast handle and knop to the stem. The goblets are of the same period and, although decorated with similar motifs, have not caught the flowing movement of the ewer.
c.1850 *Ewer £3,000 — £4,500*
Pair goblets £1,250 — £2,000

1,121. This wine ewer, in classical taste, was made in the workshops of Messrs Barnard and displays the use of medallions inspired by the decoration on ancient Egyptian terracotta vases and urns. The handle is cleverly constructed from an entwined snake motif.
c.1860 *£2,000 — £3,000*

1,121

1,120

1,118

1,119

1,122. Another ewer using the same basic shape which was very popular at this time. In this case the decoration is less effective, with an applied spiral of vine curling around the body. The application is not always satisfactory and there is some likelihood of damage. Examine very carefully.
c.1860 *£1,500 — £2,500*

1,123. The use of engraved ferns is found on a variety of silver items at this period, in this case giving the formal body much more life.
c.1865 *£1,250 — £2,250*

1,124. A fourth variation of the same theme, again with vine branch handle, but now using engraved floral posies. Examine the area around the foot carefully; in many cases it was not sturdy enough to withstand the weight of the piece when full.
c.1865 *£1,250 — £2,250*

1,125. An adaptation of the 18th century tankard chased with flowers and applied with a mask spout. This example is an original, but many eighteenth century tankards have been converted to this type of jug.
c.1870 *£2,500 — £3,500*

1,122

1,123

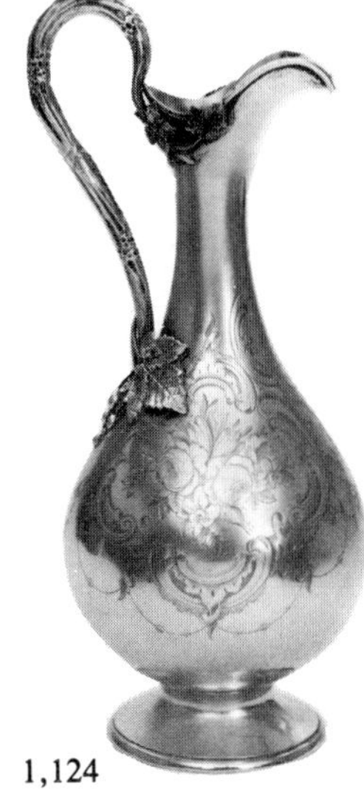

1,124

1,125

1,126. This cylindrical jug is chased with a stag hunt. 19th century craftsmen explored practically every avenue of decoration from antique styles to popular sports of the day. Note that the lid does not close properly. The hinge has been strained but this can, of course, be put right without too much trouble. Always examine the hinge however as occasionally you might find a clumsy repair which will obviously detract from the value.
c.1870 *£4,500 — £8,000*

1,127. An involved design, sometimes called 'Cellini' pattern. The inspiration is drawn from Renaissance originals, and the decoration will normally be of fine quality.
c.1875 *Single £1,500 — £2,500*
Pair £4,500 — £7,000

1,128. A ewer and six matching goblets with applied beading bordering chased foliage and matting. As already stated, many ewers of this period have an insufficiently sturdy foot and it can be seen that the foot of this example is quite badly bent. This is not necessarily disastrous, but if the metal is split will be difficult to repair satisfactorily.
c.1880 *Ewer £1,500 — £2,250*
Goblets, each £250 — £425

1,126

1,127

1,128

1,129

1,129. This popular design of ewer is often referred to as 'Armada' pattern. The inscription is later than the piece which will obviously go against value. Always examine cartouches for any thinness. This design was used over a long period, the earliest being about 1860 and the latest early 20th century.
c.1885 *£2,750 — £4,500*

1,130. Silver mounted glass claret jugs come in numerous designs, the more decorative the glass and mount, the higher the price. Always be sure that the glass is not cracked or damaged as this will practically halve the value. This type of stamped and applied grapevine is not always of the thickest gauge and there is a possibility of damage to some of the leaves or tendrils. The rampant lion finial is quite often used, and the shield held by his front paws was intended for a small inscription or crest.
c.1850 *£2,500 — £3,500*

1,131. Another example in very similar style, but with less prettily cut glass and much flatter decoration. The cover with vine tendril finial however is perhaps more in keeping with the design.
c.1850 *£2,000 — £3,000*

1,130

1,131

1,132. Plain glass bodies with star-cut bases are much less attractive and not quite so popular. The mounts are chased with vine and masks, emphasising the use of the object.
c.1870 *£1,500 — £2,750*

1,133. The illustration does not do full justice to the glass of this example which is beautifully decorated with birds and foliage, and will encourage a high price. However, the mount is not really of the same standard in this case.
c.1875 *£2,250 — £3,250*

1,134. Novelty claret jugs, this one in the form of a monkey, sometimes in the form of other animals and birds, are always extremely popular. As long as the modelling and condition are good, the price will be several times that of a more straightforward piece.
c.1880 *£5,000 — £8,000*

1,135. Much plainer glass and very simple mounts are often used at the turn of the century and later. They will of course be more realistically priced than the more attractive jugs already seen. This large type is sometimes referred to as a lemonade jug.
c.1900 *£1,250 — £2,500*
Plain claret jugs £800 — £1,600

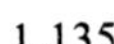

1,135

1,132

1,133

1,134

Wine Labels

There are many specialist collectors of wine labels, just as there are for vinaigrettes, and occasionally extraordinary prices can be obtained for individual examples. Unusual designs and rare names are obviously the ones to command the highest prices. However, rare provincial labels can also command a high price for their hallmark alone.

Hallmarks: ideally a wine label should bear a full set of hallmarks but prior to 1790 one is unlikely to find more than the maker's mark and lion passant. Occasionally it will be found that the town mark is omitted, even if there is a full set of marks.

Condition and Fakes: it is very important that the name or title on the wine label has not been altered. Occasionally it seems likely that this was done at the time of manufacture. It has been done in recent years to convert a common name, like sherry or madeira, to a rare or more attractive name like champagne. Any worn decoration or title is obviously undesirable and a good heavy chain is always an asset. The earliest examples will have engraved or stamped titles, many of which originally had a black wax filling, whilst the majority of later examples were pierced with the title. Smaller labels were used to hang around the sauce bottles contained in a cruet frame. These tend to be less adventurous in design than wine labels, but they are still very collectable.

1,136

1,136. The earliest wine labels of the mid-18th century were usually of shaped escutcheon form (centre bottom example of Madeira). Some however are cast and chased with two bacchanalian cherubs (bottom right). The most prolific maker between 1740-60 was Sandilands Drinkwater (a most inappropriate name!).
Left, top to bottom: Madeira, c.1790, £100 — £170 (by Hester Bateman, £225 — £335); Sherry, c.1840, £135 — £200; Port, c.1790, £110 — £200. Centre, top to bottom: W. Wine, c.1780, £90 — £145; Sherry, c.1840, £225 — £335; Madeira, c.1760, £200 — £280. Right, top to bottom: Port, c.1790, £100 — £170; Sauterne, c.1815, £170 — £225; Port, c.1750, £225 — £335.

1,137. Another selection of wine labels from late 18th/early 19th century showing a variety of styles.
Left, top to bottom: Calcavella, c.1810, £65 — £100; Malaga, c.1790, £90 — £135; Port, c.1790, £110 — £200 (by Hester Bateman, £270 — £405); Port, c.1790, £100 — £155.
Centre, top to bottom: Hock, c.1810, £225 — £335; Claret, c.1790, £135 — £225; Sherry, c.1820 (a stamped copy of mid-18th century type), £135 — £200.
Right, top to bottom: Port, c.1810, £110 — £170; Claret, c.1790, £110 — £160; Madeira, c.1790, £170 — £280; Madeira, c.1790, £100 — £155.

1,138. Further examples including Uisgebeatha.
Left, top to bottom: Port, c.1790, £110 — £200; Whiskey, c.1860, £100 — £155; Port, c.1810, £65 — £100; Brandy, c.1790, £100 — £170.
Centre, top to bottom: Claret, c.1820, £155 — £225; Sherry, c.1830, £270 — £405; Uisgebeatha, c.1810, £170 — £280.
Right, top to bottom: Port, c.1820 (a later copy of a mid-18th century type), £170 — £225; Sherry, c.1830, £170 — £225; Gin, c.1810, £65 — £100; Madeira, c.1790, £135 — £200.

1,137

1,138

1,139

1,140

1,139. A selection of wine labels, circa 1800 to circa 1820. A rare name can alter the value of a label tremendously compared with these guide lines.
c.1800-20 *Each £100 — £200*

1,140. A group of sauce labels, with four larger labels in the centre, circa 1800 to circa 1820. Hungary Water is an old toilet water prepared from Rosemary flowers. Traditionally the Queen of Hungary washed regularly with this toilet water which is said to have cured her arthritic complaints and increased her beauty.
c.1800-20 *Each £80 — £220*

Wine Tasters & Quaiches

Very few wine tasters were made by English silversmiths because wine was not a national product and the majority of wine tasters in existence are in fact French. There was however a short period in the second half of the seventeenth century when a number were produced. After this date examples are very rare indeed. In Scotland quaiches, or marriage cups, were made from the late seventeenth century through to the nineteenth century, and because of their similarity in shape, draw an interesting parallel with wine tasters.

Hallmarks: usually around the rim and should be four marks prior to 1784 and five marks between 1784 and 1890, the only exception being minor guilds and provincial towns. Avoid anything with distorted or stretched marks. Only buy with rubbed marks if the price is right.

Condition: check that handles on early examples have not been changed or pulled off so that the body has had to be patched. The simple wire handles often have original rough soldering — this is not necessarily a repair. Check the embossing for holes and lead solder repairs.

Fakes: I have come across very few. Look out for plain bases on the late seventeenth century type — this may mean the embossing became worn and a new base soldered in. I have seen one or two 'French type' wine tasters with fake marks. Beware of anything unusual unless you can obtain advice from two independent experts.

1,141. This wine taster has punched beading and lobes with typical simple wirework handles. Quite often found with contemporary 'pricked' initials and a date. Any other type of engraved initials or crests are likely to be later.
c.1670 *£1,500 — £2,550*

1,142. This wine taster displays a variation in design.
c.1670 *£1,500 — £2,550*

1,143. Another example with a slightly different design to the previous types.
c.1670 *£1,500 — £2,550*

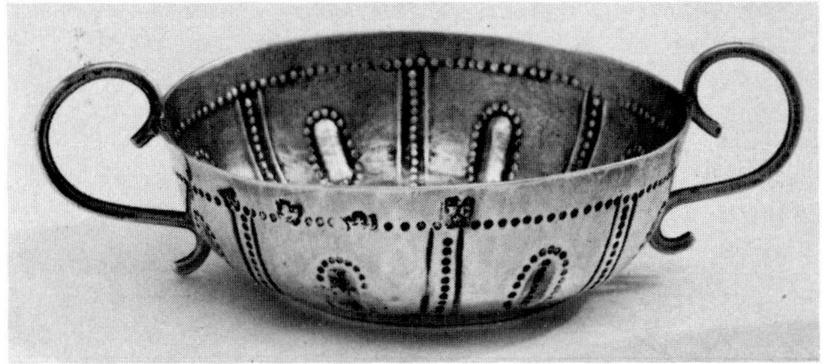

1,141

1,142

1,143

1,144

1,144. This is a rare 17th century, silver mounted wooden quaich with two sets of initials, 'IC' and 'MC' for husband and wife, and was quite probably used as a betrothal cup. It measures some 4-5ins. in diameter. The central print has some delicate stamped decoration around the armorials. Some silver mounted quaiches were made in the 18th and 19th centuries, but they vary too much to give any indication of value.
mid-17th century *£4,000 — £7,000*

1,145. An all silver quaich with engraved staves in the manner in which wooden ones were constructed. Again with initials and lug handles. This type would have a very simple ring foot, and can be made in Edinburgh, Glasgow or provincial towns.
c.1700 *Edinburgh example £4,000 — £7,000*
Provincial example, too varied

1,146. A small quaich of the type made from 1730 onwards right into the 19th century, occasionally found by Aberdeen and Inverness makers as well as the silversmiths in the main centres of Edinburgh and Glasgow.
Edinburgh and Glasgow £600 — £1,050
Provincial £1,000 — £2,000

1,147. This is the only other date when English wine tasters are occasionally found and nearly always they have flared sides. These are sometimes plain but in this case have lobed and domed centres.
c.1780-1830 *Single £1,000 — £1,750*
Pair £2,500 — £4,000

1,148. Another quaich made c.1825, still of the same basic shape but with reeded borders.
c.1825 *£450 — £800*

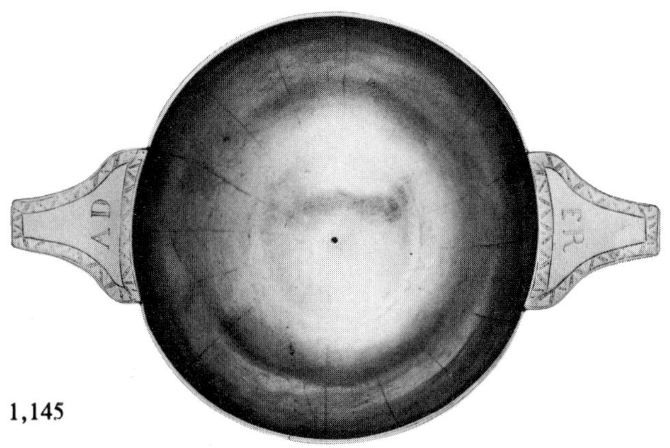

1,145

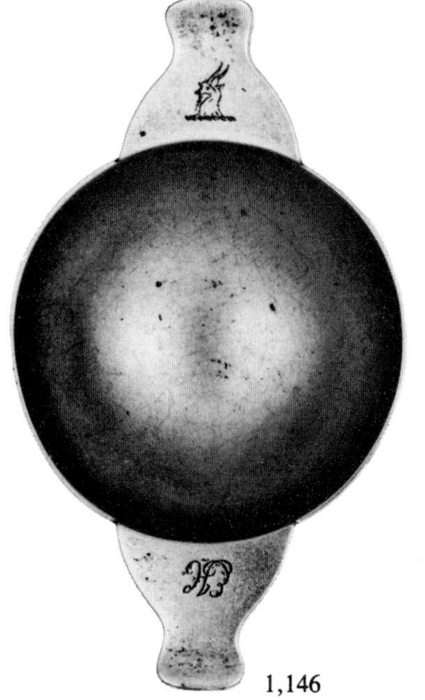

1,146

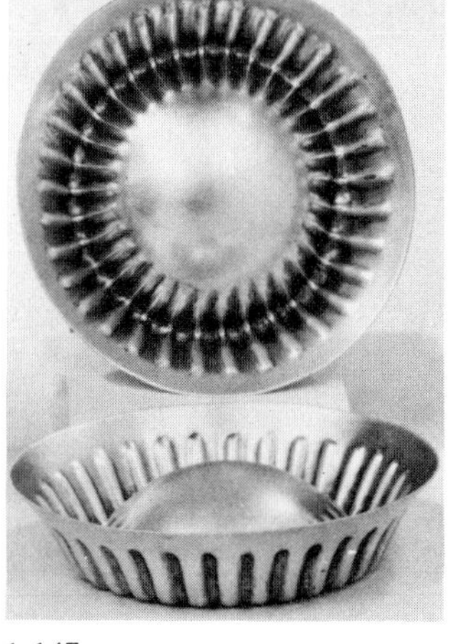

1,147

1,148

Miscellaneous

Buttons

1,149. Silver buttons sometimes appear on the market. The most desirable and collectable are those engraved with hunting scenes, dogs or foxes, and other birds or animals. The majority however are either plain, initialled or crested. If they are marked at all, they will have a maker's mark and/or lion passant, rarely any other mark. The two sets illustrated here date from the last quarter of the 18th century and are both very finely engraved. The set with wriggle work borders probably dates from about 1780, whilst the other is perhaps a slightly earlier date.

Per half dozen £900 — £1,600
Per dozen £1,850 — £3,250

Corers

1,150. A very rare early 18th century corer with a tubular handle which has an integral spice caster. Small items of this type are very collectable and although weighing less than 2oz., the price will be very high. Less elaborate examples are found c.1790 to c.1830 sometimes with an ivory handle, otherwise all silver with screw-off handle.

c.1705 *£1,500 — £2,500*
c.1790-c.1830 *£200 — £450*

Cutlery Trays

1,151. Oval or oblong cutlery trays were made around the turn of the 18th and 19th century. The majority, however, are in Sheffield plate. They are often now used as jardinières, although the example shown here has a divider down the centre which would preclude this use.

c.1820 *per oz. £45 — £70*

1,149

1,150

1,151

Fire Marks

1,152. Collecting fire marks, which are normally made of lead and other base metals, is a field on its own. There are, however, a few silver examples in existence and these are extremely rare. Fire marks were displayed on the outside of a house to show that the occupants were insured against fire. It is probable in fact that the silver examples were badges belonging to messengers or officials employed by the various insurance companies as they are normally much smaller than those in base metals. The two shown here for the Union Insurance Company are hallmarked London 1761 and London 1772.

Each £1,500 — £3,000+

1,152

Honey Pots

1,153

1,153. The honey pot was first made in the form of a skep in the last few years of the 18th century. Their design does not vary from that date onwards. This example is hallmarked 1860, but it could just as easily be of an earlier date. The earliest examples are usually either by Paul Storr or John Emes. Later ones were made by the Angells and the Barnards. Some have small circular trays which will add to the value. Others are of the same shape in cut glass with silver mounts. The lids are detachable and have bayonet lock catches.

This example £3,750 — £6,000
By Paul Storr £15,000 — £22,500
With a stand £20,000 — £25,000
By John Emms £7,500 — £12,500
With a stand £8,000 — £14,000
(Cut glass examples approximately half)

Pap Boats

A pap boat is a shallow feeding dish for a child or invalid. It is first found in the first quarter of the eighteenth century but was 'extinct' by 1840. The form varies very little. The early examples are normally marked near the rim opposite the spout. Later ones will sometimes be marked to the side of this position. Occasionally you will come across pap boats that have had three feet and a handle added to make them into small cream boats.

1,154

1,154. The plainest and simplest type of pap boat, with no decoration or applied wires.
c.1740-60 *£500 — £750*

1,155

1,155. Slightly deeper and more elongated with a small bright-cut band on the rim.
c.1780 *£450 — £600*

1,156. Similar in style to 1,155 but here with reeded border which will date it ten years or so later.
c.1790 *£450 — £600*

1,157. The addition of a reeded wire at the rim makes the piece more sturdy. The flattened oval shape will usually indicate a date around 1800 or later.
c.1800 *£450 — £600*

1,156

1,157

Rattles

1,158. In the 18th century numerous children's rattles were produced. This example is one of the earliest with octagonal shaft engraved with hatched leafage very similar to the decoration on the corer (1,150). The end is inset with a piece of coral as a teether.
c.1700 *£1,200 — £1,800+*

1,159. It is rare to find many rattles pre-dating the second half of the 18th century. The four shown here all date from the late 18th century and early 19th century. The largest example on the right is 1796, the next 1797, the third 1819 and the smallest 1821. They are all silver gilt and all but one have coral teethers. Gold examples exist but are extremely rare and can command up to ten times the price of a silver example. The first one has a mother-of-pearl teether which is probably a replacement. Often these are in a sad state because of their healthy use by their original owners! If they are found in good condition, as all these examples are, the price will be quite high. If some of the bells are missing this can reduce the price by 25%.
Each £750 — £1,500

1,159

1,158

Spoon Trays

In the first half of the 18th century when tea drinking was bccoming fashionablc, a part of thc hostcss's tca table silver would have been a spoon tray, on which she would have rested a teaspoon and a mote skimmer (see No. 794). The tea would have been poured by the hostess and there would have been a likelihood (in the absence of a tea strainer or tea bags!) that large tea leaves would get into the cup. The mote skimmer (a pierced teaspoon) would have been used to remove these from the tea cup, and with its pointed handle, it doubled as an implement to remove any tea leaves which collected and blocked the spout of the teapot. Teaspoons and mote skimmers were, however, made by specialist makers and are never found together with these trays.

Hallmarks: as you can see in the illustrations which follow, a number of these are marked on the topside, having one mark in each corner. Those marked on the base would have marks in a straight line.

Condition: these are nearly always flat based and one should therefore look for any excessive wear or holes around the base. Occasionally an example may have a small rim foot. Look for splits or repaired splits in the sides. Check for removed crests or armorials.

Fakes: I have never come across any fakes, although if one finds a so-called spoon tray hallmarked later than 1740 or earlier than 1705, one should be extremely suspicious — if it is right, it will have had a different use.

1,160. A selection of spoon trays dating from the early 18th century.

Top to bottom

c.1710	*£1,500 — £2,500*
c.1720	*£1,250 — £2,000*
c.1728	*£1,000 — £1,750*
c.1733	*£1,000 — £1,750*

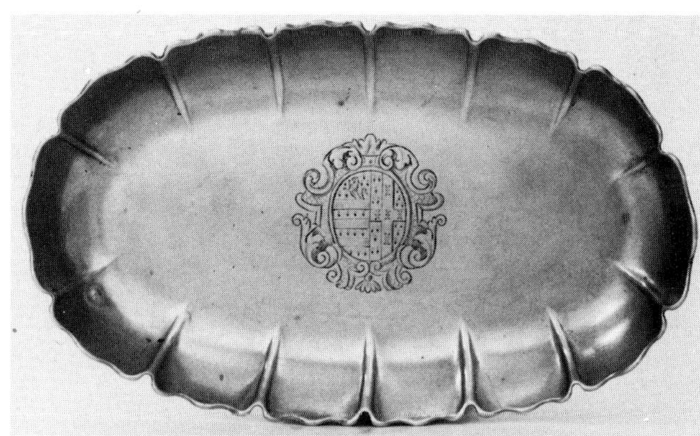

1,160

Strainers

Orange or lemon strainers were peculiar to the eighteenth century and were probably used in conjunction with punch bowls. The brewing of punch in the late seventeenth and eighteenth century was a popular custom, hence there are many punch bowls, not necessarily silver, in existence. The strainers are normally marked in the piercing in the centre of the bowl and should have a lion passant on the handle(s).

1,161. A particularly pretty example with more unusual concentric piercing than might normally be found. The handles are cast and chased with portrait medallions, matting and chasing.
c.1730 *£3,500 — £5,000*

1,162. An unusually plain and simple example, purely functional, no great merit in the design.
c.1755 *£750 — £1,250*

1,163. This is the most commonly found type of strainer and is found with both one and two handles. The former sometimes have a small tongue or lug on the opposite side of the handle which may have been used to hook it on to the side of the punch bowl.
c.1760 *£800 — £1,500*
Single handled examples £600 — £1,000

Table Decorations

1,164. From the late 19th century up to modern times models of animals and birds have been very popular as table decorations. Many are usable as casters, peppers, etc. (see **Casters** pp. 94 and 95), others are purely ornamental. English made examples are of high quality and very well modelled. This swan jardinière was in fact made as recently as 1971 and weighs well over 100oz.
c.1971 *per oz. £50 — £70*

1,164

1,163

1,161

1,162

Toast Racks

Toast racks are not known until the late eighteenth century. Prior to their introduction, toast must have been served on a dish or perhaps wrapped in a napkin. Some of the earliest examples have oval or oblong tray bases. These have wire bars which are attached to a frame base with lugs which fit into slots in the tray and are then fixed with silver wire skewers. The use of a tray base was not of long standing and within a decade or so the openwork toast rack, very much in the form of modern examples, became the norm. They are on the whole very basic items of household table furniture and rarely have any merit in design or quality.

Hallmarks: the detachable bars must be marked with the lion passant and maker's mark, otherwise a possible conversion from a teapot stand or salver would be suspected.

Condition: the bars are usually flimsy and are often broken or repaired where they join the base. As long as any repair is competently executed, the value will not be substantially decreased.

1,165. A toast rack with an oval tray base. The base of this example is very similar in design and size to a teapot stand.
c.1785 — *£750 — £1,250*

1,166. A close examination of this example shows a number of broken bars.
c.1795 — *When restored £400 — £800*

1,167. Another late 18th century example.
c.1795 — *£400 — £800*

1,168. An up-market, silver gilt toast rack displaying the very fine, heavy decoration of the Regency period. This was made by Paul Storr for Rundell, Bridge and Rundell and has an oval base to which the six section frame is bolted. It should be marked on both pieces.
c.1810 — *£3,500 — £5,500*

1,165

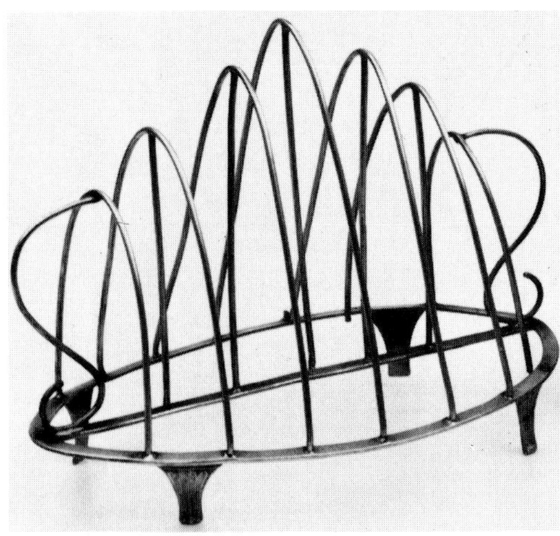

1,166

1,167

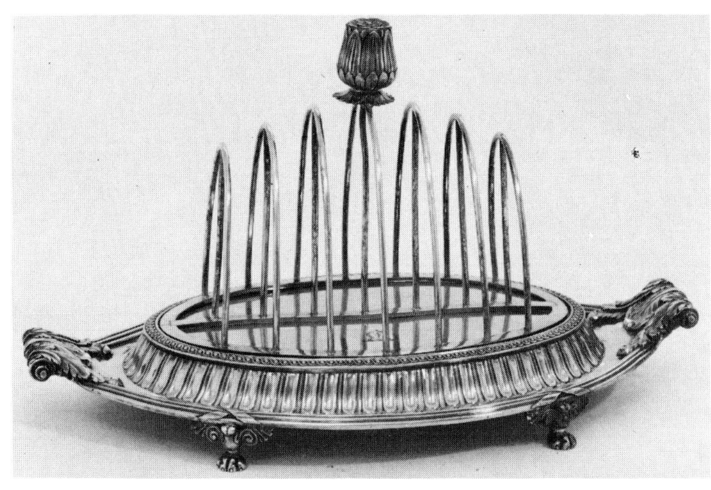

1,168

1,169. An example of the mid-Victorian period displaying the revival of Gothic designs.
c.1860 *£800 — £1,600*

1,170. A simpler example of the same period as 1,169, still displaying a heavier quality than the earlier Georgian examples. The bars are, however, still likely to be damaged where they join the base as so much strain is put on them when washing or cleaning.
c.1860 *£500 — £950*

Trinket Boxes

1,171. This circular box and cover is made by Messrs. Comyns who were perhaps the most prolific manufacturers of dressing table accoutrements. It is likely that it was intended for use as a powder jar or trinket box. The profuse decoration will mean added value in some quarters. The quality and weight is just in excess of 16oz. and this will help to dictate the price.
c.1890 *£900 — £1,600*

1,172. This square box was probably intended for use as a jewellery case or trinket box. It again has die stamped decoration with the sides being cut from a strip and then soldered together at the angles. More often than not these are velvet lined. 8ins. wide.
c.1905 *£1,000 — £2,000*

1,172

1,171

1,169

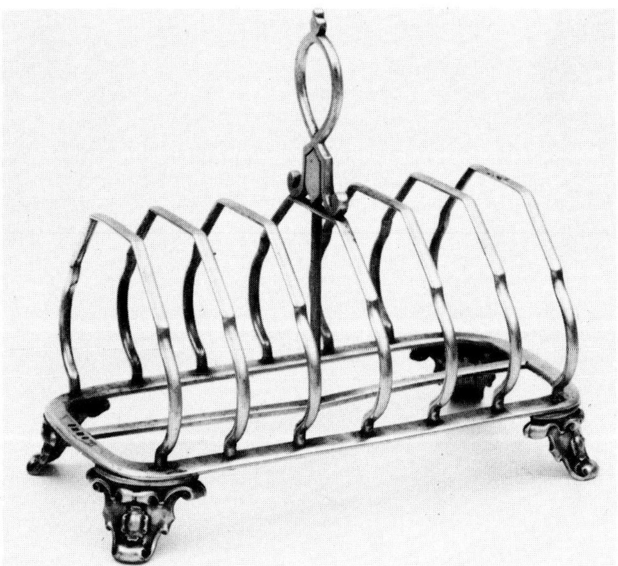

1,170

Makers

The following is a list of some of the better known makers arranged chronologically with the approximate dates at which their marks are found.

1697-1719 : Pierre Platel
One of the premier Huguenot silversmiths, renowned for silver of the highest quality. **Paul de Lamerie** (see below) was apprenticed to him.

1697-1728 : David Willaume I
Another Huguenot silversmith who was fairly prolific. Until recent years he was thought to be one and the same as **David Willaume II,** his son (1728-c.1746).

1713-1751 : Paul de Lamerie
The most famous of all silversmiths working in London and the greatest exponent of the rococo style, although his workshop also produced many straightforward items. His finest pieces can fetch thousands of pounds per ounce, whilst the more domestic items may command only hundreds per ounce!

1722-1747 : James Gould
A specialist candlestick maker. His son, **William Gould,** was also a candlestick maker (1732-1756).

1731-c.1750 : Robert Abercrombie
He specialised in making salvers.

1733-c.1773 : Samuel Wood
The best known of the specialist caster makers. He was apprenticed to **Thomas Bamford.**

1738-c.1780 : Ebenezer Coker
Mainly produced table candlesticks, but also some chamber candlesticks and salvers.

1740-1757 : John Cafe
Another specialist candlestick maker who produced chamber candlesticks and snuffers trays as well as table candlesticks. **William Cafe,** his brother, took over the business in 1757, his mark being found from that date until c.1775.

1744-1773 : Samuel Taylor
Best known for his sets of tea caddies.

1761-1790 : Hester Bateman
Perhaps one of the most universally known English silversmiths. By the 1770s the Bateman workshop was producing vast quantities of domestic silver. Pieces bearing Hester Bateman's mark have been avidly collected for some time, a craze which started because of many people's fascination with the novelty of a female silversmith. When she retired the business was carried on firstly by **Peter** and **Jonathon Bateman** (sons), Peter and **Ann Bateman** (son and daughter-in-law), Peter, Ann and **William Bateman** (grandson), and finally by **William Bateman II** (great-grandson).

1763-1811 : Robert Hennell
Probably the best known of the Hennell family. His father, **David Hennell,** specialised in the making of salt cellars. Robert Hennell worked in partnership at different stages with both of his sons, **David Hennell II** and **Samuel Hennell.** His grandson, **Robert Hennell III** was working until 1868.

c.1765-c.1780 : John Carter
Best known for table candlesticks and salvers. His mark, together with London hallmarks, are often found struck over Sheffield marks on loaded candlesticks.

c.1770-c.1800 : Andrew Fogelberg
He was Paul Storr's master and is perhaps best known for his use of cameo-like medallions. He was in partnership with **Stephen Gilbert** between 1780 and 1793.

1773-1809 : Matthew Boulton
The premier Birmingham silversmith who opened a highly productive factory in 1784 making various unusual and high quality works of art in Sheffield plate, ormolu and silver, as well as producing more mundane items such as buttons and buckles in cut and polished steel. It is mainly due to him that an assay office was established in Birmingham, and also to a certain extent in Sheffield. The company continued for thirty-five years after his death.

1776-1796 : John Schofield
Undoubtedly one of the finest makers of the last quarter of the 18th century. His craftsmanship and fine designs put him a head above any of his contemporaries. This is not always reflected in the price.

1786-1810 : Henry Chawner
Produced good quality domestic items, mainly teapots and associated pieces. He was in partnership with **John Emes** from 1796 until 1810 (see **Messrs Barnard**).

1792-1818 : Robert Garrard
He is known for good quality pieces. A tradition still continued by the famous London firm of the same name. His son, **Robert Garrard II,** was working from 1818 to 1853.

1792-1838 : Paul Storr
Second only to **Paul de Lamerie** (see above) in the 'high price stakes', he produced many gargantuan creations for **Rundell, Bridge and Rundell** as well as some of the prettiest and most delicate pieces. Much of his work was inspired by the finest designers of the period such as Flaxman and Theed. **John Samuel Hunt,** who died in 1868, took over from Storr when the firm became **Hunt and Roskell,** late **Storr and Mortimer.** The quality of his work is comparable with that of Paul Storr.

1802-1818 : Benjamin Smith
His firm worked almost exclusively for Rundell, Bridge and Rundell. The quality and craftsmanship are equal to that of **Paul Storr** (see above). He was in partnership with **Digby Scott** and later his brother **James,** and finally his son **Benjamin.**

1811-1824 : Joseph Angell I
Best known for the production of tea and coffee sets. **Joseph Angell II** took over in 1824 and was in partnership with his nephew **John Angell** from 1831 until c.1850.

1813-1835 : Edward Farrell
Produced some fantastic items based on Dutch paintings in the style of Teniers, as well as copying from 17th century designs. Perhaps one of the first people to use the fussy florid decoration so often associated with the Victorian period.

1822-c.1840 : Charles Fox II
The son of **Charles Fox I,** he produced many fine quality individual pieces, many copied in the Dutch style. **George Fox,** a descendant, also produced unusual items (working c.1860 to c.1900).

1829 onwards : Messrs. Barnard
Were responsible from this date onwards for the production of many important centrepieces, candelabra and cups as well as various less impressive pieces of high quality. Their predecessors, **Rebecca Emes** and **Edward Barnard** (1808-1829) and **John Emes** (1796-1808) are also known for their production of good quality silver.

1840 onwards : George William Adams of **Chawner and Co.**
Together with **Francis Higgins and Sons** the most prolific makers of cutlery in the 19th century.

1843 onwards : Elkington and Co. of Birmingham
The firm is primarily associated with electrotyping and electroplating. Together with **Messrs. Barnards** (see above) they are probably the best known 19th century manufacturers producing pieces of individual design.

Bibliography

Bennett, Douglas, *Irish Georgian Silver* (London, 1972).

Bradbury, Frederick, *Bradbury's Book of Hallmarks and Old Sheffield Plate Makers' Marks 1743-1860* (Sheffield, 1975, pocket edition).

Bradbury, Frederick, *A History of Old Sheffield Plate* (Sheffield, 1968; reprint of the 1912 edition).

Clayton, Michael, *The Collector's Dictionary of the Silver and Gold of Great Britain and North America* (London, 1971).

Grimwade, A.G., *London Goldsmiths 1697-1837. Their Marks and Lives* (London, 1976).

Grimwade, A.G., *Rococo Silver 1727-65* (London, 1975).

Hayward, J.F., *Huguenot Silver in England, 1688-1727* (London, 1959).

Heal, Ambrose, *The London Goldsmiths, 1200-1800* (Newton Abbot, 1972).

Hughes, Gerald, *Modern Silver* (London, 1967).

Jackson, Sir Charles J., *English Goldsmiths and their Marks* (New York, 1965; first edition London, 1921).

Jones, Kenneth Crisp, ed., *The Silversmiths of Birmingham and their Marks. 1750-1980* (London, 1981).

Oman, C.C., *Caroline Silver* (London, 1970).

Oman, C.C., *English Engraved Silver, 1150-1900* (London, 1978).

Penzer, N.M., *Paul Storr* (London, 1971; first edition, 1954).

Rowe, Robert, *Adam Silver* (London, 1965).

Taylor, Gerald, *Silver* (London, 1965).

Index

INDEX

Other Books on Silver from

Antique Collectors' Club

Starting to Collect Silver *by John Luddington*
Describes in an easy-to-read manner the many problems and pitfalls which face the novice. Superb illustrations and a clear analysis of the valuation of individual pieces provide the reader with a much clearer understanding of the complex factors which make up the assessment of quality of a piece of silver.
11 x 8½ in./279 x 216mm. 228 pp., 345 b. & w. illus.
ISBN 0 907462 48 0

Silver Flatware: English, Irish and Scottish 1660-1980
by Ian Pickford
A reference to the many patterns which have been produced. Examines the stylistic development, production, history and makers and deals with the patterns. The author also discusses quality, repairs, forgeries, alterations and marks.
11 x 8½ in./279 x 216mm. 232 pp., 396 b. & w. illus.
ISBN 0 907462 35 9

Pocket Edition Jackson's Hallmarks *edited by Ian Pickford*
Based on the new, revised edition of *Jackson's Silver and Gold Marks of England, Scotland and Ireland.* Includes a selection of over 1,000 makers whose work is of particular interest. Complete cycles of silver marks are given for all the important assay offices. This *Pocket Edition* has been updated to 1991 to include current assay marks and is the most accurate and up to date guide on the market.
8½ in. x 4¾ in./215 x 120mm.
172 pp., over 1,000 marks.
ISBN 1 85149 128 7. Hardback
ISBN 1 85149 169 4. Paperback

Jackson's Silver and Gold Marks of England, Scotland and Ireland *edited by Ian Pickford*
For over 80 years this has been the essential book on antique silver used by dealers, scholars and collectors. This new edition contains some 10,000 corrections to the original material and an enormous amount of entirely new information. In view of the sheer extent of the changes, many treasured but battered copies of the original must be replaced.
11 x 8½ in./279 x 216mm. 766 pp., 400 b. & w. illus., 15,000 marks. ISBN 0 907462 63 4

19th Century Australian Silver *by J.B. Hawkins*
The first comprehensive book on the fascinating but hitherto neglected wares of 19th century Australian silversmiths. An essential reference as without it, a good deal of Australian silver, usually many times more valuable than its European equivalent, will go unrecognised or wrongly ascribed.
11 x 8½ in./279 x 216mm. 2 volumes. Vol. I 344 pp. Vol II 376 pp. Over 80 colour plates. Over 700 b. & w. illus. ISBN 1 85149 002 7

Antique Collectors' Club

5 Church Street
Woodbridge, Suffolk, IP12 1 DS
Tel: 01394 385501
Fax: 01394 384434

Market Street Industrial Park
Wappingers' Falls, NY 12590, USA
Tel: 914 297 0003
Fax: 914 297 0068